39.95

Toward a New Synthesis
John Fowles
John Gardner
Norman Mailer

Toward a New Synthesis
John Fowles
John Gardner
Norman Mailer

by
Robert J. Begiebing

Research
Press
Ann Arbor / London

813.09
B41t

Produced and distributed by
UMI Research Press
an imprint of
University Microfilms Inc.
Ann Arbor, Michigan 48106

Library of Congress Cataloging in Publication Data

AL **Begiebing, Robert J., 1946-**
    Toward a new synthesis : John Fowles, John Gardner, Norman
Mailer / by Robert J. Begiebing.
    p. cm—(Challenging the literary canon)
    Bibliography: p.
    Includes index.
    ISBN 0-8357-1947-2 (alk. paper)
    1. American fiction—20th century—History and criticism.
2. Ethics in literature. 3. Magicians in literature.
4. Postmodernism (Literature) 5. Fowles, John, 1926- —Criticism
and interpretation. 6. Gardner, John, 1933- —Criticism and
interpretation. 7. Mailer, Norman—Criticism and interpretation.
I. Title. II. Series.
PS379.B414   1989
813'.54'09353—dc19   88-34076
                                                               CIP

British Library CIP data is available.

For Linda
and for Brie and Kate

Contents

Acknowledgments

In any scholarly book the author's debt to others is of course enormous, and any reader will find that such is the case here. I do want to single out, however, a few people who have been extraordinarily helpful to me. I wish to thank Professors Samuel Chase Coale, of Wheaton College, and Andrew Gordon, of the University of Florida, for their helpful and encouraging readings of major portions of this book in, its first typed draft. One is lucky and thankful indeed to have distant colleagues so willing to devote their own time to help one through struggles with the early phases of a manuscript. I would also like to thank my colleagues and the academic administration of New Hampshire College, who granted me a sabbatical leave in 1983 to begin work on this book, and Jackie Hickox for her typing labors and her sharp eye for errors. And of course I am again greatly indebted to my wife, Linda, for all of her work with the manuscript and for her encouragement and patience throughout the entire process.

1

Introduction

Our relativist minds made by a relativist world make a relativist world. And there is no Truth in us.
Betty Jean Craige, *Relativism in the Arts*

Fiction and theories about fiction today are shaped by renewed debates over ancient issues—means versus ends, form versus function. The factions are diverse and numerous, and as Elizabeth Bruss points out in *Beautiful Theories,* lack of consensus is the order of the day: no single program has gained such widespread support that its speculations "take on the look of simple common sense." And as Alan Wilde argued in *Horizons of Assent,* there is likewise no monolithic program among Anglo-American authors, whether modernist or post-modernist. There are only tendencies. Although it may be even more difficult to name schools of theory that have achieved prominence among fiction writers and poets than it is to name the various schools of theory themselves, self-reflexive tendencies have flourished in imaginative literature that parallel prominent ideas in theoretical scholarship. Yet, as Wilde points out, certain authors often considered post-modernists struggle beyond and transform the limits set forth by the theoreticians.[1] At the center of the contentious, rootless environment in which fiction writers work, however, is a debate (to use Robert Scholes' terms derived from Edward Said) over the *hermetic* and *secular* powers of art and perception. The hermetic position tends to view the novel as a closed system or word game, while the secular position tends to view the novel as a moral force in the world.

Vincent Leitch has suggested one reason for renewed debate: our post-romantic philosophical heritage that calls into question traditional Western concepts of being, truth, and consciousness.[2] Alan Trachtenberg has identified roughly a dozen factors contributing to the breakdown of any predominating intellectual or moral schema in the post-War world, ranging from the "ethic of abundance" and the sexual revolution to the scientific revolution in quantum physics and cosmology.[3]

Equally important is the radical dissociation of art from idea among twentieth-century avant-garde artists in Europe. From Dada, through Existentialism, to what Claude Mauriac has called Aliterature, avant-garde writers in Europe and America have created a "post-modern fiction" that Raymond Federman describes as: "fiction that tries to explore the possibilities of fiction . . . challenges the tradition that governs it . . . exposes the fictionality of reality . . . and admits that no meaning pre-exists in language. . . . This creature will be totally free, totally uncommitted to the affairs of the outside world . . . irrational, irresponsible, irrepressive, amoral, and unconcerned with the real world." Other writers such as William Gass have argued, in more moderate language, that a writer is best when he does not believe in ideas, that the chief value of the novel is not moral judgment but aesthetic quality and elegance, and that the only moral activity for a writer is to contribute to the world objects of beauty worthy of contemplation in themselves.[4] But in public debate over the function of moral vision in art with his friend William Gass (whom he admires), and more notably in *On Moral Fiction* (1978), John Gardner represented an opposing (secular) view. He argued, essentially, that the novel can affirm what is "good" and "true," can move the reader toward affirmations of value, can raise questions of how to live and of moral judgment.

My purpose here is not to describe this debate in detail, nor to trace the history of such controversies, nor to define at length the techniques and concerns of "metafictionists,"[5] nor to map advanced literary theory. These tasks have been undertaken by many others. I do need to offer here, however, a reminder (or, for those unfamiliar with it, an explanation) of the debate sufficient to understand that element of post-modernism to which John Fowles, John Gardner, and Norman Mailer are responding. I shall undoubtedly simplify and do a certain violence to the complex post-modern ethos by focusing on what is a kind of temperamental bias, which Scholes identified as the "hermetic" tendency in post-modernism. It is true that the various expressions and emphases of post-modernism depend on a given practitioner or theoretician. Yet this hermetic temperament or tendency is, by the testimony now of many analyses, fundamental to Anglo-American post-modernism and therefore to our understanding of it. Moreover, this hermetic tendency is the particular issue that most engages the three subjects of this study, and that is the central reason for our attention to it here. These three authors directly address contemporary questions about whether imagination and perception are separate from the world or cosmos, and whether art can or should point to moral dilemmas and struggles that resonate in our political, professional, and life conduct.

One could argue that a number of Anglo-American writers have taken up a secular, even ethical, position against the hermetic. Candidates in America might include Bellow, Malamud, Updike, Cheever, Ellison, and Beattie—to suggest a few—and in Britain Greene, Golding, Spark, and Burgess—to suggest a few more. My main purpose here, however, will be to examine extensively how three particular novelists have vigorously entered the debate, how they have constructed a new fiction that serves as an indicator of humanity's moral condition, and how they have all used at the center of their work the device of the magician and the theme of restructured consciousness through moral revelation. Moreover, each of these writers employs a similar structural principle: the dialectical narrative of a hero's or narrator's encounters with the magus figure. Such narrative expresses the dialectic of quest, allegory, and romance as psychomachia—the debate and fight for mind or soul.

Didactic Moralism versus Moral Responsibility

At times, authors who have concerned themselves with the *ends* of art rather than the *means* have led the way toward preachiness, authoritarianism, or outright repression. Certain of the Puritans come immediately to mind, as do some of the lesser Victorians. And of course medieval English literature is by and large the moralizing literature of Catholicism. In our own century the literature of state Marxism, to suggest but one example, has exercised its totalitarian power. With ample justification theorists and readers concerned with technique have warned against or ridiculed the excesses of overzealous moralists. The late twentieth century is not a vantage point of innocence, and most intelligent people these days have a healthy scepticism for pompous or self-righteous zeal. We don't need many reminders of the tyrannies that have had their day because a person, or a group, or an institution, or a nation has claimed privileged knowledge of one or another religious, social, or political absolute, whether such privilege has appeared in the guise of patriarchial Victorian Christianity or in the mask of the devourer—a Nazi madman.

But a common error is to mistake the posing of ethical dilemmas, the suggesting of moral responsibilities, or the raising of ethical issues for the dangers of didactic moralism, cliché, and authoritarian zeal. Gerald Graff notes a similar leap of logic, using Susan Sontag and Richard Gilman as two of his examples. For both Sontag and Gilman works of art are greatest when they are "self-sufficient, self-justifying universes without secondary connections to the world." Making such "secular" connections, their logic continues, between art and life, form and content—"those old Mediterranean values"—has led to the horrors and tyrannies of Faustian Western man.

Alasdair MacIntyre considers a similar logical leap in other contemporaries:

There are a series of later writers—J. L. Talmon, Isaiah Berlin and Daniel Bell are examples—who see in this republican commitment to public virtue the genesis of totalitarianism and even of terror. . . . It was rather, so I would claim, the ways in which the commitment to virtue was institutionalized politically . . . and not the commitment itself which produced some at least of the consequences which they abhor; but in fact most modern totalitarianism and terror has nothing to do with *any* commitment to virtue.[6]

The problem with mistaking ethical content or question for authoritarian moralism and zeal is, simply, the error of confusing values or ideals with our failures to meet them at obvious historical moments. One might end up blaming Goethe for Hitler. Surely "the enemy" lies elsewhere. Are not the conditions of twentieth-century life requiring of us greater sophistication, and even more basic distinctions between cause and effect?

We need to understand, first, what three frequently misunderstood writers—Fowles, Gardner, Mailer—who connect art and consciousness to an actual world or cosmos, or even to history, are *not* approaching in their work. Then we will also be more prepared to define, as the subject of this book, what their work *is* approaching. Generally they have sought to combine certain of the least restrictive and most flexible elements of our classical, romantic, and existential heritage. These three writers have not, therefore, devoted their careers to the production of literal precepts to live by, nor to the production of moralizing platitudes, nor to the foolish moralizing of such artistic criteria as "poetic justice" that certain rigors of Christian neo-classicism in the seventeenth and eighteenth centuries produced. Nor have these three authors presented a series of unbreakable rules of unity or form. Neither has Fowles, Gardner, nor Mailer accepted that other facet of neo-classicism which has tended toward its own fanaticisms: the philosophical rationalism rooted in Descartes, Spinoza, and Leibniz. That is to say, these three contemporary writers have not argued for some innocent confidence in the ability of human reason to find and systematize the unalterable laws of nature or the regulations of God. If at their worst Fowles, Gardner, and Mailer can at times seem preachy, it is more a preachiness of tone than of substance. And in their better, more typical, moments, that preachiness belies the experimental, even tentative, nature of their quests.

These three writers have drawn, above all, their very sense of the purpose of art and the role of the artist from the ancient springs of classicism. Fowles, especially in *The Aristos,* Gardner, in *On Moral Fiction,* and Mailer, in *Cannibals and Christians* and throughout his nonfiction, all argue that art seeks elusive but significant truths, persuades and nurtures the mind and soul, and leads toward greater personal integrity, toward "virtuous" growth. Viewed from the hermetic position, they are contemporary heretics because they have drawn on primitive roots by connecting form with ideas associated with the form, have viewed art as *psychagogia,* and have, even through the most experimental forms, still returned to the conviction that the form implies the value and the idea. Fundamental to form for all three writers is the concept of "man *in via,*" as Alasdair MacIntyre puts it, or of human life as a narrative structure of quest or journey. Every classical and medieval view of virtue is "linked to some particular notion of the narrative structure of human life," to the individual's ability "to survive evils" on his or her "historical journey." MacIntyre writes specifically of Gardner, but he might have been writing of Fowles and Mailer when he continues on this point:

> It is in the course of the quest and only through encountering and coping with the various particular harms, dangers, temptations, and distractions which provide any quest with its episodes and incidents that the goal of the quest is finally to be understood. A quest is always an education both as to the character of that which is sought and in self-knowledge.
>
> The virtues are therefore to be understood as those dispositions which will not only sustain practices, but which will also sustain us in the relevant kind of quest for the good . . . and which will furnish us with increasing self-knowledge and increasing knowledge of the good.[7]

These three artists work on the assumption that art is rhetoric, to borrow Frank Lentricchia's terminology in *Criticism and Social Change,* that the artist (or theorist) has a choice to work on behalf of the dominant hegemony or to work "counter-hegemonically as a violator." I find myself hard put to think of three other contemporary Anglo-American authors who see their work so much as an effort (in Lentricchia's phrasing) to reeducate or inform, to aid the birth of cultural revolution or transformation, and to create a body of work that can stand as a "redemptive social project."[8]

Moreover, we are considering in this book three authors whose central, prototypical novels express secular themes through techniques and characters that arise out of a tradition in English literature—the dramas, metadramas, and masques of the magus. During the fifteenth through the early seventeenth centuries the magus became a symbol of the possibilities open to humanity. As Barbara Howard Traister puts it, the human being becomes an opening through which the "inexhaustible richness of being" may pour, even though the magician—as teacher, master of revels, and metadramatist—is always "precariously balanced upon the margin of an absolute risk." If the magicians of medieval romance with their spectacles and role-playing for the discomfort, edification, and entertainment of spectators came to be associated also with the creative artist, this association increased as Tudor-Stuart drama developed, just as the philosophical tradition of magic increasingly informed the fictive tradition.

The magicians of Renaissance drama raise moral questions of "how much achievement, power, or knowledge is permitted to man, and what are his possibilities and his human limitations." Likewise, the magicians of court masque, if more stereotypical and inhuman, were central figures in moments of transformation, in elaborately staged "internal conflicts." If magician figures could not survive the rationalism and scepticism that began to dominate English intellectual life in the seventeenth century, Fowles, Gardner, and Mailer restore the metaphorical, psychological, philosophical, and spectacular powers of magicians and their "magic" to literary art. Once again, the magus plays a role in "explorations of the nature of man and his place in a world he comes painfully near to controlling."[9] Once again three authors, through the magus figure, return their readers to the referential terrains of history, of life lived in the society of others, of moral consequence and responsibility.

Though at times Gardner and Mailer, especially, have been erroneously singled out as reactionaries who accept what is "right" only because it is established, they have, on the contrary, tried to discover what it is in human conduct and life that leads to freedom rather than repression, to individual growth rather than diminution, and to life rather than death. No three contemporary writers have, moreover, been so deeply concerned about the growth and psychology of the individual amidst the totalitarian impulses of twentieth-century cultures. And therein lies their second chief artistic resource—their roots in our rebellious romantic and existential heritage. Basic to Fowles, Gardner, and Mailer is their belief in the potential of the individual to assess means as well as ends in life and art. All three authors also emphasize the significance of psychological reality, emotion, and originality in the development of humanity's moral sense. And by their works, these three writers hope to suggest possible avenues to freedom amidst the labyrinths of established or "revolutionary" oppressions. But they are not willing to substitute the labyrinths of word-game for the labyrinths of oppression. By their definitions of freedom, Fowles, Gardner, and Mailer would transcend the restrictions and the ethical limitations of either kind of labyrinth. Though these three writers have used, variously, such typically post-modern and metafictional techniques as multiple choice endings (or plots), embedded tales, parodied mythic and fabulative texts, "false" characters who address readers, multiple contradictory points of view, labyrinthine games, speculations about fiction *in* fiction, the deliberate confounding of fact and fiction, the parody of popular genres, irony directed at both characters and writers, and improbable coincidences, they are not prepared to accept such techniques as an intervention *only* in other fictions (or writing) or to accept fiction *only* as a symbolic system of signs and relationships without connections to the world.

Philosophical Relativism and the Human Sciences

Besides the disruptions of the Second World War and the world that followed it—from Vietnam, to political terrorism, to corporate waste dumps that poison the waters of life (among the scores of crises that have been and are before us)—a separate element in contemporary thought has added to the confusion and debate about what we can and cannot know, and how we should or should not define ourselves, our political systems, our conduct toward one another, and our art. That further element in contemporary speculations is structuralist and "post-structuralist" thought in linguistics and the human sciences. One might speculate that the influence of structuralist theory on contemporary Anglo-American fictional practices is akin to the influence of Freud and Freudianism on the British and American literary mind during the first forty years or so of the twentieth century. The lines of influence are being traced out by other critics. Robert Scholes focuses our attention on one important parallel when in *Fabulation and Metafiction* (1979) he writes that modern fabulation is connected to structuralist thought by its rejection of the "empirical concept of history" as something that may be retrieved "by objective investigations of fact." The "fabulative histories" of Pynchon or Barth adapt history "to the artifices of daydream and fabulation."[10]

The similarities between the post-war experimental fiction—by metafiction, nonreferentialism, fabulism, surfiction or any other name—and the radical subjectivism in certain structuralist theories, especially as those theories have taken root and flourished in the American academy, are by now commonplace observations of the critical canon. But I need to emphasize the drift of powerful and persuasive elements in late-twentieth-century theory and fiction so that we begin to understand the magnitude of the challenge, indeed the sheer audacity, of writers who persist in regenerating through practice and critique a contrary view of fiction as moral force. Despite the at one time appropriate revolutionary claims of the post-structuralists, one of the most heretical and philosophically disturbing things a writer can now say is that human consciousness and hence art as the expression of that consciousness are attached to an actual world where historical processes are not only knowable and valuable in some degree, but are processes that create an arena where humanity still tests its own ethical dimensions and still grows either farther from or closer to its responsibilities to itself, to history, and to the earth.

In his search for the ways in which the literary intellectual can participate in the radical work of social transformation, Frank Lentricchia arrives at a similar view of the hermetic tendencies in current theory. Using Paul de Man as his example of the "undisputed master of deconstruction in the United States," Lentricchia writes: "I would wager that he [de Man] will be rediscovered as the most brilliant hero of traditionalism, the theorist who elaborated the cagiest argument for the political defusion of writing and the intellectual life. . . . The insidious effect of his work is not the proliferating replication of his way of reading . . . but the paralysis of praxis itself: an effect that traditionalism . . . should only applaud." Throughout *Criticism and Social Change* Lentricchia places as de Man's great theoretical antagonist Kenneth Burke—he who connects gnosis with praxis (Mailer would be our chief novelist counterpart here), he who restores to art its antinomian force, and he who reverses the tendencies of "aesthetic isolationism" since the late eighteenth century toward a political and social (i.e., historical) "aesthetic pragmatism." If Burke insists on the potential efficacy of the engaged life, de Man insists that we cannot know enough to intervene as activist intellectuals or artists (or worse, that all intervention is doomed to failure); if Burke argues for the possibility of historical consciousness, de Man argues for its impossibility; if Burke implies we can be agents of change, de Man implies we can be only agents of the status quo. Lentricchia concludes that, because for de Man there can be no revolutionary change on the terrain of history, then de Man's claim expresses "the postulation of the most genuine meaning of political conservatism. . . . This is the effect of his theory; this is his social work; this is the message of post-structuralism in the United States."[11]

Earlier, in *After the New Criticism,* Lentricchia had emphasized the two general principles that, from Saussure to Barthes, arise out of the structuralist movement: first, that the self is an intersubjective construct formed by cultures and not controlled by the individual and, second, that the text is a formless space where shape is imposed by structured modes of reading.[12] The whole movement of post-structuralism and deconstructionism continues to argue for the loss of an "identifiable center" or a "privileged position" for any body of knowledge, any particular meaning, or any ethic. Indeed, the only center now becomes the "centerlessness" of all texts, and the only positive value the "free play" of mind in creator and reader. The work of art becomes an enclosed labyrinth without reference to "reality," history, absolutes, or center. Hence the terms *non-referential* and *decentered* in recent discourse on fiction and theory. Now the self has become rootless, and the thing "signified" has no meaning beyond a rootless "signifier."

Yet the "issue of whether or not signifieds are purely arbitrary or partly grounded upon phenomena," writes Robert Scholes in *Textual Power,* "is an issue of great importance." Scholes positions Umberto Eco as a reasonable corrective to post-modern theoretical excesses because Eco argues for the interdependency of verbal and nonverbal worlds. It is, for Scholes, reference—"a dimension of the human use of language"—that has been "systematically repressed or ignored by structuralist and hermetic theoreticians." In short, the "hermetic view of textuality inhibits any attempt to criticize either the text or the world." Although Scholes applauds such elements in the deconstructive analysis as the correcting of "naive empiricisms of all sorts," his critique is very close to Lentricchia's. It is to this recoiling "with horror from contamination by praxis," to this "wide-spread phenomenon of deconstructive paralysis, a permanent state of equivocation before the bridge that leads from thought and writing to consequential action," that Scholes is likewise unsympathetic. "The foreknowledge of guilt leads to an abdication of responsibility." Ultimately, Scholes argues, as does Lentricchia, that the problem with hermetic attitudes is their tendency to accept and foster the "quietistic acceptance of injustice." Scholes' theoretical project (and our three authors' fictive project) is to "rehabilitate reference" and "rescue the referent" without falling into "naive assumptions about the empirical object."[13]

One upshot of post-modern theory, then, is a pervasive contemporary vision of reality as universal disorder, and any vision of ideals, ideas, or values (old or new) as mere supports of relative, repressive ideologies. The only order, if there is any, exists within language itself, and the body of fiction thereby becomes an enclosed world of pure contemplation where all ideas may be entertained as of equal value and as without external consequence. That relativity and lack of consequence is what has been called the "self-deconstructive quality" of the text; it is what makes fiction very like a game, nothing like moral force, certainly not a substitute for dead religions and past ethics.

Structuralism and its theoretical offspring, then, are certainly disenchanting. To the extent that humanity has needed disenchantment, we can understand the desirability of espousing such theory. As Michel Foucault has argued, the potential of advanced linguistic theory and analysis is the disillusioning of historical vision through the process of learning to see history as a series of revolutionary orders imposing themselves and their game rules on one another. It is this vision of history, to Foucault, that frees humanity to question all values continually, including and especially the system of values within which one lives, even though there is no final answer, cause, or value to be discovered. But as Lentricchia points out, this "deconstruction" of history, with all its healthy ramifications for individual action and responsibility within the larger world, has not been the predominant direction of transplanted structuralism, via, above all, de Man.[14]

Some, including Graff as early as 1973 and Karl Kroeber a decade later, have gone so far as to connect post-modern theory to the general "bureaucratization and technicization" of university education. It is, Kroeber argued, simply the "smashing academic success of the natural sciences" that has so tempted literary critics to "found the kind of academic specialization that empire builders need in our bureaucracy of criticism." It has been for us, Kroeber argues, all too easy a step from the bureaucratization of our intellectual life and our progressive desacralization of life generally to "the idea of art's autonomy" or triviality, because "an object without relation to other phenomena *is* by one definition unimportant."

Whether one agrees with Kroeber's analysis, the limitations of advanced theories and fictions have gradually become clear. I have noted certain of Scholes' and Lentricchia's reservations. Even in his search specifically for the "ethical control" in contemporary fantasy, Scholes concluded with a similar reservation, and he later argued in *Textual Power* for the importance of literary studies in the classroom as a corrective to students' lives in the most manipulative of cultures. Graff, to take another example, argues that the whole "post-modern movement within contemporary literature and criticism calls into question the traditional claims of literature and art to truth and human value," and thereby tends to render literature increasingly "meaningless in the classroom." And Jacques Barzun, extending his critique to prevailing movements in art and culture, has questioned our tendency to substitute revulsion and nihilism for disinterested critical judgment; and he has questioned our narcissistic tendency to create "this train of images in which individual responsibility is lost," art is dissociated from history and biography, and art's "energy of emancipation" is dissipated."[15]

As we will see, there are important correspondences between this theoretical critique of the limits of post-modern hermeticism—however wrong-headed that critique may seem from the post-modern position—and the critical reactions and fictional practices of Fowles, Gardner, and Mailer.

The Avant-Garde: Roots of the Post-Modern Novel

In addition to our modern philosophical heritage, the global disruptions during and after World War II, and influential aspects of structuralist thought, the literary avant-garde itself, as it responds to all of these developments, makes a further contribution to the milieu in which Fowles, Gardner, and Mailer have lived and worked. If each of these writers has to some extent employed the literary techniques that developed within a post-modern milieu, each has also reacted against the most relativistic and hermetic orientations within that milieu.

One more threat to the possibilities of equilibrium in human nature and the social order, one more challenge to the assumptions of humanism, the avant-garde in Europe in its revolutionary stance against traditional art forms and culture has furthered the detachment of consciousness from history, the disintegration of "reality," the conversion of man to automaton, and the substitution of artifice for life. Finally, the avant-garde has turned art against itself. The roots of the movement go deep.

In *The Dismemberment of Orpheus,* for example, Ihab Hassan argues that the "Dionysiac frenzy" of surrealism and post-modern literature is manifest early in romantic irony and—through Heine and Mallarmé—moves imagination toward its abolition. Art is persuaded of its own impossibility. The avant-garde that Hassan traces through Sade to Hemingway and Kafka, and finally to Genet and Beckett, is a "literature of silence" that "de-realizes the world" and then either "turns consciousness upon itself" or condemns it to the solipsist drama of self and anti-self, to the autism of an "ambivalent semantic."[16]

The *nouveau roman* of Nathalie Surraute, Alain Robbe-Grillet, Michel Butor, Claude Simon, Jean Cayrol, and others, Hassan argues, seeks nothing short of a complete transformation of the idea of the novel that would render past genres alien, or at best, quaint. These writers embrace a vision of life's futility in a universe without established norms. In France, the post-modern novel is neutral. It rejects protest, denies the possibility of analysis, abhors ideology. It has become notorious for its vision in life as a depthless surface that is essentially trivial and banal, and for its stylistic flatness or *"matisme complet,"* as Roland Barthes calls it. The fictional labyrinth, the structure or form, again becomes, as Robbe-Grillet argues, the principal value of the work. This value Robbe-Grillet gladly limits further to the total subjectivity of superficial perceptions, or *"écriture."* And if, for Hassan, Genet takes us all the way back to Sade's transvaluation of values and the resulting denial of the ethical differences of all symbols—from swastika to cross—then Beckett, the "supreme post-modern artist," gives us the ultimate literature of "solipsistic drone," consciousness separated from matter, of that solitary game the human voice plays with itself, of, finally, human "consciousness spinning loose of history" (160–69, 177–209, 210–47).

This growing emphasis on surface as opposed to depth in continental literature of which Hassan writes, Alan Wilde places as one of the most fundamental reversals of modernism at the hands of late modernist and post-modernist authors. Ivy Compton-Burnett is Wilde's model transitional figure in English literature. Compton-Burnett's early approaches to the reflexive, reductive, and anti-referential adumbrates certain later tendencies and themes, as does the "morally and psychologically claustrophobic ambience," the narrow range of human possibility, and the "acid bath" of irony in her novels (108, 122).

Toward a New Synthesis

I want to suggest at this point that in much of our theoretical debate we may be missing the central issue. Few would argue seriously with what Scholes identifies as the unbridgeable "Borgesian" gap between language and reality—a veritable cliché of modern epistemological and poetic theory, generally called "formalism." But Scholes argues that despite the wide acknowledgment of this gap, Borges himself does not turn his back on reality for a purely verbal universe. Scholes sees in Borges a willingness to acknowledge the "ungraspable reality" while to some degree defining it through complex allegory, rather than through a single reducible truth.[17] What Scholes is saying about Borges and Eco's bridging of the gap between signifier and signified—whether through allegory, historical irony, or theoretical discourse—does parallel a synthesis that Fowles, Gardner, and Mailer have begun to construct. This synthesis, as we will see, is perhaps closer to the spirit of an international genre of historically engaged metafiction and ethically challenging experimentation (represented also by Márquez, Calvino, and Fuentes) than to the spirit of Anglo-American post-modernism of the 1960s and 1970s. The central issue, however, may be that the debate over slice-of-life realism versus reality-denying metafiction is by now a conflict of strawmen. The theoretical and fictional issues are more complex.

Graff seems to suggest this complexity when he considers the politics behind such debates: "Before we can even argue about such concepts (reason, ethics, objectivity) it seems necessary to free them from false politicization. . . . Until this is done, debate can hardly get off the ground, since what is being attacked is not 'reason' or 'realism' itself but a caricature that has been set up in order to be quickly disposed of" (28). As Graff puts it, of course: "The choice having been reduced to one between defensive Puritanism and open-minded creativity, not much remains to be argued about" (82).

I think the issue worth pursuing now is the difference between amoral and ethical fiction (whether realistic, fabulative, or metafictional). Who, for example, can seriously argue that chronological plot development has been the only true form of fiction for the past two hundred years? Yet some post-modern critics and fiction writers still treat plot development as their chief bogey, with "characterization" and "setting" standing just behind plot like a row of effigies awaiting the torch. Sukenick gives us one example of the level of this debate:

> Realistic fiction presupposed chronological time as the medium of a plotted narrative, an irreductible individual psyche as the subject of its characterization, and . . . the ultimate concrete reality of things as the object and rationale of its description. In the world of post-realism, however, all of these absolutes have become absolutely problematic. The contemporary writer . . . is forced to start from scratch: Reality doesn't exist, time doesn't exist, personality doesn't exist.[18]

The problem with such absolute expressions of the nonexistence of reality warring against absolute expressions of objectively verifiable reality is that they both are like shooting fish in a barrel. They are too easy. And they are off the real target. By the late twentieth century few are willing to support (or need bother to support) dusted philosophies of nominalism, or of the absence of reality. There *are* no innocent fictional forms anymore. What serious contemporary writer would argue that his work is a priori the only "frame" on reality?

To my mind, the more important question is one of seriousness of purpose *within* experimentation of form and technique. That is a question which leads to the examination of the ethical control of design. To put it another way, what Fowles requires of a novel is that the design direct our attention to the ethical content, to the question of what the individual's responsibilities to self and others are. What Gardner requires is that the novel be morally alive, that it explore the subtle, shifting connections between self and others and history. What Mailer requires of a novel is that it be above all "philosophically disturbing." But Sukenick requires only that a novel be written in the new style, or "Bossa Nova" as he calls it, that the novel represent only itself through the techniques of opacity, abstraction, and improvisation. "Opacity implies that we should direct our attention to the surface of work . . . calling the reader's attention to the technological reality of the book . . . keeping his mind on that surface instead of undermining it with profundities" *(Surfiction,* 45). To the "surfictionist" then, the greatest enemy beyond plot and character is, as Marcus Klein put it, "didacticism of any sort, with its implication of the possibility of social and philosophical certainties beyond the work of art." Only by remaining "rigorously detached" from his material will the author achieve his avant-garde effects and style.[19]

But the issues grow more complex still when sympathetic critics like Scholes set out to find precisely the ethical content in experimental fiction. Scholes asks: What is the nature of the ethical concern, where is it vigorously denied, and, finally, how does such denial of ethical value differ from the affirmation of ethical value in particular works? It is part of Scholes' final question that I try to answer in this book chiefly by examining three related affirmations of ethical value in the contemporary novel.

The very process of Scholes' search for the "ethical control" in works by Barth, Fowles, Murdoch, Barthelme, Gass, Vonnegut, Coover, Hawkes, and Southern might suggest, however, just how sparse the ethical dimension in most of these novelists is. Scholes discovers a hint of ethical order in Gass, who seems to portray "object man" becoming sentient, harmonious man, and Ishmael Reed, who returns to social satire through fabulation. Scholes can say of John Fowles alone that he writes "precisely about" the relationship between the aesthetic and the ethical.

If there is to be a new synthesis through a new fiction, Fowles, Gardner, and Mailer show one direction that synthesis may take. Not only do they regenerate certain classical, Renaissance, romantic, and existential literary traditions through their work, and not only do they employ some of the most current fictional techniques and theoretical concerns, but they also attempt to integrate some of the most productive affirmations and scepticisms of modernism and post-modernism. If like post-modernists these three are chary of solutions, doubtful of the self's integrity and identity, open to randomness and contingency (what Fowles calls our environment of "hazard"), and conscious of a chaotic world, they have not given up the traditionally modernist concern with psychological and metaphysical depth for post-modernist surfaces, nor have they sought to demystify life but, on the contrary, to return to life its mystery. They long, like modernists, to bridge the gaps and discontinuities of life through, first, their art. They long, in Wilde's phrase, "to restore significance to the broken world," not to catalogue a world and selves beyond repair. Out of these concerns arise their redemptive themes and symbols, including their heroes who—however small or ordinary their heroisms may at times seem—cut strange figures in the disjunctive and anti-heroic terrains of so much post-war fiction.

For Fowles, Gardner, and Mailer, the small, rare assents of post-modern-ism, as Wilde defines them through the examples of Elkin, Apple, and Barthelme, remain insufficient in moral and antinomian force as well as in the energy of emancipation. It is not enough for these three subjects of my study, for example, merely to participate in or accept the world of disorder and chance to be able to enjoy its small pleasures for oneself. It is not enough merely to recover one's humanity within disillusionment, and it is not enough merely to express the range of one's "minor, banal dissatisfactions," to continue with Wilde's definition, or to express "not anomie or accidie or dread but a muted series of irritations, frustrations, and bafflements" amidst that death of con-sciousness, a death which "may explain the concern with the apocalyptic in much recent fiction or with the self-abnegations of the minimalist and the alea-tory in painting and music" (15–16, 129, 165, 170–78). And that is why the current "minimalist" fiction of, say, Raymond Carver or Frederick Barthelme— sometimes seen as the proper successor to post-modernism—seems to pale beside the new synthesis Fowles, Gardner, and Mailer have been approaching since the 1960s. Such "minimalism" (and I want to include here those variants that Gardner identified in *The Art of Fiction* [1983] arising from the suppression of technique or style—or any artistic modification of reality—as well as the suppression of sublimity, ideology, or morality by a kind of surface, "super"- or "photo"-realism) is closer to the hermetic spirit of post-modernism, not nearly so bold a challenge to that spirit nor so dynamic an adaptation of technique.

The interest and scepticism of Scholes and Hassan, among others, are important because they help us to understand the direction in which the work of Fowles, Gardner, and Mailer seems to be taking us. These sceptical critics are of course sometimes writing about different authors and literatures, they discuss in the course of their books a variety of issues, but on the issue of historical engagement as bold, ethical challenge they generally agree. From one point of view the sceptics may be wrong, but their positions on that issue—their desire to "rescue the referent" and return art and theory to praxis—are similar. As Scholes expresses it in *Fabulation and Metafiction:*

> The lesson is clear. . . . Alienation is simply the price we pay for civilization. . . . Having reached the point where we understand this, we can see that the great task of the human imagination for the present time is to generate, in literature and in life, systems that bring human desires into closer harmony with the systems operating in the whole cosmos. . . . It is now time for man to turn civilization in the direction of integration and away from alienation, to bring human life back into harmony with the universe.

This is the task Fowles, Gardner, and Mailer have undertaken with varying degrees of success, and it is this undertaking that makes them worthy of our choice and attention if we are to understand the themes and forms that may be superseding post-modernism itself. Scholes continues: "For fiction, self-reflection is a narcissistic way of avoiding this great task. It produces a certain kind of pleasure, no doubt, this masturbatory reveling in self-scrutiny; but it also generates great feelings of guilt—not because what it is doing is bad, but because of what it is avoiding" (213–18).

If Scholes sees "signs of faith in something" in the "obsessive ingenuity" of Pynchon, the anger of Coover, the energy and inventiveness of Barth, he also sees the birth throes of a new artistic epoch when these "marvelous monsters, like leviathans and pachyderms" will go the way of woolly mammoths whose environment grows "more hostile to them every day." As the time of these "great and gaudy creatures" ends, humanity seems increasingly aware that "history is real and . . . we are in it": a condition of consciousness that grows more alien to self-reflexive fiction every day (209, 212).

Likewise, Hassan's similar scepticism is expressed in the conclusion of his study of the avant-garde, *The Dismemberment of Orpheus*. Hassan believes that the necessary "reign of terror, wonder, and burlesque in our age," which culminated recently in America, connects contemporary fiction to the whole post-modern spirit in Western art, politics, science, and morality. But that spirit is itself merely the birth throe of a new epoch. We are witness in America and Western culture generally, Hassan argues, to "the renewal of shapes" that strain "the structure of human life." Hassan concludes:

> I can only hope that after self-parody, self-subversion, and self-transcendence, after the pride and revulsion of anti-art will have gone their way, art may move toward a redeemed imagination, commensurate with the full mystery of human consciousness. Neither more nor less. Our revels then will have ended. Everyone then his own magician, and no man a magician alone. (256)

2

John Fowles: The Magician as Teacher

> *Cöet had been a mirror, and the existence he was returning to sat mercilessly reflected and dissected in its surface . . . and how shabby it now looked, how insipid and anodyne, how safe. . . . One killed all risk, one refused all challenge, and so one became an artificial man. The old man's secret, not letting anything stand between self and expression; which wasn't a question of outward artistic aims, mere styles and techniques and themes. But how you did it; how wholly, how bravely you faced up to the constant recasting of yourself. . . .*
>
> *He had a dreadful vision of being in a dead end, born into a period of art history future ages would dismiss as a desert; as Constable and Turner and the Norwich School had degenerated into the barren academicism of the midcentury and later. Art had always gone in waves. Who knew if the late twentieth century might not be one of its most cavernous troughs? He knew the old man's answer: it was. Or it was unless you fought bloody tooth and fucking nail against some of its most cherished values and supposed victories.*
>
> John Fowles, *The Ebony Tower*

Few fiction writers in England or America have met the challenge of "nonreferential" contemporary fiction and theory in such a head-on manner as John Fowles. One would be hard put to find another major British writer who is so dextrous in his use of metafictional and fabulative technique, yet who is so determined to attach technique to the moral dilemmas and choices in our world.[1] If such later fictions as *The French Lieutenant's Woman* (1969), *The Ebony Tower* (1974), *Mantissa* (1982), and *A Maggot* (1985) further displayed Fowles' knowledge of avant-garde theory and his skill in technique, *The Magus,* written in the 1950s, first published in 1965, and revised in 1977, is in the vanguard of post-war British experimental fictions. Fowles created in this instance a modern fable of one man's personal transformation through moral awakening. Moral regeneration and its attendant values in this novel (e.g., individual freedom, responsibility for others, love, and integrity through self-knowledge) are expressed through an intricately structured drama in which the reader—tempted, fooled, and led through a labyrinth of conflicting "realities"—shares in the fictional hero Nicholas Urfe's confusion, manipulation, and growth. In this early novel Fowles establishes the relationship between structure and ethic and lays the foundation for his future themes and narrative devices.

There are numerous passages in Fowles' work where he addresses the problems of abstraction versus realism, life versus art, form versus content, and theory versus practice. I'll take three examples from *The Aristos, The Ebony Tower,* and *Mantissa* to demonstrate Fowles' sustained concern for contemporary theoretical issues and his hope that art, like "whole species of feeling" as the magician will say in *The Magus,* not die out of human life, not become meaningless, detached technique.

In *The Aristos: A Self-Portrait in Ideas* (1964/1970), a collection of aphorisms that serve as indicators of the thematic issues in Fowles' fiction, Fowles admits that neither science nor art creates *the* reality (a vast disconnection and incoherence). But he does look to art as *a* reality, as an interpretation in some degree of the collective reality that so deeply concerns us. An artistic reality represents a structuring or making of a human reality within the larger incoherence. Yet as soon as we reduce an artistic reality to one system or formula, as soon as we "scientize" art, we reduce it to something less mysterious and complex than it really is. And what it is "constantly surpasses whatever science or the craft of the art might have foretold."[2]

Like the search for a single best system of analysis, the search for a unique style and form at the expense of content—what Fowles calls the "new rococo"— is a means of dangerously distancing ourselves both from apparent incoherencies of cosmic reality as well as from man-made social realities. Fowles argues for the possibility that art comes deeply from "humanity, history, time," and is infinitely more complex than either the scientific or the therapeutic. Our recent preoccupation with style, Fowles believes, devalues thought and "human moral content." "Even in didactic art the pursuit is much more of the right aesthetic or artistic expression of the moral than the moral itself"; therefore, Fowles argues, morality "becomes a kind of ability to convey" (146–47).

> The great eighteenth-century rococo arts were the visual and aural ones; the style was characterized by great facility, a desire to charm the bored and jaded palate, to amuse by decoration rather than by content—indeed serious content was eschewed. We see all these old tricks writ new in our modern arts, with their brilliantly pointless dialogues, their vivid

description of things not worth describing, their elegant vacuity, their fascination with the synthetic and their distaste for the natural. . . .

We have used words in all the extreme ways, sounds in all the extreme ways, shapes and colours in all the extreme ways, all that remains is to use them within the bounds of the extreme ways already developed. We have reached the end of our field. Now we must come back, and discover other occupations than reaching the end of fields. . . . What will matter finally is intention; not instrumentation. (200, 203)

The conflict between the rococo (or decorative) and the expressive, as a part of the theme of the separation of art from life, is developed further in *The Ebony Tower*. In the title story, a young artist-critic David Williams reflects on what he has learned from several days of exposure to Henry Breasley, an infamous old master painter and renegade from the modern artistic and social scene:

Perhaps it was happening in the other arts—in writing, music. David did not know. All he felt was a distress, a nausea, at his own. Castration. The triumph of the eunuch. He saw, how well he saw behind the clumsiness of the old man's attack; that sneer at *Guernica*. Turning away from nature and reality had atrociously distorted the relationship between painter and audience; now one painted for intellects and theories. Not people; and worst of all, not for oneself. Of course it paid dividends, in economic and vogue terms, but what had really been set up by this jettisoning of the human body and its natural physical perceptions was a vicious spiral, a vortex, a drain to nothingness, to a painter and a critic agreed on only one thing: that only they exist and have value. . . .

One sheltered behind notions of staying "open" to contemporary currents; forgetting the enormously increased velocity of progress and acceptance, how quickly now the avant-garde became *art pompier;* the daring platitudinous. It was not just his own brand of abstraction that was at fault, but the whole headlong postwar chain, abstract expressionism, neoprimitivism, Op Art and pop art, conceptualism, photorealism . . . *il faut copuer la racine,* all right. But such rootlessness, orbiting in frozen outer space, cannot have been meant. They were like lemmings, at the mercy of a suicidal drive, seeking *Lebensraum* in an arctic sea; in a bottomless night, blind to everything but their own illusions.[3]

More recently in *Mantissa* Fowles parodies the post-modern novel—complete with its writer-persona Miles Green, who lies in bed recovering from a brain aneurysm throughout, who steps out of the book and points to the very page number the reader is on, and whose own gray matter is the only setting for the novel. Perfectly in tune with its object, this parody is at once a discourse on current fiction and on his own writing in particular. To be sure, it is a *mantissae* ("an addition of comparatively small importance, especially to a literary effort or discourse," as Fowles' footnote tells us), just as the post-modern novel itself may be. Yet this little addition is revealing. Fowles enumerates and spoofs his own techniques. The novel is full of allusions to the characters and plots of his own novels; and in spoofing them, he treats his own work as if it were one more system of nonreferential (or intrareferential) texts. Fowles is also aware of the wide-ranging negative criticisms he has attracted, and the way Fowles glories in cataloguing them is one of the most humorous qualities of this playful little tour de force: he is backward in his regard of love as opposed to sex, he is a hopelessly outdated male chauvinist, his women are mere archetypes and *Doppelgängers,* his values are anachronistic, he studs his work with elitist allusions, he is crudely repetitious, he is incapable of adjusting to contemporary realities, and so on. But Miles' defense of post-modernism is perhaps the best comment on Fowles' real feelings (ironically presented) about the state of the novel today:

> What do you think modernism is about? Let alone post-modernism. Even the dumbest students know it's a reflexive medium now, not a reflective one. . . . Serious modern fiction has only one subject: the difficulty of writing serious modern fiction. First, it has [to be] fully accepted that it is only fiction, can only be fiction, will never be anything but fiction, and therefore has no business at all tampering with real life or reality. . . . Second, the natural consequence of this is that writing about fiction has become far more important. At the creative level there is in any case no connection whatever between author and text. . . . The deconstructivists have proved that beyond a shadow of a doubt. . . . Our one priority now is mode of discourse, function of discourse, status of discourse. Its metaphoricality, its disconnectedness, its totally ateleological self-containedness.

"I dislike so much the general literary climate in Britain," Fowles said in one of his most recent interviews, "that criticism here doesn't bother me much."[4]

Unlike his character Miles Green, Fowles has devoted his work to attaching art (the realm of internal realities) to external realities. As a sort of Ur-text that expresses an ethic to which experimental form is still subordinated, *The Magus,* through its metafictional design and themes, amounts to a careful definition of what in human behavior today we may begin to see as immoral and moral. In *The Aristos* Fowles clarifies his distinction between traditional codes of behavior (those which society or authority imposes as absolute without justification beyond tradition) and existential codes of behavior (those which reject the merely traditional in favor of the personal discovery of moral commitments, discoveries he associates with Socrates, Kierkegaard, and Sartre).[5] If the world represents the responsible person's stage for moral action, art is the aesthetic arena in which that person may *discover* avenues of self-definition and moral action.

Fowles argues, then, in *The Aristos* and *The Magus,* against that relativism that Alasdair MacIntyre identified as "emotivism." It is all too easy, on the one hand, to confuse local moral utterance at Cambridge, the Hanoverian court, or any other time or place with moral utterance as such; just as it is too easy to deny, on the other hand, the possibility of any impersonal moral standards that can be rationally justified. Emotivism, that denial of standards, has itself become a localized ethic (local to late twentieth-century Anglo-American thought) taken to be universally current: all moral argument is nothing but a mask of personal preferences. MacIntyre calls this currency "a grave cultural loss" and "degeneration" most of all because it obliterates any genuine distinction between "manipulative and non-manipulative social relations," and it validates the self-less, role-playing persona. He connects this phenomenon of emotivism, beyond Nietzsche and Sartre, to the social science methodological canon, which argues for the separation of "fact" from evaluation. That canon thereby negates the possibility of recognizing the "fact," for example, that someone failed to be courageous or just.[6]

In *The Magus,* Fowles ridicules an ethic of voguish avant-gardism (i.e., emotivism), a simplistic anti-establishment pose like that of the Oxford Les Hommes Revoltes with whom the hero Urfe once drank sherry and mistook "a certain kind of inconsequential behavior" for existentialism. Fully aware, however, of the current confusion between Sunday-School moralism and the more sophisticated morality the twentieth century seems to demand of us, Fowles repeatedly establishes in *The Magus* that level of local ethical consciousness which he is *not* espousing: the simple-minded boarding-school moralism of social intercourse and class mannerism which, indeed, can blind one to deeper ethical perceptions. It is that simple-minded morality that Gerald Graff also has in mind when he writes of "the genteel schoolmarm theory of literature" and "prettified didacticism" that is so easily (and rightly) ridiculed.[7] Urfe refers to this level of ethical consciousness as his own "quaint morality," a form of self-delusion that precedes his personal awakening through the magician's masque. This quaint level of ethical consciousness is typified by a host of minor characters in the novel. One example is Urfe's military father who "in lieu of an intellect . . . accumulated an armoury of capitalized key words like Discipline and Tradition and Responsibility" to "kosh" anyone who disagreed with him. Likewise, the ex-officer Mitford with his class-snobbish "barbarism," his mask of tics, preenings, and "mess mannerisms" (which Urfe admits "caricature certain qualities in myself") is another example, both early and late in the novel. Similarly, the succession of principals, teachers, and interviewers from the British boarding school system, as well as the Embassy Officials—who promote the old roles and games of "Old Country, the Queen, the Public School, Oxbridge, the Right Accent, People Like Us"—all serve to warn readers away from exactly the conventions and moralisms so often charged against "referential" or "moral" novelists. As Urfe says, even the setting plays its role on this point. "Greece . . . made conventional English notions of morality, of what was moral and immoral ridiculous."[8] But more important to the design of the novel, Urfe's reaction to his latest lover Alison suggests this distinction of moralities best. He is astonished that her honesty in relationships could be coupled with her capacity for petty theft and sexual license. Her breaches of social decorum are what trouble him more than his own emotional isolation from Alison, his own pretenses in their relationship, and his desire to "hurt her." As Mrs. de Seitas will say near the end of the novel, by such "Queen Anne morality" of received ideas and manners excusable in less dangerous times, even Conchis' whole masque would be immoral.

It is this quaint morality and pious arrogance—so readily mistaken, or set up, for ethical consciousness—that Fowles uses as a foil to the alternative kind of ethical vision he expresses in *The Magus* as a positive though hard-earned human value. That sophisticated level of morality will be defined throughout this long novel, but it is (if I may summarize at this point with some risk of oversimplifying) defined in part by its opposite, by the truly sinister behavior Urfe will discover as he participates in Conchis' masque. Fowles' definition of immorality is twofold. A series of unconscious, mechanical, and selfish characters, first, depict for us concretely that hardened egocentricity which is particularly blind to interrelationships between people, things, and events. Such characters take the reader closer to the heart of the matter by clarifying the distinction between social piety and personal evil. Before his awakening begins, the hero himself is such a selfish character who views love as a merely pleasing sexual game he despises, who "narcissistically" mistakes "dropping a girl" for "love of freedom," and who wears his "Chesterfieldian mask" to manipulate a succession of lovers through neat beginnings and endings of liaisons, and whom Alison describes as: "a filthy selfish bastard who can't even think of anything except number one. Because nothing can hurt you, Nicko. Deep down, where it counts. You've built your life so that nothing can ever reach you" (21, 274).

More sinister yet is that truly destructive behavior which violates others either by removing possibilities of freedom or, in its extreme development, by that outright imprisonment and torture which have always marked tyranny. Perhaps we can see already how closely these two kinds of "immorality" are connected, and how, indeed, each level of ethical unconsciousness feeds the other. The person stuck in his or her Sunday-School morality, for example, is likely to be unconscious of any morality beyond social manners and piety. Such mere moralism is best maintained by one unaware of any deeper connections, or responsibilities, between oneself and others. And such selfishness in turn makes the violation of others easier than does a heightened awareness of the rights, aspirations, or the life in other human beings. The clerk Clegg in Fowles' *The Collector,* for example, assumes he is thinking "nothing nasty" about his captive Miranda, but is also able to imprison the object of his fantasies in his "priest's chapel" and cause her death. Or, in *The Magus* the extreme development of the selfish and deadened automaton is the Nazi Colonel Wimmel in whose eyes there is no sympathy, nothing but "assessment and calculation . . . the eyes of a machine," even an educated machine who claims love of Shakespeare, Goethe, and the musical genius of Germany, but who as a machine can learn nothing from them.

It is Maurice Conchis (pronounced "conscious"), creator of the masque, who reminds Urfe of the disastrous results of such moralism, egotism, and ignorant arrogance combined. It is, for example, the simple-minded adaption of cultural fantasy, ideal, and slogan that led to both world wars and all their horrors:

> I saw that this cataclysm must be an expiation for some barbarous crime of civilization, some terrible human lie. What the lie was, I had too little knowledge of history or science to know then. I know now it was our believing that we were fulfilling some end, serving some plan—that all would come out well in the end because there was some great plan over all. Instead of reality. There is no plan. All is hazard. And the only thing that will preserve us is ourselves. (128–29).

Our preservation, that is, depends on human constructions of evil or good, on the choices we make, on the "history" we cause and live.

Fowles at times treats his characters' immoral tendencies and their levels of ethical unconsciousness with the subtlety of a novelist of manners, but he also makes it difficult for readers of even the most literal and relativistic tempers to avoid the ramifications of his thematic point. For at the heart of the novel lies Conchis' parable of the monstrous Nazi occupation of Greece. Here the hero journeys to that heart of darkness where human evil is absolute, where the definition of evil—extreme immorality—might grab the most philosophically hardened among us as if to say: Look at this, feel this! And then tell me all human acts are relative, all moralities "cultural constructs," all realities mere solipsistic modes of perception.

In the underworld of the masque the point is appropriately melodramatic against our prevailing relativism and solipsism. Here in the beast's maw lies the final evil in the human heart, ever awaiting its release into the world of human affairs and institutions. Conchis tells Urfe of his own descent into a Nazi torture chamber during the occupation of Greece.

> I think anyone but a doctor would have fainted. I should have liked to have fainted. The room was bare. In the middle was a table. Roped to the table was a young man. The cousin. He was naked except for a bloodstained singlet, and he had been badly burnt about the mouth and eyes. But I could see only one thing. Where his genitals should have been, there was nothing but a black-red hole. They had cut off his penis and scrotal sac. With a pair of wire-cutting shears.
>
> In one of the far corners another naked man lay on the floor. His face was on the ground and I could not see what they had done to him. He too was apparently unconscious. I shall never forget the stillness of that room. There were three or four soldiers—soldiers! of course torturers, psychopathic sadists—in the room. One of them held a long iron stake. An electric fire was burning, lying on its back. Three of the men wore leather aprons like blacksmith's aprons, to keep their uniforms clean. There was a disgusting smell of excrement and urine. . . .
>
> I turned round and looked at Wimmel. The extraordinary thing was that he seemed the most human other person in the room. He looked tired and angry. Even a little disgusted. Ashamed at the mess his men had created.

He said in English, these men do this for pleasure. I do not. I wish, before they start on that
murderer there, that you will speak to him. . . .
He asked me if I thought he enjoyed such scenes. I did not answer. Then he said, I should
be very happy to sit at my headquarters. To have nothing to do but sign papers and enjoy the
beautiful classical monuments. You do not believe me. You think I am a sadist. I am not. I
am a realist. (425–26, 428)

It may be safe to assume that most readers surface as I did from that
moment in the novel, and several others such as the rape and disembowelment
of peasant women, blinking with horror. Fowles is asking whether we are
beyond the point where we can be suddenly awakened from our armchairs to the
knowledge that such things can be, indeed are even now as we read. Have we
arrived at the point where we deny the human choices behind such acts and
blame cosmic absurdity and mass insanity? Can we still make distinctions between the good and evil that human beings can do? Perhaps our answers to
Fowles' questions depend on our personal experiences of good and evil, or our
insulation from them. As Conchis put it to Urfe in speaking of Hitler's Germany:
"That was the tragedy. Not that one man had the courage to be evil. But that
millions had not the courage to be good" (132).
It is precisely this inability to distinguish between good and evil, between
humanity and monstrous inhumanity and all the subtle beginnings that lead to
such ends, that historically results in something far more sinister and destructive
than a cultural relativism; it results in the unleashing of every excess, every
horror mankind has witnessed or dreamed: "One of the greatest fallacies of our
time is that the Nazis rose to power because they imposed order on chaos,"
Conchis argues.

Precisely the opposite is true—they are successful because they imposed chaos on order. They
tore up the commandments, they denied the superego, what you will. They said, you may
persecute the minority, you may kill, you may torture. You may couple and breed without
love. They offered humanity all its great temptations. Nothing is true, everything is permitted.
(428)

Fowles' torture chamber scene is meant to reach us on two levels of experience and thereby to combine those two levels. It is his assumption as much as
it is Conchis' that the spectator's contemplation of the aesthetic object leads to
the spectator's contemplation of his or her life and the world in which that life
is lived. The two worlds are connected by Conchis, eventually by Urfe, by
Fowles over all, and finally, perhaps, by the reader. The connective agency is
the imagination, its memories, its powers of depiction and revelation, its power
to stir emotion.
Colonel Wimmel and his *die Raben* band of sadists are but the extreme yet
plausible result of that mechanical egotism, arrogance, blindness, and lack of

consciousness typified by Urfe's father, by Mitford, by Demetriades, by the boarding-school representatives, by political and theological slogans, and even by Urfe himself. But it is Urfe in this case who will be made to endure the lessons of history and the lessons of personal suffering at the hands of the magus who will help him transform himself into what, with all the limitations of the modern world and its theories of consciousness, might still be called an ethical being.

What are the sources of Urfe's transformation? The first source is of course his benefactor, Maurice Conchis. Conchis is the manipulator of realities and the creator of the enlightening art form. To the extent that Urfe is incapable of self-transformation, some magician/artist is required to guide the transforming process. And it takes a dedicated, thorough, and masterful artist to make the necessary drama. Conchis' fundamental assumption is that some new art form is required to renew art's power. His masque or "Metadrama" is a means to an ethical end—the moral regeneration of the hero who will, if he passes the tests, return to the world a new man, capable of gaining self-knowledge and ethical vision. This new art, like Greece itself, is like a mirror. "It makes you suffer," as Conchis puts it. "Then you learn." When Urfe responds, "To live alone?" Conchis replies, "To live. With what you are" (99). "Stupidity"—lack of self-knowledge, blindness to interrelationships—Conchis will later add, "is lethal." In this new art form it will be necessary to deal with the literal-mindedness of modern people, to temporarily turn fiction into "fact," as Conchis puts it, so that the fiction-fact can finally serve as metaphor for wider realities of self and world. Like a "novelist without a novel," Conchis will create a living drama to overcome our handicapped imaginations.

"I do not object to the principles of fiction," Conchis explains. "Simply that in print, in books, they remain mere principles. . . . What I am employing is a very new psychiatric technique . . . situation therapy" (231). If Conchis borrows techniques from psychiatry, he uses them as a necessary therapy with those for whom the written word no longer holds power. Earlier Urfe had reflected on the same problem for himself:

> We were equally tired, in mid-century, of cold sanity and hot blasphemy; of the over-cerebral and the over-faecal; the way out lay somewhere else. Words had lost their power, either for good or evil; still hung like a mist over the reality of action, distorting, misleading, castrating; but at least since Hitler and Hiroshima they were seen to be a mist, a flimsy superstructure. (19)

If, as Conchis says, the novel (and by extension any literary form) is to us "as dead as alchemy" (96), then the magician, like the artist Fowles, must also remove us temporarily from the contemporary world. Perhaps we are no more susceptible now to the necessary trials and wisdom in contemporary London than through the epic, novel, or drama. Urfe—a representative modern *and* mythic man—is but the first of Fowles' characters for whom some removal from Western urban culture is necessary. That removal—whether in *The Magus, The Ebony Tower,* or *Daniel Martin*—is not into a closed labyrinth, but into an aesthetic system that, as we will see, tends ever outward to external life. Conchis' domain at his Bourani estate is a world where the game is not only a game but a momentarily living metaphor ("the masque is only a metaphor," he reminds Urfe) for the processes by which one earns wisdom about one's place in and relationship to a larger community or world. Phraxos is "the world before the machine." And as Michael Bellamy has pointed out, the pastoral convention here is obvious. But Fowles, like Conchis, is combining the pastoral with the heroic. Both conventions remove the hero to a domain where we sense the "mysterious yet profound parity in all existence," as Bellamy puts it, that reconciles the enclosed private world and the public world.[9] It is this sense of parity, I would add, that also reconciles art or imagination with life. Stripped of his modern identity, marooned at sea or in hell, Urfe compares himself to Crusoe and to Adam, prepared for his journey in the labyrinth.

In his preface to the revised edition, Fowles makes this connection between the game and the world for his readers. He had considered calling the novel *The Godgame,* he tells us, in which Conchis would be a kind of god-as-gamesman. "I did intend Conchis to exhibit a series of masks representing human notions of God, from the supernatural to the jargon-ridden scientific. . . . And I wish there were some super-Conchis who could put the Arabs and the Israelis, or the Ulster Catholics and Protestants, through the same heuristic mill as Nicholas" (10).

That "heuristic mill" necessary in a cynical and literal-minded twentieth century is both a psychological process and an aesthetic process translated to modern conditions. It is, then, a mythic process of rebirth as well as a therapeutic adjustment of modern psychosis; it is based on the assumption that the surest road to psychic balance is through some process that reaches the human being's deepest roots of primitive terror, fantasy, and symbolic image-making. For example, the underlying structure of the novel, which lends aboriginal meaning to the masque, is the ancient quest of the hero.[10] That by-now-familiar seeker of enlarged consciousness who journeys in strange realms and underworlds suffers so that he may emerge with the boon to regenerate his decadent, atrophied race. Comparing himself to Ulysses, to Theseus, to Oedipus in search of his identity, Urfe is a man for whom a whole realm has been created so that he may regain his capacity for genuine, not merely abstract, feelings of excitement, mystery, and dread. This primary archetypal structure with all its traditional associations is Fowles' conscious craft, as he tells us in his preface when he writes of "the obvious influence of Jung, whose theories deeply interested me at the time" and from whom he was seeking "the deep pattern, and mood, of

such books" that remain with us "long after their initial impressions and memories wane" (6). We can begin to see now that if in *The Magus* Conchis is the
first source and cause of the hero's education and transformation, then the nature
of the archetypal journey itself is the second.

Earlier in *The Aristos,* Fowles has argued that our necessary "synoptic
education" (one that makes for a "world view" of connections and interrelationships) must take place in our own "mental territory" where our psychic body of
emotions, ideas, and beliefs (akin to the Jungian complex) that governs our
social behavior lives and hides from us. Inward education will finally make us
ask who we are, what our duties are to ourselves and others, what we mean by
love and guilt, and how well we strike a balance between extremes. It is the
discontent that follows such education that gives us a sense of "moral purpose"
(181–182).

To take a later example of inward education through quest, Dan and his
past lover Jane will discover in *Daniel Martin* (1977) on their journey—another
quest for wholeness of vision, life, moral awareness—that the modern man or
woman is ever forced to move into some retreat or domain, some forest of the
mind, some (once sacred) territory where the hero, a kind of latter-day Robin
Hood in flight from the vanities of science and modern life, finds the ancient
rituals of self-transformation. This later novel is Fowles' journey to Egypt, his
own retelling of the Isis-Osiris myth, which again opposes the merely playful,
the timely, the conventional, the pretended, the merely formalistic, to the moral,
the timeless, the risky, and the genuine. Likewise, the moral problem before the
hero and heroine is to reconcile their past, present, and future into a timeless
whole reflected by the few transcendent moments recalled during the story.
Such moments are represented by the sense of ecstatic unity Dan, Jane, Nan,
and Anthony experience during their night swim at Tarquinia, as well as by
what Fowles calls "the archetypal moment" of the English imagination—the
moment of the retreat of self into the sacred valley, be it Tsankawi, New
Mexico, a Devon farm, or some psychic parallel of the *bonne vaux*. During the
novel first the hero and then the heroine move through a series of such momentary retreats from the temporality of the urban machine age. Their retreatings
climax with their journey together to Egypt and, ultimately, to Palymra in Syria,
the ruined city of the dead where they meet the magus-Tiresias (in the guise of
Prof. Kirnberger). Here, at the furthest point of the journey, as Susan Klemtner
put it, all dualisms are integrated into a nonpolar whole, the moral center of the
quest.[11]

But here again that retreat is not an escape, not a fleeing of the world any
more than fiction is. What Lentricchia called Kenneth Burke's and Antonio
Gramsci's argument for the "socially and politically enmeshed character of the
intellectual" is Fowles', and his character Dan's, final attitude. Like Burke,
Fowles extends the alienation of Marxism beyond the economic and working

class levels to include the political and cultural, the intellectual and the artist. This extension of alienation is what Dan (like Urfe) experiences and works through, and it is in part what the novel's epigraph from Gramsci refers to: "The crisis consists precisely in the fact that the old is dying and the new cannot be born; in this interregnum a great variety of morbid symptoms appear."

Simon Loveday, in his excellent study *The Romances of John Fowles,* contributes to the points I am developing here. Fowles' relationship to the romance tradition helps us to better understand his uses of intensity, mystery, polarization, myth, and magic. More importantly, we might understand that the quest narrative is also the classic romance narrative, the goal of which is redemption. Moreover, as the genre of dissidence, romance expresses alienation and discontent and, I might add, responds by its very nature to stasis and hegemony.[12]

Ancient elements of the quest encourage the transformation of perception and consciousness. Like his mythic progenitors, Urfe journeys in a new world. From the moment he arrives in Greece, he feels like one who has journeyed to Mars or taken a trip through the looking glass, "as gladly and expectantly disoriented, as happily and alertly alone, as Alice in Wonderland." Here are strange new beauties, new harmonies of nature, new premonitions of health, he tells us. As if about to undergo "an interrogation under arc lights" he already feels his "old self began to know that it wouldn't be able to hold out" here. On Phraxos itself, he meets his guide. Trickster, fool, teacher, master of revels, compared variously to Zeus, God, and Prospero, Conchis is the wise old man who will guide the hero to self-awareness, the acceptance of hazard and mystery, the self-less understanding of freedom and love, and the sense of responsibility such knowledge and acceptance give to the individual alive in a richly interconnected world.[13]

Yet a third source of transformation must reside within the hero himself as a potential, a ripeness for personal evolution. Urfe had gathered so many personal illusions about himself—he is a poet, the best approach to life is cynicism, etc.—that even long before the masque as far back as Oxford he sensed that he was "not the person I wanted to be," that he was seeking some "Socratic honesty," something more that mere revolt "against one's past," some person or thing to love. "I needed a new land, a new race, a new language" (15, 17, 19). His potential, therefore, to reconstruct a self or identity is enormous from the start, and from the beginning of his removal to Greece, everything from British morality to his own contemplated suicide (a "Mercutio death" or aesthetic pose) seems ridiculous and devoid of moral content (61–62).

It is in part 2 of the novel, the book of mysteries, that the restructuring of the self begins in earnest when Conchis introduces Urfe into the domain of Bourani (translated as "skull" or "Death and Water"). At this stage it is the carefully placed passage from Eliot, which Urfe "discovered," that foretells the goal of the quest:

> We shall not cease from exploration
> And the end of all our exploring
> Will be to arrive where we started
> And know the place for the first time (69)

The next five hundred pages will take the reader with Urfe through the process of exploration, but in the conclusion of the tale Eliot's lines will reverberate, just as the nature and process of the quest reverberates in Pound's "discovered" lines:

> This sound came in the dark
> First must thou go the road
>   to hell
> And to the bower of Ceres' daughter Proserpine
> . . . to see Tiresias
> Eyeless that was, a shade, that is in hell
> So full of knowing. . . .
> Ere thou come to thy road's end (60–70)

It is, then, to Lily's bower, daughter of Ceres-de-Seitas, and the domain of Tiresias-Conchis that Urfe, at the mythic level of the text, must go. Here the magician will be the True Father, the teacher who opposes the False Father, Urfe's dogmatic and obtuse father whose early death freed the orphaned hero to seek a wise father and a true identity. The old man as a true benefactor will spare no expense, no care, no wit, no pain to create the aesthetic and psychic realities for transformation. Conchis is a man who has come back from the underworld of human evil, a rare survivor with a rare message (so full of knowing), as are many survivors of Nazi and other historical horrors. He chooses to turn his resources to the creation of a fictive world that will teach the same lessons, one by one, as Mrs. de Seitas ultimately tells Urfe, to a series of men whom he discovers to be ready for regeneration. One might do worse, less comprehensible things with one's personal fortune. Compared to what Conchis and the Greeks suffered under the Nazis, the successive heroes in the masques endure their moral transformations in relative safety. Their psychological and existential anxieties in the process most of us would choose over torture, murder, and oppression.

Unlike Clegg in *The Collector* who traps and manipulates Miranda to fulfill his puerile fantasies, Conchis runs his heroes through the mill for their own and society's benefit. Conchis leads Urfe to a level of consciousness that Urfe himself has blunderingly sought and that is finally applicable to our daily lives and relationships. Such wisdom is earned or suffered, but that suffering mirrors the very suffering Urfe has inflicted on others. What he suffers at Lily's hands—temptress, virgin, whore, "eternal source of desire . . . without . . . physical and psychological flaw," as Urfe describes her, the *anima* of the archetype—duplicates both Alison's ordeal at Urfe's hands, and the ordeals we humans inflict on one another.

What I have called the primary archetypal structure of *The Magus,* the mythic quest motif, Fowles makes relevant to twentieth-century conditions through a secondary layer of structure: the structure of Conchis' masque, which Urfe calls "the strangest maze in Europe." This secondary structure is likewise essential to the transformation. It is also the greatest technical achievement of the novel, for it has a remarkable aesthetic unity and it is delicately interwoven with the primary structure. This secondary structure of the masque operates on at least two levels of dramatic representation itself: (1) a series of specific tests or trials based on certain realities of the modern world, and (2) a series of parables operating like *entràctes* within the stages of the labyrinthine drama and drawing connections between the hero's trials, moments in modern history, and moments in Urfe's personal history. Urfe's past, his guilt, his ignorance, his selfishness, are all clarified and examined by Conchis' allusiveness, his hints at connections between the past, Urfe's life in London, and the artificial labyrinth he has created for his apprentice.

On the first level of dramatic representation, the trials of the labyrinth take the hero through a series of four acts, or successive "realities," that lead outward toward the masque's ultimately heuristic goal. The first act, roughly the first two hundred pages, disrupts, disorients, and resonates to the primary or mythic level of the transforming process. A series of mythic characters and situations inspire in the hero "a distinct primitive terror" (as does the Priapus in the garden), and introduce the important theme of the mystery in artifice and in life.

With its affirmation of life and its heightening of perceptions, mystery supplies that source of energy which opposes modern cynicism. Such at least is Conchis' early hint when he takes Urfe snorkeling: "For him it [the undersea] was like a gigantic acrostic, an alchemist's shop where each object had a mysterious value, an inner history that had to be deduced, unravelled, guessed at. He made natural history sound and feel like something central and poetic; not an activity for Scoutmasters and the butt for *Punch* jokes" (145). One duty of the masque will be to restore that which modern humanity has lost: "Remember that you have paid a price: that of a world rich in mystery and delicate emotion. It is not only species of animal that die, but whole species of feeling," Conchis says (149). Such loss has debilitated our psychic energy for the task of attaining higher consciousness, for the final value of mystery is that "mystery has energy. It pours into whoever seeks an answer to it" (235). In *The Aristos* Fowles had affirmed his belief that the best possible situation for us is to live in mystery. Like hazard, mystery is fundamental to our awareness of any reality beyond ourselves and a source of power to us. Mystery is, therefore, an evolutionary necessity. It provides increased self-knowledge and ethical vision (20, 108, 118). The mystery theme in Fowles also provides another example of where his craft and themes coincide with post-modernism. One commonly repeated goal of post-modern thought is to "defamiliarize" the familiar so that we can see it new, reexamine it. The magician is both traditionally and, in this case, a perfectly suited strategy to "defamiliarize" what we take for granted or truth.

As important as the mystery theme in this first act of the masque are two parables that will draw parallels between Conchis' development and Urfe's, and prepare the hero for the next corridor of the labyrinth. First, Conchis' "fairy story" of his love for Lily and the horrors of the First World War, followed by his test of Urfe with poisoned molars, establish the hero's "passion to exist" despite the psychosis and absurdity in the modern world. Second, the parable of Deukans, the aesthete, collector, and recluse, demonstrates the way in which detached aestheticism "extinguishes the moral instinct" and makes men like Deukans "the most abnormal" of all. Conchis argues that such a life breeds psychosis, social inequity, greed, and mass mediocrity (186).

The second act of the masque or labyrinth begins after the first two hundred pages when "Lily" is unmasked and presented as "Julie," and with her twin sister becomes a mysterious double figure Julie-June. Believing, as most readers would, that this change represents cessation of the masque, Urfe becomes more infatuated with the woman now, his Ariadne, his ideal-woman-in-reality. Conchis begins to look like a crafty old fool who gets his joy from the voyeuristic pleasures of the metadrama. But that vision rests on tenuous beliefs because here Conchis hypnotizes Urfe, and quite possibly drugs him, into a state of mind where Urfe experiences the ecstasy and power of psychic transformation, a "fountain" of pure energy through which one feels "the total inter-relationship of the all." So not only is the energy of mystery further confirmed in this act, but Urfe experiences the first feelings of an important lesson to come: ultimately reality is simply Being, but it is only human beings who can create social order, meaning, good, or evil within amoral Being (238–39).

An equally important event in this second act is the first movement of the masque outward toward the external world, toward a point where world and masque interact and reflect one another, and where the hero's readiness, or need, of further trials is tested. Urfe goes to mainland Greece to meet Alison. But fascinated by the Julie-ideal, he is unable to accept reality-as-Alison. She is too weak, too human, too real. "Don't always sit so in judgment on everything I say, everything I do," Alison pleads. "I can't help being what I am" (252). As trapped by the fantasy of the masque as by his inability to confront reality honestly, lying to Alison about syphilis so that he can control the terms of their reunion, Urfe still imagines "lying in the same position with Julie, and I thought

I knew it would be infinitely disturbing and infinitely more passionate; not familiar, not aching with fatigue, hot, a bit sweaty . . . some cheapened word like randy; but white hot, mysterious, overwhelming passion" (263–64).

Urfe is therefore found wanting amidst his trials and tests, not *conscious* enough to return to the world and act upon lessons learned and perceptions gained in the living metaphor of his ordeal. Though Parnassus was a place where "anything but the truth [was] a mind sore" and where love is a risky part of truth, it "rushed on" him that he still: "wanted to keep her *and* . . . to keep—or to find—Julie. It wasn't that I wanted one more than the other, I wanted both" (269–70).

Unable to accept what Alison calls the "dreadful responsibility of having to live with someone who loves you," unable to tell the truth about his Parnassus experience to Conchis and Julie upon his return to Bourani, Urfe is equally unable to distinguish between the gift, the meaning if you will, that the artificial bears *to* the real. Conchis had earlier spoken of that gift when showing Urfe a Bonnard: "Sunlight. A naked girl. A chair. A towel, a bidet. A tiled floor. A little dog. And he gives the whole of existence a reason." At that moment Urfe sees it too: "It was an unforgettable painting; it set a dense golden halo of light round the most trivial of moments, so that the moment, and all such moments, would never be completely trivial again" (97). Conchis intends that each selfish young man passing through the masque-ordeal should become aware of such moments, see even the masque itself as "one of those experiences [that] so possesses you that the one thing you cannot tolerate is the thought of their not being in some way for ever present" (310)

Urfe enters the third act of the magician's masque upon his return to Bourani. Now Julie will play schizophrenic to Conchis' psychiatrist. But Conchis' commentary on her illness reflects the mental instability of the hero more than of the woman, for it is Urfe who has proven his inability to distinguish between the work of art and the lived life: "She will make her first valid step back towards normality when one day she stops and says, This is not the real world. These are not real relationships" (282). Through a series of false endings and Alison's pretended suicide, Urfe comes to understand in this third act his own "crime and guilt" both in violating the love and trust of others and in violating the metaphorical and moral connections between the aesthetic domain and the world he lived in. There will be no escape for the conscious man from the responsibilities imposed by the experience of the godgame.

In this stage of the labyrinth the events and parables both become increasingly more threatening and, through the false endings, move the hero and the reader ever closer to the external reality. The first parable is of Henrich the blind hermit who is visited in his lunacy by God. Here the hero learns of one approach to enlivening reality, "that great passive monster," with the "mysterious vigor" of the eternal in the present: the total, "lunatic" immersion of one's identity in the eternal moment that "endures when all the other noises, objects, all the dull street, have sunk into dust and oblivion," as Conchis earlier had described such moments. If one may be able thereby to cause a mysterious reality "to break through the net of science," to defeat the "vanities of our age" (our rationalism, our psychoanalysis, our classifications, our aetiologies) one must follow the path of a blind hermit to do so, and deny any mystery in the mundane, man-made world as much as one's ethical responsibilities toward it.

The second parable in this third act, the Nazi occupation that all of Urfe's later investigations and feelings will suggest is the only one based on real incidents from Conchis' life, ramifies the historical consequences of that selfishness, hollowness, egotism, and self-deception that has characterized Urfe's personal past. Both the parable of atrocities and the news of Alison's death work together now to teach the hero a new definition of freedom. The Nazi phenomenon proves that freedom is the only priceless thing, the "Eleutheria!" of the tortured guerrilla's screams. It is the condition from which all choices are made. If hazard represents the principle in the essence of things and in inhuman order beyond morality, the freedom to choose, operating within hazard, is the fundamentally human act which makes order or disorder of reality.

In *The Aristos* Fowles calls freedom "man's magnetic north," and the highest human good. Fowles argues that freedom is the source of human evolution and survival. Between the limits of hazard, the purpose of which is to "force us to evolve," and the limits of totalitarianism, the human and social tendency toward "unipolar conformity," we have "relative freedom" to evolve toward greater relative freedom. But in order to so evolve and to survive, we need more training in what is good and what is evil. That training, of course, is the function of the godgame. Our judgments may be meaningless beyond the human sphere, Fowles argues, but they are crucial within it. So it is part of our evolutionary function for Fowles that we exercise our freedom to choose between good and evil. A good act is an act that "institutes more freedom," and such acts are the basis of a just society. Acts against injustice and inequality are acts of "hygiene" (26, 42, 61, 76–77, 80–82, 121).

Later in his career, Fowles will develop the theme of freedom especially in contemporary social contexts. If again in *Daniel Martin* the hero Dan and heroine Jane are wiser in the end, they still must continue the journey to self-knowledge and choose freely each day a moral life. But the timeless values sought are not some version of an existential present; the values are a more mystical, more primitive, and simple past-present-future toward which Fowles' heroes and heroines more recently journey. Whether this goal is a reflection of Fowles' studies of Zen Buddhism is open to speculation. *Daniel Martin,* though its critics agree it is flawed, does represent a continuing development of previous themes, particularly the theme of the relationship between the individual and the community, hence the presiding spirits of Lukacs and Gramsci. In this novel Fowles emphasizes more emphatically the dangerous insufficiency of existential freedom. Such freedom is no longer enough; it is too exclusively obsessed with personal destiny. It is our obsession with personal destiny in all its forms that Fowles now argues is guaranteed to make us "stink in the nostrils of history." The wholeness Fowles seeks, however, is still best sought through art by the individual imagination. It is in the voyage into self, through the vehicle of art (here the book that Dan is writing and we reading) that one discovers the unity that reality seldom provides, but in which one also discovers relationships and responsibilities beyond the self. That is also the point of the Seferis quote (echoing Urfe) near the end of the novel. Morally, as magnetically, there is only one pole "in the geography of the mind's total being; and even though it is set in an arctic where no incarnate mind can exist."[14]

In the earlier prototypical novel, Urfe also learns that freedom is not the selfish fleeing of relations or love, not the "emotional triumph" of "escape," as he once defined it, from the quotidian or from honesty and fidelity toward others. On the contrary, such escape is violation and death. Deep in the maze news of Alison's death affects Urfe powerfully ("to my horror I began to cry") and leads him to a more clear-headed mistrust of all the enchanting players in Conchis' troupe. "And a great cloud of black guilt, knowledge of my atrocious selfishness, settled on me. . . . My monstrous crime was Adam's, the oldest and most vicious of all male selfishness: to have imposed the role I needed from Alison on her real self" (399–400). But his education through act 3 is far from complete, for he is still able to divorce the moral from the aesthetic two days later: "I had begun to absorb the fact of Alison's death; that is, had begun to edge it out of the moral world into the aesthetic, where it was easier to live with. . . . By this characteristic twentieth-century retreat from content into form, from meaning into appearance, from ethics into aesthetics, from *aqua* into *unda,* I dulled the pain of that accusing death" (491–92).[15]

As Conchis now puts it, "You do not know my meaning yet," and hence the necessity of act 4. Beginning with one more pretense that the revels have ended, and finishing with the disintoxication ceremony, this final stage returns Urfe to his beginnings in the maze: "I knew I had returned to the beginning. . . . In terms of hard fact I knew no more of this girl than when I had first set eyes on her naked figure" (467). When Urfe is torn from his lovemaking with Lily and thrust into the underground disintoxication ritual, when he sees now that Conchis refers to him as a "young man," and Lily looks at him "like a surgeon who has just performed a difficult operation successfully," he loses his last illusions about the masque and its characters. He is in this way prepared for the final disillusionment about himself before returning to the world as a man responsible for himself and aware of the reality of reality—if I may coin such a phrase—or of the human significance of reality. "But I clung to reality. I clung, too, to something in Alison, something like a tiny limpid crystal of eternal non-betrayal. Like a light in the darkest night" (493).

If the disintoxication ritual begins on the primitive magical level of a "Dr. Crowley," it ends on the modern, scientific, and psychoanalytical level, further from the primitive world of the masque Urfe is leaving and closer to the modern world he will have to reenter.

Both the primitive and scientific qualities of the ceremony have truths for the seeker, but both qualities will have to be used, balanced by the seeker in such a way that he learns from them both, yet goes beyond each, in making for himself a more sophisticated moral consciousness. The ceremony itself has elements to help the seeker make such a synthesis, and to connect the lessons of the labyrinth with his personal past. One of Urfe's revelations during disin-toxication in act 4, for example, is the sudden realization that his past actions are both metaphorically and actually connected to the choice one has to violate others or allow them their own freedom:

> Then suddenly.
> I understood.
> I was not holding a cat in my hand in an underground cistern, I was in a sunlit square ten years before and in my hands I held a German sub-machine-gun. And it was not Conchis who was now playing the role of Wimmel. Wimmel was inside me, and in my stiffened, back-thrown arm, in all my past; above all in what I had done to Alison. (518)

Even as earlier in the masque Urfe had understood Conchis' definition of the freedom to choose as opposed to Urfe's definition of it, now Urfe has experi-enced first-hand that knowledge of freedom. "He had simply guessed that for me freedom meant the freedom to satisfy personal desire, private ambition. Against that he set a freedom that must be responsible for its actions" (440–41).

Urfe will also now understand that each of us must choose good or evil within the cruel arena of disordered existence: "for him [Conchis] the smile was something cruel, because freedom is cruel, because the freedom that makes us at least partly responsible for what we are is cruel. So that smile was not so much an *attitude* to be taken to life as the *nature* of the cruelty of life, a cruelty we cannot even choose to avoid, since it is human existence" (531).

After the disintoxication ceremony which ends the masque, Urfe (this mythic and modern hero) emerges from the labyrinthine underworld of his journey. At the threshold, apocalyptic images abound. Stranded high in the decaying old city at Monemvasia, feeling like "the last man on earth" in some "medieval Hiroshima" or "city of the dead," Urfe refuses the suicide offered by the loaded pistol and experiences again the simple passion to exist—"the taste of coffee, the taste of bread, of cold lamb sprinkled with origan and lemon

juice." He has indeed now a new freedom: "I had this: being obscurely victorious. Being free again, but in a new freedom . . . purged in some way" (533).
He has, as foretold, returned to his beginning, as an old woman he passes asks
him "the old Homeric questions": "Who are thou? Where goest thou?"

We have seen already the kind of morality Fowles is definitely not espousing, and we have had through the hero's experiences in the labyrinth a clear
indication of the more sophisticated and open ethic that Fowles, through Conchis, suggests. There is, however, a final brief portion of *The Magus*, part 3,
the return home. This concluding section completes the primary level of the
narrative structure—the mythic journey—and makes it fully relevant to the
secondary structural level—the labyrinth of tests and parables of Conchis the
magician. The masque will now serve Urfe as a kind of timeless moment that
informs, with the help of a final guide named Lily de Seitas, his future choices
and acts. In short, what the hero has learned and the level of consciousness
toward which the whole adventure has been tending define the moral vision of
Fowles' novel. Part 3 confirms this vision.

The level of consciousness part 3 confirms begins with the acceptance of
"reality" as the only arena in which we live, or perhaps are condemned to live.
It is here, finally that we must choose, act freely, make our lives. "All my life
I had tried to turn life into fiction, to hold reality away," Urfe realizes. Conchis'
masque was a painful fulfillment of that wish. And now Urfe realizes that above
all reality is represented in Alison: "because I knew she was a mirror that did
not lie; whose interest in me was real; whose love was real. That had been her
supreme virtue: a constant reality" (539). As Mrs. de Seitas tells Urfe, that is
what so distinguishes Lily, an actress in a psychodrama, from Alison: "My
daughters were nothing but a personification of your own selfishness" (601).
Urfe has been "tormented . . . till he lives," to use the phrase he discovered
among Lily's papers; that is, tormented in the ordeals of Conchis' mill until he
no longer needs metaphors, fictions, or metafictions, until he sees the awesome
mystery of living and making choices *in* reality itself, until, in the lines of Lily's
poem, he comes to see that there is "Mystery enough at noon." As the fable of
"The Prince and the Magician" suggests to Urfe, each person must become his
own magician, and will, once he realizes his only choice is between death or the
full mystery and ordeal of life. It is for whatever gods may be "simply to be and
to constitute," Urfe realizes when he looks a last time at the statue of Poseidon;
it is for mankind to shape its life through individual freedom of choice, self-
knowledge, and the acceptance of vital reality, especially the vital reality of
others. This burden, as Fowles argues in *Mantissa,* is the burden post-modernism wishes to avoid.

If the first element of the hero's new consciousness is the acceptance of a
mysterious reality within which one is free to create either ethical order or
amoral disorder, the second element of new consciousness is that power of

vision which sees interrelationships and accepts responsibilities within the net of interrelationships. If the experience of suffering in the labyrinth leads Urfe to that first quality of consciousness, it is the experience of love that leads him to the second. Here too it has required the masque-goddess Lily's torments as well as the honesty and reality of Alison to bring the hero to such vision. As Mrs. de Seitas puts it, Lily's role has been "to teach you that physical pleasure and moral responsibility are two very different things" (627). Had Urfe, as a modern Everyman, had the capacity to learn from love, it might have been his first and last teacher and the masque would have been unnecessary.

Love teaches Urfe that in all human relationships it is self-deception, pretense, and violation of others that lead in their ultimate logic to *die Raben*. "The noblest relationship," Fowles writes in *Aristos,* "is marriage, that is, love. Its nobility resides in its altruism, the desire to serve another beyond all the pleasures of the relationship; and in its refusal ever to regard the other as a thing, an object, a utilizability" (175).

At one point in the masque Conchis had commented on the Nazi occupation parable to emphasize the larger dangers of blindness to responsibilities that arise from relationships between people: "I should like you also to reflect that its events could have taken place only in a world where man considers himself superior to woman. . . . That is, a world governed by brute force, humorless arrogance, illusory prestige and primeval stupidity. . . . That is the great distinction between the sexes. Men see objects, women see the relationships between objects. . . . I'll tell you what war is. War is a psychosis caused by an inability to see relationships" (413). Mrs. de Seitas in returning the issue to the more personal world of love between a man and woman tells Urfe that sex is one part of love and "the essential part is truth, the trust . . . [built] between their minds." The "real infidelity," she adds, "is a lie" (602–3).

This ethical concept of interrelationships and responsibilities is what Alasdair McIntyre meant in *After Virtue* by the "moral particularity" of one's moral identity. Each individual is inextricably attached to history, not divorced from it. Personal, social, and historical identity coincide at that point where an individual inherits the debts and responsibilities of family, tribe, city, and nation. Moral identity, then, according to McIntyre, exists in community (205–6).

Part 3 of *The Magus* defines the new consciousness, or ethical vision, but it also clarifies the wisdom gained through the ordeal of the labyrinth. Again with Mrs. de Seitas' help, Urfe comes to understand the primal sin in modern life, that essential immoral act, if you will, which breeds the lesser and greater evils of our time: the violation of others through outright ignorance or sadistic torment. "Lily de Seitas had told me her version of it. . . . I had taken it as a retrospective thing, a comment on my past. . . . But I saw now it had been about my future. . . . I began to feel the force of this super-commandment, summary of them all. . . . I had to choose it, and every day afresh, even though I went on failing to keep it. . . . Adult-hood was like a mountain, and I stood at the foot of this cliff of ice, this impossible and unclimbable: *Thou shalt not commit pain"* (641). That, Urfe decides, is the only historically viable commandment left. And it is that commandment that binds us together, Urfe comes to believe, in a complicated, delicate moral web that is merely unseen by the selfish or the automatic man, the aesthete, the political ideologue, and the sadist alike. In simplified terms, that last historical commandment summarizes the moral regeneration of the hero—a transformation of consciousness—and the moral vision of Fowles' mysterious novel.

John Fowles writes novels with the same goals in mind as Maurice Conchis when he creates his labyrinthine metatheatre. Fowles has said that for him "writing is a form of teaching."[16] The manipulation of realities, the successive debunkings of the fictional world, the skilled unity and integrity of a complex fictional structure, and the dense allusiveness of this single novel to a vast linguistic "system" of literary works—Shakespeare, Lawrence, Alain-Fournier, Richard Jefferies, Dickens, Honoré d' Urfé, the Utopian literary heritage, and the classical hero myths and epics, to suggest a few—all associate *The Magus* and Fowles with the "metafictional" concerns of twentieth-century European and Anglo-American fiction. But as we have seen, such concerns and techniques are not for Fowles the end of art; they are his acknowledgment and use of the advances in literary form and theory, and they are a means to an end. Fowles has embraced the idea, expressed by Conchis, that modern consciousness is unable to see in traditional dramatic or fictional forms alone the relationships between art and reality. He plays variations on the modern theme that we have joyfully eliminated all traces of the heuristic and the ethical in art by our characteristic philosophical relativism, formalism, and solipsism. But he is a different breed of artist, a renegade indeed, because he can appropriate and manipulate all the aesthetic and theoretical baggage of our time and *still* sail into the prevailing philosophical and theoretical winds. For Fowles, as for Conchis, the new art form, whether metadrama or metafiction, is transformed itself into a source of the old, now lost, powers of art. "Do you really think we do this just for you? Do you really believe we are not . . . charting a voyage?" Lily de Seitas asks Urfe. "All that we did was to us a simple necessity. . . . The days of simple experiments are over" (604).

For Fowles, as for Conchis who is the central vehicle for Fowles' theme, what is dying out now like some endangered species is precisely our inner potential for any ordering of life within hazard and against every limitless excess. It is loss of love, loss of truth, loss of self-knowledge, loss of freedom, loss of that vision which sees interrelationships between people and nations that all characterize the condition of mankind in the contemporary world. We have had other chances, tried other experiments, and we have failed. The great social experiments of Democracy and Communism, the Utopian communities and visions, the Wellsian hopes and blueprints for a scientific-ethical elite that will manage the world and save us from ourselves—these prospects we can no longer naively look to for order or salvation. Conchis parodies them himself by demonstrating his youthful membership in "The Society of Reason" and its dream of a "scientific and ethical elite" of "moral supermen."

In short, for Fowles no social management or legislation can create a human order within an inhuman, hazardous cosmos. If there is any hope for order and survival, we might better look for it in some revolutionary and relevatory process that lies at the heart of each individual's psyche, a psyche that has been touched by art for thousands of years. It is the imagination and its capacity to see the relationships between people and things and its capacity to live, feel, and learn vicariously that Fowles chiefly values. That psychic self, imagination, precedes society yet nourishes it; that self is the basis of Fowles' radical humanism traditionally expressed through romance, allegory, and myth. It is in this sense that he still draws upon a tradition while being a fictional innovator himself.

Fowles, like Conchis who has a line of Urfe's predecessors going back to at least the 1930s, goes to each reader one at a time with a rattling good tale and a tenuous experiment. The tale carries the reader through all the limited attitudes of modern consciousness, but it also presents a contrasting series of metaphors for a reality in which we can be free to choose and to collaborate in the creation of some new level of consciousness. Or, like Mitford, we are free to deny it. The greatest difference between Fowles and Conchis is that Fowles still believes the arts have the power to awaken imagination, whereas Conchis believes it may be awakened now only through a threateningly live drama, or therapy, where reality is temporarily but totally controlled by the master magician and director. But the purpose, like Fowles', is to help each initiate—hero, heroine, reader—reach a more independent destiny. As he says in *The Aristos,* "the true destiny of a man is to become a magician himself" (202).

Each creator, then, is looking to his experimental and existential program with a sceptical yet hopeful urgency. For in the wings of the metatheatre or the metafiction, as near and as far in our world, *die Raben* await their every opportunity, and a tragic future for humanity everywhere contends with a living future.

For Fowles, as for his old magician, we simply cannot afford to choose ignorance, solipsism, moral blindness, and the inhuman disorder of behavior without limits. No more can we afford to deny the ancient power of art and imagination, nor to valorize aesthetic form without purpose, content, or reference beyond the wit of its parodies and the beauty of its elegance. As he puts it in *The Aristos,* the new kind of ominous intellectual is not merely dangerous for poetry or for art, he is dangerous for humanity, for any hope of amelioration of the psychic diseases and social barbarities of history and our own time. This new intellectual is "chiefly interested in art, in cinema, in photography, in dress fashions, interior decoration and the rest. His world is bounded by colour, shape, texture, pattern, setting, movement; and he is only minimally interested in the properly intellectual (moral and sociopolitical) significance of events and objects. . . . [He] does not *feel* a rioting crowd being machine-gunned by police; he simply sees a brilliant news photograph" (211). There has to be a human meaning beyond the joy of adventures in the labyrinth or the godgame, "because," as Mrs. de Seitas puts it, "there is no God, and it is not a game."

In a world where a God, a Conchis, or an artist must finally abscond to leave each of us to ourselves, the choice we face is Urfe's in the end. Shall I be one more anti-hero for whom "the smallest hope, a bare continuing to exist, is enough. . . . Leave him says our age, leave him where mankind is in his history, at a crossroads, in a dilemma, with all to lose and only more of the same to win; let him survive, but give him no direction, no reward; because we too are waiting . . . for this girl, this truth, this crystal of humanity, this reality lost through imagination, to return; and to say she returns is a lie"? Or, shall I cling "to the something I had never seen, or always feared to see, in [Alison's] grey eyes, the quintessential something behind all the hating, the hurtness, the tears. A small step poised, a shattered crystal waiting to be reborn" (645, 655)?

Urfe's admission that he will never be more than "half a human being" without Alison, and all she has come to represent as masque-symbol and reality, is enough to clarify in which direction the positive choice lies. "All waits suspended . . . fragments of freedom, hazard, an anagram made flesh" (656). It also makes it clear that Urfe has undergone a change. Although Fowles has left the reader to construct the meaning of the whole, as he warned in his preface, and although here, as in *The French Lieutenant's Woman*, Fowles draws on the avant-garde in physics as well as in art for a kind of "constructivist theory" of meaning, as Ernst von Glasersfeld argues in the *Georgia Review*, Fowles does not end on a note of utter relativity, or "constructivism," that would place all meaning, event, object in the observer's own substance any more than he wants the reader to end up believing no external reality exists.[17] On the contrary, our choice as readers depends now, like Urfe's, on what we have learned in the labyrinth about our lives. Have we at least learned, as Fowles expresses it in *The Aristos*, the difference between the *aristoi* ("the best") and the *hoi polloi* ("the mass-man") in each of us? The former represents the passion to choose "intelligent and enacted goodness," to become not the manipulated object of a conjurer, but, finally, magicians ourselves. "To accept one's limited freedom, one's isolation . . . this responsibility, to learn one's particular powers, and with them to humanize the whole: that is the best for the situation" (212–14).

In his themes—the personal discovery of good and evil, the tension created by our passion for the ideal and our need to live within the limits of the real, the limitations of post-modern art—Fowles himself is aware of a certain repetitiousness throughout his work. In *The Ebony Tower* he speaks of "variations both on certain themes in previous books of mine and in methods of narrative presentation." In this collection, thematic and design variations include the hero's choice between two women, the domain where much of the action takes place, the relationships between life and art, and the artistic necessity of risk-taking. The collection is at the same time highly artificial in a contemporary sense— from the ebony (shit) tower of modern art in the first story to the sodomy in the last, from the self-reference to earlier works and the repetitions of themes to the speculations of Barthes. Fowles also speaks of the primal expression of "behavior and moral problems" through dialogue, action, setting, and theme that he believes to be "seminal in the history of fiction" and best represented by the "forest . . . of Celtic romance generally" and by the *Eliduc* of Marie de France particularly. It is the depiction of "human emotions and their absurdities" as well as the depiction of the dangers of "passionate excess" that Fowles finds most original in Marie de France (119–20). One might condemn Fowles' repetitiveness, as Karen Lever does. Or one might view it as one sign of greatness in a writer, as Richard Poirier does in his study of Norman Mailer when Poirier argues that the importance of a writer comes from his or her ability to develop creatively while tracking certain major themes throughout his or her life.[18] You may take either position and still see *The Magus* as Fowles' inceptive work.

Throughout this chapter I have tried to suggest connections between *The Magus* and Fowles' larger body of work. At this point I want to emphasize further some ways in which *The Magus* is especially prototypical of themes and structures in two later fictions. Both novels are especially shaped by the quest for a greater consciousness that arises from moral revelation and that ends in the conscious choices that follow revelation.

In Fowles' next novel, *The French Lieutenant's Woman* (1969), the differences between moralism and moral vision, the quest for freedom and the terrors of choice, and the evils of cultural or personal manipulation of others are again the principal themes. Here too the structure of the novel derives from such older fictional conventions as the "good story," nineteenth-century authorial intrusions and high rhetoric, and the heroic quest. But the novel's structure is again also derived from the conventions of the *noveau roman,* metafiction, and postmodernism generally. More accurately, the structure derives parodically from Fowles' reactions to the dogmas of post-modernism.

To take the themes I have mentioned first, we find, as in *The Magus,* that Fowles quickly establishes in his next novel the kind of moralism he is not recommending. Such moralism in its most degenerate form is of course embodied by Mrs. Poultney. Chapter 9, which Fowles devotes to his depiction of her as the epitome of autocratic conventions, rigidity, and moral blindness, has to be one of the funniest portraits Fowles ever penned. The very caricature of acculturated or localized morality, Mrs. Poultney stands as the representative of all the worst elements of Victorianism that Sarah and Charles must battle in their efforts to attain freedom. "The moral question," that Charles finally asks Dr. Grogan is "Would you have me live a lifetime of pretense? Is our age not full enough as it is of a mealy-mouthed hypocrisy, an adulation of all that is false in our nature? Would you have me add to that?"[19] The question Charles begins to put before Grogan and the reader is the question of distinguishing between relative or timely "truths" and human or timeless truths. For what any age, epoch, culture offers us, like the Victorian period in England where so much became exaggerated, is "totally without love or freedom . . . but also without thought, without intention, without malice, because the deception was in its very nature; and it was not human, but a machine." To the extent that Charles has accepted his age, become it, or been influenced by it, "he had become while still alive, as if dead" (362–63).

What is of timeless value, however, is the freedom of self-definition amidst cultural and personal manipulations. Each emancipation begins the restoration of freedoms to all, as the epigraph of the novel from Marx argues: "Every emancipation is a restoration of the human world and of human relationships to man himself." Such freedom is embodied in Sarah, who in this novel comes, after all, to be associated with the ageless "ethical elite," to borrow Fowles' phrase, or "the elect" (to use Conchis') who live outside their particular cultures. The "link" they all hold in common, as Fowles reminds us, is that "they all rejected or reject the notion of *possession* as the purpose of life, whether it be a woman's body, or a high profit at all costs, or the right to dictate the speed of progress."

MacIntyre, in *After Virtue*, makes a similar distinction between the "tradition of virtue" that is, especially, outside the modern order of economics and systematic politics, an order characterized by "its acquisitiveness and its elevation of the values of the market to a central social place" (237). Charles is in this sense "a man struggling to overcome history"—his particular time and place in it—and "to preserve personal identity" enough to make moral choices. He may fail or, as in the third alternate ending, he may be "reborn" and become a child again who "has at last found an atom of faith in himself, a true uniqueness, on which to build." But his struggle, like Urfe's, is to choose between the "heroism" or adulthood of self-knowledge and moral vision, on the one hand, and the static, coddled adolescence offered by his epoch's morals and conventions. And given "the moral enormity of his privileged economic position," the challenge to Charles is overwhelming (290–97). If like Alison, Lily, and Conchis before her, Sarah deceives the hero—she is a virgin, she has no limp—such deceit is not the evil. Rather, deceit is the source of liberation from the amoral and even immoral life, as Charles realizes when he finally sees that Sarah has used "strategems to unblind him" (368). Like Conchis, Sarah comes to symbolize "the pure essence of cruel but necessary (if we are to survive—and yes, still today) freedom" (366). Like Conchis also, she is the representative of mystery, that force which activates the quest. As Peter Wolfe suggests, Sarah is this time the arch-dramatist, the one who, magicianlike, creates a mysterious reality about herself, a metadrama, within which the hero acts. Part of her mysteriousness is that she represents passion and instinct in an age that suppressed those qualities. Furthermore, Wolfe rightly notes that Fowles keeps the reader ignorant of Sarah's personality. She, like Conchis, is the only one of several major characters into whose mind we never see. Yet, inexplicably to my mind, Wolfe counts our sharing of Sarah's mysteriousness as the major flaw of the book, a flaw that somehow "obscured the book's moral basis and disjoints narrative writing" (151–53, 155).

Freedom is the main theme again, responsible freedom. In the scene where a devastated Charles kneels in church and carries on a dialogue between his best and worst selves (Matthew Arnold, like Thomas Hardy, provides the melody for many a variation in this novel), the question before Charles is the question of choosing one's freedom and accepting the responsibilities that come with freedom. He now realizes how much every step of his way he has been choosing Sarah, if less than fully conscious that he has been doing so. Yet he has not had the courage to face the consequences of such a choice because, as he tells himself, "you lack the courage to give her back her gift." For "being free is a situation of terror" (341, 360–61).

The dilemma Charles faces he has caused himself by the deadly combination of moral blindness and the desire to transcend his culture. As with Urfe, lack of self-knowledge is the source of blindness. "What is to blame is a blindness in myself," he writes to Ernestina in the truest line in the whole letter, "as to my own real nature." Ernestina is the victim this time. She suffers if he rejects her now after a long courtship filled with his hypocrisies; she suffers equally if he marries her now and lives with her as an "imposter" in a marriage every day of which is a lie. As Dr. Grogan says, it is "suffering [that] is evil." And to be aware of the suffering we cause others and to reduce it are of course the difficulties in attaining moral vision and the reason why only maturity through self-knowledge can guide us through a moral life. Charles has before him the choice of being either comfortably safe and hypocritical or free and crucified (i.e., cast out). What good would his strength do in the world? He can only find the answer in the crucified Christ he contemplates in the church. This agnostic scientist, this analytical collector and classifier, this dilettante in life, comes to represent us all, perhaps, in his moral dilemma and in his answer to that question. The moral truth in Christianity is ageless, Charles realizes, and it is a far cry from the Christianity of the world and the Mrs. Poultneys. As in the example of Christ, the moral purpose of Christianity is to bring forth "the peace of victory brought about by, and in, living men and women," in short, to uncrucify (262–63), even if they be outcast, even if they be crucified by the representative intelligence of their particular epoch.

If there is a flaw in the construction of *The French Lieutenant's Woman,* it is not that in the final, most ethically challenging of the three endings Charles must begin again from scratch to build a morally responsible life in the aftermath of his sufferings and lessons, "all to be recommenced, all to be learned again!" The flaw is, perhaps, that Sarah, who "embodied the freedom" from his age, his ancestry, his class and country, practices her freedom of choice by being merely the associate, model, and amanuensis of men who, as she says, do indeed live their lives as artists pursuing "honorable endeavor" and "noble purpose" larger than themselves or their accumulated possessions. Sarah's "new self-knowledge and self-possession" might be more convincing, or at least more forceful, were she more *active* in her own honorability of endeavor and nobility of purpose, more of a George Eliot than an Elizabeth Siddal. But at least she has solved for herself, as Charles has to learn to solve all over again, the problem of avoiding a life of "nothingness, an ultimate vacuity, a total purpose-lessness" that surely submission to the relative judgments of epoch and convention would doom him.

Although as I have said the evil in the world is identified, as in *The Magus,* as the suffering we cause others, that evil is further defined in *The French Lieutenant's Woman* as the waste of human potential, or more simply of humanity, caused by the extent to which we accept and live by the local conventions of economic and class privilege. Echoes of Marx fill this novel as much of the echoes of Arnold and Hardy. Though many an epigraph and author-ial meditation on Victorianism, to say nothing of the scenes of the London underworld of prostitution, keep our noses in the dirt of economic privilege and arrogance, it is Charles and Sarah who are the most particular examples of such waste. Sarah exemplifies this "sense of waste" that Charles feels as he contem-plates the social ostracism of a woman of such fine intelligence whose chief talent seems to be the ability to see through the absurdities and social evils of convention and hypocrisy—the very quality her age most needs. "The feeling was not of male envy: but very much of human loss." Sarah's potential to make a creative contribution to her society is lost when her "passion and imagination" are "banned by the epoch" (181–82, 189). Charles exemplifies the human loss himself when, later, he realizes he has been incapable of rising to the challenges of his best instincts. "Indeed it was hardly Sarah he now thought of—she was merely the symbol around which had accreted all his lost possibilities, his extinct freedoms, his never-to-be-taken journeys. . . . There was no doubt. He was one of life's victims, one more ammonite caught in the vast movements of history . . . a potential turned to a fossil" (332–33). Moral vision is not sufficient; indeed it can destroy one. One must live and act, finally, in accordance with that vision, to some nobility of purpose, or submit to a living death defined by one's country and one's time.

In his use of the conventions of metafiction and post-modernism Fowles again has structured his novel in a way that seems to transfer authority from the writer to the reader. His sudden breaks of plot to impose his philosophical-aesthetic musings, often ironically, about the "unreality" of fiction and his three alternate endings to the novel—the dewy ending of Victorian convention where Ernestina and Charles pledge their troth; the hardly less sentimental ending where Sarah, Charles, and child are finally united to the tortured sounds of a lady practicing Chopin; and the final and most ethically challenging ending where Sarah and Charles part company and we are left with Charles as he is about to reenter the world like a child who must learn to live all over again—have caused the most critical comment.

Maurice Beebe points out, quite as Fowles did long before in *The Aristos*, that there is nothing particularly new about transferring authority or responsibility to the audience and thereby reflecting the reader's consciousness as much as, or more than, the author's. Indeed, that transfer is a literary convention that, in English fiction, dates back at least to the eighteenth century. What is new, as Beebe says, is the extreme to which post-modernism takes that convention in every manner of "do-it-yourself art." Such experiments are beginning to seem almost commonplace," Beebe wrote in 1976. What Beebe did not seem to notice is that in *The French Lieutenant's Woman* Fowles was using and parodying the new conventions and Victorian fiction.[20] The irony of Fowles' use of post-modern conventions seems to be clear enough the first time he interrupts his tale to tell us all how aware he and we must be, since Robbe-Grillet and Barthes, that a story is only a story, a character only a creation of the author. Yet in this interchapter, so to speak, Fowles ends up mocking, if using, the theoretical basis of post-modern fiction when he argues that the created world must be as much an organism independent of its creator as a real world. As soon as characters become flat puppets, as soon as the novel becomes a machine, it is a mechanism, a game, an artificial labyrinth, and therefore a dead thing. "The novelist is still a god, since he creates (and not even the most aleatory *avant-garde* modern novel has managed to extripate its author completely); what has changed is that we are no longer the gods of the Victorian image, omniscient and decreeing; but in the new theological image, with freedom our first principle, not authority." The definition of the novelist is that he is a "freedom that allows other freedoms to exist" (96–97).

A Maggot (1985), another amalgamation of the oldest and most current techniques, may be Fowles' most experimental fiction yet. His lengthy epilogue suggests his own uncertainty about the success of the experiment, an uncertainty shared by the reviewers. Much of the experimentation is typically contemporary. Point of view shifts constantly through a series of contradictory voices. An external third-person narrator is, early on, a strangely cameralike observer reporting only surfaces of character and action, but this same narrator later takes on the prerogatives of traditional, omniscient third-person narrators. The fiction uses and parodies, among other forms, the historical novel, the supernatural novel, science fiction (the only *deus ex machina* or "other world" we moderns can accept?), Faust dramas, and, in the words of one character, "legendary romance." The series of depositions, letters, and documents from all the investigations of lawyer Ayscough suggest the detective novel as well, perhaps as an overriding generic structure. We can see that *The Magus* is prototypical even here, for it too supports numerous plot types from, as Simon Loveday points out, social comedy to *Bildungsroman,* fictional autobiography, detective story, novel of ideas, and *roman a tiroirs* (a series of self-contained, inset tales that stop the main narrative).[21] And all of the points of view in *A Maggot* unveil only speculations about the never-resolved mysteries: What happened? Who was His Lordship?

If *A Maggot* is one of his most experimental novels, it is also, and more importantly, one of his most political, as Pat Rogers points out.[22] Even more overtly than *The French Lieutenant's Woman,* this novel is concerned with the dialectic of social stasis and antinomian force. Again the novel is ostensibly historical, and again a central character is an outcast woman who comes to represent rebelliousness, change, and freedom to choose. Fowles tells us in his epilogue that the "underlying approach and purpose" in his novels follow Defoe's. That historical comparison is instructive if it is not construed too superficially, nor "politics" too narrowly. It is true that Fowles, as Defoe, presents what seems to be a factual account of the extraordinary. Likewise, Fowles bases his fiction on his varied reading and experience. Furthermore, he uses techniques such as historical commentary, real and imagined documents and characters, and painstaking replications of period language. But as Fowles points out, such fictions are "immensely different" from documentary history,[23] not the least, I might add, because *A Maggot* reclaims Defoe's purpose—persuasion. This novel allies Fowles clearly with the dissenting Defoe, the didactic Defoe, the debunker of entrenched injustice and the purveyor of economic and educational reform. As always, Fowles bases his ideas about potential reform on individual transformation and freedom, both of which might *lead* to social reform. The narrative follows this quest, as in *The Magus,* for redemption and rebirth. Christ is the archetype here, and his example is a clear presence in the novel. Like Defoe, Fowles understands in a radically Christian sense the necessities built into the social forms that carry impoverished men and women "by need," as the central character puts it, to crime, reminding us of *Moll Flanders,*

Colonel Jack, or even *Roxana.* And like Defoe, again, Fowles' own interest in magic in part creates the unresolved mystery at the heart of the novel.

The magus here is His Lordship, unnamed son of a powerful Duke. His willing-unwilling apprentice is Rebecca Hocknell, later Lee (alias Louise, alias Fanny), a visionary ex-prostitute and ex-Quaker infamously known as the Quaker Maid. For such apparently poor but potentially rich material as Rebecca does the alternately friendly and cruel philosopher-magician direct his stage shows, revels, and terrors. He fits the literary tradition of the magician especially in his doubleness (both white and black magic are suggested, and he has an earthly "other," the deaf mute Dick); in his changeable cruelty and helpfulness; in his trickster's disguises and "elaborate subterfuges" or dramas (complete with hired actors and naively participating novice); in his alternating scorn of cosmos or fate and humility before powers greater than he; in his portrayal by others as alternately Faustian seeker driven to suicide and Christlike redeemer of the lost and outcast. Rebecca will finally say, not unlike Urfe of Conchis, "what I took for his cruelty was his kindness, though I saw it not at first. He was not Christ of the Book but of His spirit," in short, the restorer of a cruel freedom (417–18).

He is also revolutionary, and in that guise most unsettles Fowles' representative eighteenth-century men, the Duke and his investigator the lawyer Henry Ayscough. "For how might a better world come if this one may not change?" the actor Lacy reports His Lordship to have said. "Change that is my purpose," the regenerate Rebecca will later echo, particularly referring to her daughter Ann Lee who later becomes the founding Mother Ann of Shakerism (136, 424). Likewise will Rebecca echo the Duke's son in her final testimony that the basis of change is the individual's freedom to move and choose, just as Christ would have us free to choose him or not (136–37, 419). This is the revolutionary spirit of the magician and his transformed heroine. Like Urfe, Rebecca must be, first, freed of London, then placed in another domain, tested, tried, and denied her freedom so that, finally, she may assert greater freedom and gain enlightenment. (Light in this novel, as in the domain of Conchis, symbolizes new consciousness.) Both her Lordship's and her own antinomian spirit struggle peaceably but without compromise against the hegemonies of the age embodied in politics, hypocritical class structure, and familial hierarchy (see especially 136–37).

As Victorian England served in *The French Lieutenant's Woman,* early eighteenth-century England serves in its own way as another exemplum of social stasis, privilege, narrow moralism, and corruption in *A Maggot.* Fowles sees it as another time "united only in a constipated hatred of change of any kind." If we have not the disastrous class slavery, starvation, poverty, and waste of industrial capitalism on the scale of Victorian England, we have suffering and a world "abominally prescribed," a world of largely fixed personal destinies that to us would seem intolerable and "totalitarian in essence." It is the hegemony of caste, of appearances before realities, of the "idolatry of property," and of the reactionary horror of change, against which the Duke's son and finally Rebecca will struggle. It is ultimately a social hegemony opposed, for Fowles, not only to change but to rebirth. Answering an outraged Ayscough, Rebecca puts it this way:

> Christ's kingdom is not must. If a thing must be it is not of Christ. A harlot must be always harlot, is not Christ. Man must rule always over woman, is not Christ. Children must starve, is not Christ. All must suffer for what they are born, is not Christ. No must by this world's lights is Christ. It is darkness, 'tis the sepulchre that world doth lie in for its sins. . . . [We must obey Christ] if first we are free not to obey Him; for He would have us choose Him freely, therefore we must be free also to choose evil and sin and darkness. He tells us man may change of his own will; and by His grace, so be redeemed. (419–20)

Through the testimony of others—their letters and depositions make up most of the novel—we understand His Lordship's ironies and scepticisms against such a system too. But he is, in another sense, a more traditional magician figure as well as a redeemer figure, for his researches into numerology, mathematics, astrology, and so on have a Faustian edge to them. Like Christ in the temple he can teach the philosophers much, but he would also seek powers never granted to inhabitants of this world—his rebellion is larger than social and religious, it is philosophical and spiritual. He seeks some secret of nature, some certainty of belief, some "great light" of the Ancients. He would go beyond Newton and Leibnitz and probe the secrets of eternal time and motion, which secrets the "dance of the Gogs and Magogs" at Stonehenge seem to represent and reveal. He would pierce time, tell the future, and demonstrate that Providence is not responsible for our worldly miseries. He would cross uncrossable boundaries, "his Rubicon." "All this," Ayscough will say, "is most dangerous doctrine" (see especially 142).

Indeed, but whether he is damned for these ambitions or redeemed (even what his ambitions really are) is never resolved in the novel. He remains an even greater mystery than Conchis. He might be Faustian, Satanic, or in touch with other beings in the universe, or a completely unearthly being himself returned from "heaven" in search of one who can shed new light. "You are she I have sought," he tells Rebecca, and she agrees he changed her sinful life forever. All possibilities are explored in the novel, though there is more evidence for our modern sensibilities (including four separate testimonies: Jones, a shepherd, Rebecca, Stephen Hales) that suggests the flying saucer hypothesis, a possibility I'll admit with a number of reviewers that may undermine rather than enlarge the "credibility"—the relationship between fictional theme and praxis—of Fowles' novel. But finally His Lordship's true nature is unimportant, as was Conchis'. For the antinomian themes are carried by the dialectic of

Ayscough and Rebecca, of that prescribed world and the radical Christian light that would break it. The sources of her enlightenment are less important thematically than the intention and force of enlightenment.

Fowles makes his own sympathies in the debate clear. His epilogue not only provides some much-needed background for the confused reader; it is a kind of philosophical-thematic appendage, like *The Aristos,* which most novelists abhor, but to which Gardner and Mailer are likewise given. Fowles confesses deep sympathy with Mother Ann Lee. In his novel Ann is born at the very end and it is her purely fictional mother Rebecca whose story, spirit, and sources of vision we have followed. It is Rebecca's visions in the cave within the "maggot" that are the basis of her daughter's own radical vision of agricultural utopia.

The author praises certain aspects of this vision that his heroine has found. The vision is a sort of feminist Manicheanism (Christ-Antichrist, darkness-light) set against orthodox theology, capitalism, sensual-narcissism, and, later, communism and sexism. It is that emotional rather than intellectual side of the Enlightenment Fowles found worth exploring in this novel. Ann Lee, despite her charismatic personality, ecstacies, visions, and rigors does, Fowles argues, provide a practical vision of what was wrong with the world, just as Christ in another time did. And Fowles argues that her effort to escape "mere science, mere reason, convention, established belief and religion" and all the "powerful social gods" is one avenue to a "more humane society." Her message falls on deaf ears even today. If she foresaw the hegemony of Mammon that would one day threaten to destroy the world, if she called for more "simplicity, sanity and self-control," her too-plain, too-radical faith is beyond us. We are of the many where she is of the few, of an ethical elite, as Fowles put it in *The French Lieutenant's Woman* and in *The Aristos.*

But even more important for Fowles is the presence of any dissent. Dissent, he argues in his epilogue, is "a universal human phenomenon" and Northern Europe's and America's "most precious legacy to the world." Dissent, as antihegemonic force, is both a religious and biological need in us and, echoing *The Aristos* again, an evolutionary necessity. This dissent mechanism we need now more than ever, and hence the relevance of his quasi-historical text. We have not, Fowles goes on, "progressed one inch" in a morality that "justifies the flagrant injustice and inequality of human society." Sounding more than a little like Frank Lentricchia, Fowles identifies our particular hegemony in the West as obsession with self and every excess promoted by all the interworking mechanisms and metaphors of Mammon and established religion. Dissent is that "refusal to believe what those in power would have us believe . . . in all ways from totalitarian tyranny and brutal force to media manipulation and cultural hegemony" (see 449–55).

Looking back in his 1985 interview with Carol Barnum, Fowles responds to her question about his previous "political" ambitions for the novel to alter society this way:

> I said that a long time ago, and would now call it a totally unfulfilled hope. I know I may have helped a little in altering people's view of life—if I can believe their letters. I now think that this is the only practical "political" ambition a novelist can have. I should certainly like our present societies to become much fairer and more equal in economic terms; not so outrageously selfish, aggressive, and stupid in their supposedly Christian principles as America and Britain today. Western society is now in my view far too dominated by the middle-class ethos—anything goes, so long as the bourgeois way of life is preserved. The rise of this subtle tyranny—Gramsci's "cultural hegemony"—over the last forty years seems to me the most striking historical development of the century—and something very similar has happened in Russia also, of course. What fills me with gloom is that in the West people like Reagan and Thatcher are elected by *majorities*. (188)

Like Urfe at his worst, or Smithson, or Ayscough, we are, Fowles argues finally in his epilogue, too clever, too selfish and multiple, too dominated by the great I, too pledged to our own convenience, too tired, too indifferent to others, too frightened—in brief, I would add, too immoral—to dissent. What we have lost of value is not so much Mother Ann Lee's specific spiritual program or her utopian agrarianism, Fowles suggests here; we have lost her spirit, her courage, and her imagination for dissent. But he has not given up. He more modestly now hopes to rekindle the spirit of scepticism and dissent in some of his readers, as Conchis did, one at a time. The novel, as he said in his Barnum interview, "can't change society," but "it can push people a little bit or show them the way" (192).

As in his previous fictions, Fowles exploits current technique ironically and parodically; more important to him are his ethical themes as they are revealed through structure (and nonfictional discourse). If critics like Beebe seem unaware of this element of irony and parody, Beebe nonetheless suggests a new direction in literary art that Fowles (to say nothing yet of Gardner and Mailer) has already taken. "Before long our better novelists may return to old-fashioned assumptions about their responsibility to control and structure their work, improving upon the realness of their unreal fictive worlds instead of merely becoming absorbed within them." Of course, we might well doubt that the return will be merely to "old fashioned assumptions"; we might rather expect, as Fowles' work demonstrates, that a more vital use of old and new conventions will supersede, as it even now is, the fictional forms and themes of the post-modern movement itself.

John Gardner:
The Magician as Fool

*In art, morality and love are inextricably bound: we affirm
what is good—for the characters in particular and for humanity
in general—because we care.... This is the final point John
Fowles makes in his novel,* Daniel Martin: *"No true compassion
without will, no true will without compassion." Without will—
the artist's conscious determination to take his characters seriously—no artist can achieve real compassion. And without compassion—without real and deep love for his subjects (... and
by extension all human beings) no artist can summon the will to
make true art; he will be satisfied, instead with clever language
or with cynical jokes and too easy, dire solutions like those
common in contemporary fiction.*

John Gardner, *On Moral Fiction*

*The great secret of morals is love; or a going out of our
nature, and an identification of ourselves with the beautiful
which exists in thought, action, or person, not our own.*
The great instrument of moral good is the imagination.

Shelley, *A Defence of Poetry*

In John Gardner's fourth published novel, *The Sunlight Dialogues* (1973), another mysterious magician, through seemingly inexplicable antics and teachings, provokes new consciousness in those people whose lives he alters. Like
Fowles' magus, Gardner's is an artist himself who manipulates reality to run his
chosen apprentice especially through an heuristic mill that will change the
apprentice's conception of himself, others, and human relationships. Unlike
Fowles' magus who isolates his "heroes" for the process of transformation,

Gardner's magus enters the world to effect the process. Even though Gardner's magus-teacher exposes the weight of his own guilts and weaknesses to the reader, both magi are nevertheless masters of metafictional ceremonies who, in the course of their personal journeys, lead others through journeys and transformations of their own. In the course of his narrative, Gardner, who admires Fowles, questions the nature of fiction (largely through parody of metafiction) and demonstrates delight in the virtuosity of his art. Yet both authors, more importantly, take pains to connect their fictions to history and to compare deadening with living visions of human community and evolution. In Gardner's case most reviewers accepted this connection and comparison with some degree of understanding. But Gardner's later essays on fiction, followed by *On Moral Fiction* in 1978, distorted the general understanding not only of *The Sunlight Dialogues* but of Gardner's work and ideas.

Especially misunderstood are Gardner's purpose and his process of writing fiction. He brought on some of the misunderstanding himself. *On Moral Fiction* critiques, perhaps too frankly, many of Gardner's contemporaries. And Gardner acknowledged certain oversimplifications by redefining "moral fiction" in numerous subsequent interviews and in two posthumously published books—*On Becoming a Novelist* (1983) and *The Art of Fiction* (1984).

Two critics' reactions are particularly representative of positions taken against Gardner's argument for "moral art." First, Joe David Bellamy's response in 1973 to Gardner's article in the *New York Times,* "The Way We Write Now," misses Gardner's real point and takes the easy way out. Bellamy resorts to caricature and ridicule. If Bellamy is nearly right that nobody today is asserting that "style is life's only value" (i.e., that Gardner is setting up easy strawmen of his own), Bellamy is not correct in arguing that Gardner attempts to "reduce . . . multiformity to a single spurious unifying principle," or to recommend throwing back fictional character and style to Austen and James, or to adhere "to the historically discredited idea that art should provide moral exhortation." Bellamy believes that Gardner is making an "aesthetically retrograde argument" for "a sermon, or, at best, a Victorian novel with a message, characters as moral exemplars, and a coherent system of universals." Quoting William Gass' statement, "I distrust people, including artists, who make pretentious claims for literature as a source of knowledge," Bellamy prefigures John Barth's reaction by holding Gardner up as one more emerging Right Winger who has placed himself "squarely in the same camp with Plato and Nixon." John Barth, my second representative, phrases his response similarly: "a Proposition-13 mentality pervades the medium; our literary Howard Jarvises are in ascendancy, preaching 'the family novel' and 'a return to traditional literary values.' And, in Reagan country . . . one may expect more of the same: The decade of the Moral Majority will doubtless be the decade of moral fiction."[1] If Gardner erred in the strategies of his essays and in *On Moral Fiction,* such respondents erred themselves in resorting to gross caricature and misreading.

Fortunately for Gardner's credibility, he continued to clarify and sharpen his position, and as he did so the tone of his theoretical comments and books became more even-tempered and just. Even in *On Moral Fiction,* however, Gardner repeatedly emphasizes that, "Didacticism and true art are immiscible." Moral art, he takes care to assert, is neither doctrinaire nor moralistic. Recognizable by its "careful, thoroughly honest search for and analysis of values," true art, Gardner explains is "not didactic because, instead of teaching by authority or force, it explores, open-mindedly, to learn what it should teach." In *On Moral Fiction,* as in numerous interviews, Gardner also repeatedly emphasizes his acute awareness that "morality" is a dangerous term not only because devils keep using it, but because it has been historically misused as a means, a cover, for oppression and self-righteous brutality.[2] Yet in the face of so much misunderstanding, it is important for us to grasp the nature of Gardner's ideas about the process and purpose of fiction before we examine the process at work.

Gardner nowhere argues that art should be reduced to preaching from a privileged, conservative position. On the contrary, Gardner sees writing fiction as "a kind of philosophy" where the writer tests his or her "abstract ideas in the real world." This testing is a process of discovery for the writer, and for Gardner "the joy of it is that I reach discoveries." As Simon Loveday pointed out about Fowles, so does Gardner *think* in fiction; both writers derive hypotheses about life shared between writer and reader. The philosophical statements that result and appear in such books as *The Aristos* and *On Moral Fiction* are what Northrop Frye called "existential projections" from fiction (particularly romance) into the field of philosophy.[3]

For Gardner, "serious philosophical questions" are best raised and discoveries best made through "the human drama," as he put it in his *Paris Review* interview. Indeed, it is in the process of writing fiction, Gardner explains, that one discovers the complexity of moral issues and debates: "I always start out with a position I later discover to be too simple. . . . In everything I've written I've come to the realization that I was missing something, telling myself lies." The process of discovery through fiction is essentially dialectical, represented by conflicting characters' debates and opposing approaches to life and to moral dilemmas. To some extent this process expresses the nature of Gardner's own character, as he suggests when comparing the "battle in my own fiction between the hunger for roots, stability, law, and another element in my character which is anarchic." Yet the process also expresses Gardner-the-medievalist's adaptation of the "dialogue" form, the agon born of ancient epics, and his continuation of the historical debates between Dante, Malory, and the great fictionists through the ages. "My subject really is . . . human history—the conflict of ideas and emotions through the ages." This dialectical approach also arises, as Samuel Coale points out in *Hawthorne's Shadow,* from what Richard Chase called the "radical disunities in American culture" that have always informed the dialogues and melodramatic confrontations of the American Romance ("however scintillant with post-modernist artifice" today) right down to Mailer and Gardner in our time. Gardner is still, Coale argues, "mining the soul's disharmony" as Hawthorne did.[4]

The fiction writer, Gardner argues, best works out the dialogue of conflicting visions by creating characters that thoroughly and sympathetically present their particular positions in the dialectical exchange, an exchange through which one or more characters may develop and reach a new synthesis. The synthesis, when there is one, may represent the author's own discovery or development, but it must be founded, Gardner advises, on the writer's willingness and ability to give each character his or her due and to admit each character's frailties.[5] In the *Paris Review,* Gardner sums the point up: "No ideas but in *energeia* . . . the actualization of the potential which exists in character and situation" (49–50). This process is what Gardner means to suggest in *On Moral Fiction* when he writes: "Art is the means by which the artist comes to see; it is his peculiar, highly sophisticated and extremely demanding technique of discovery." What the reader discovers, Gardner adds, is "the dramatic equivalent of the intellectual process he [the writer] himself went through." This dramatic equivalent is another way of defining the novel's suspense. The dialectic of discovery works throughout the artist's career too: "Healthy fiction is dialectic: the writer's understanding increases with each book he solves" (91, 108, 198).

If the dialectic of fully presented yet representative characters is the essence of Gardner's fictional process, the essence of his fictional purpose is that fiction has at least the potential to affect life and, through the various models it presents, to provide avenues for the humane and sentient evolution of civilization. "The greatest model in all our civilization is art," Gardner says in his interview with Marshall Harvey, and he argues that "art always affects life." Gardner further suggests here that his collection of stories *The King's Indian* (1974) is about just this possibility of literary form to become "a vehicle of vision" and the artist to become the creator of "new and wonderful possibilities" (77, 81, 84).

That texts, fictional and nonfictional, can and have become vehicles of vision is what Scholes means by "textual power." In *Textual Power* Scholes puts it this way: "We care about texts for many reasons, not the least of which is that they bring us news that alters our way of interpreting things. If this were not the case, the Gospels and the teachings of Marx would have fallen upon deaf ears. Textual power is ultimately power to change the world" (165). Every artist, through his art, is then potentially in the traditional position of the shaper, the poet or *scop,* as he is in *Grendel.* As shaper, the artist chooses either to enhance life or affirm death, to speak only of the abyss, or to speak of it and help prevent the collapse of everything human into it.

This is the point Gardner has in mind earlier in *On Moral Fiction* when he speaks of art's sworn opposition to chaos and art's "civilizing influence." Like D. H. Lawrence, who continually probed the conflict between life-affirming and life-denying values, and who spoke in *Lady Chatterley's Lover* of the function of the novel as leading "the flow of our sympathetic consciousness" toward life and away from "things gone dead," Gardner continually says in *On Moral Fiction* that the novel's function is to clarify life; art "carefully judges our right and wrong directions, celebrates and mourns." He continues: "It does not rant. . . . It designs visions worth trying to make fact." It seeks "to assert significant coherence in human experience: to assert that some beliefs and attitudes are beneficial for the flowering of sensation and consciousness, while others, to a greater or lesser degree, constrict and tend to kill." Since morality is too complex to be knowable or reduced to any code, fiction is, for Gardner, the most appropriate ethical vehicle because it "deals in understanding, not knowledge," in consciousness rather than code. And art's function, as he announced it in his introduction to *On Moral Fiction,* is therefore to rediscover "generation by generation, what is necessary to humanness" (6, 14, 50, 100, 135, 146, 177). Gardner puts it more concretely in his *Paris Review* interview:

> If you believe that life is fundamentally a volcano full of baby skulls, you've got two main choices as an artist: you can either stare into the volcano and count the skulls for the thousandth time and tell everybody, "There are the skulls; that's your baby, Mrs. Miller." Or you can try to build walls so that fewer baby skulls go in. It seems to me that the artist ought to hunt for positive ways of surviving, of living. You shouldn't lie. If there aren't any, so far as you can see, you should say so, like the *Merdistes*. But I don't think the *Merdistes* are right. (46–47)

In order to agree with Gardner on this point, you have to hold the belief, as Fowles does, that the imagination connects the aesthetic to the historical through its power, in Gardner's words, "to transform and redeem." This is the belief, Gardner says in *On Becoming a Novelist,* that demonstrates the "major influence" of William Blake on his ideas. You also have to hold Gardner's view, as Mailer does, that "what happens in real fiction is identical to what happens in a dream." This view Gardner develops in the *Paris Review:* "As long as we have the right to wake up screaming from a nightmare, we have the right to worry about character" (51). Indeed, like Mailer and Fowles, Gardner "got tired" of pure realism early, as he explains in his *Chicago Review* interview (80), and like them, Gardner has often been criticized and misunderstood when his books have departed from realistic conventions. Like these other two writers, the last thing we can charge Gardner with is that he creates traditionally realistic characters and plots. Contrary to recent criticism of "reflective" fiction as mere realism, Gardner's *The Sunlight Dialogues* is certainly not mere realism. Like most of his novels, *Sunlight Dialogues* is much closer to the pastoral and allegory and, as Gardner said of his fictional preferences since he was a child, to fable and tale.[6] David Cowart has noted those purely fabulistic elements of the novel's structure—the author's use of myth, legend, and epic from Homer, Dante, and Malory especially. The most obvious antecedent is the epic form with its twenty-four books, parallel plots, and epic themes and tricks.[7]

One of Gardner's chief values in good fiction is its ability, through a variety of techniques, to create this sense of dreaming on the part of the reader, a value he calls *profluence* or "the vivid and continuous dream" the writer creates and the reader "falls into." As Gardner describes this dreamlike movement of imagination in *On Becoming a Novelist,* profluence also provides for the reader "the sense that things are moving, getting somewhere, flowing forward." He does, nevertheless, maintain one fictional value associated with realism—"the novel's unashamed engagement with the world." It is the result of this value that the author employs "the myriad details that make character come alive" and that give the setting, however unreal, the feel of existence (7, 9). It is the value of detail, in turn, that helps define Gardner's sense of moral art.

We have seen that what Gardner means by moral art is certainly not right-wing politics and still less didacticism: "The didactic writer is anything but moral because he is always simplifying the argument, always narrowing away, getting rid of legitimate objections. *Mein Kampf* is a moralistic book—a stupid, ugly one. A truly moral book is one which is radically open to persuasion, but looks hard at a problem, and keeps looking for answers." Two criteria, finally, make a work "moral." The first is the writer's ability to start with the perception "that life is better than death" and to hunt "for avenues of life." A novel "succeeds if we're persuaded that the focal characters, in their fight for life, have won honestly or, if they lose, are tragic in their loss, not just tiresome or pitiful." The second criterion of the moral work is the dialectical process itself. Moral works "study values by testing them in imagined/real situations, testing them hard, being absolutely fair to both sides. The real moral writer is the opposite of the minister, the preacher, the rabbi. . . . He [the writer] should, if possible, not be committed to one side more than the other. . . . If he favors the cop, he must understand the arguments for life on the side of the robber."[8]

Having worked the ground of moral art so often in interviews, in articles, and in *On Moral Fiction,* Gardner returns to it in his last two books, written as guides and handbooks to would-be professionals. Here, as one might expect, his definitions are more well-wrought. Good fiction, or moral art, "does not deal in codes of conduct . . . ; it affirms responsible humanness" and it is "intellectually and emotionally significant." This responsible humanness, which the characters may or may not seek, is an essential element of profluence: "in the final analysis, real suspense comes with moral dilemma and the courage to make and act upon choices. False suspense comes from the accidental and meaningless occurrence of one damned thing after another."[9]

In *The Art of Fiction,* Gardner continues his analysis of the moral by explaining to young writers that good fiction must eventually lift from the particular to the universal—especially the universal affirmation, but that universal "is likely to be too subtle, too loaded with qualifications to be expressed in any way but the story's way; it may be impossible, that is, to reduce to any rule of behavior or general thesis. We *understand* the value . . . but even the shrewdest literary critic may have trouble formulating it in words and thus telling us the story's 'message.' "[10]

On the other hand, what one also realizes in reading Gardner's last two books is how much value he does place on technique. Again and again he advises new writers not to seek to discover a set of aesthetic laws, but to achieve "artistic mastery"—the masterful, conscious control of technique. It is simply that for Gardner, either calling attention to such mastery or questioning technique through fiction has never been his principal purpose. Like Fowles, he distrusts technique for is own sake or as its own end. "In texture alone there *is* no process; there is only effect," he writes in *On Moral Fiction.* In that earlier book he describes the lost artist as one who puts all his money on texture or on some easily achieved or faked structure. What Fowles has called the "new rococo" (or predominating texture), Gardner likewise believes "is king in all the arts" today (51, 57, 65). "A basic characteristic of all good art," Gardner later argues in *Art of Fiction,* "is a concord of ends and means, or form and function" (55), which is to say the concord of seriousness of purpose and mastery of technique. Gardner contends here that there is nothing particularly new about metafiction ("fiction that, both in style and theme, investigates fiction") and deconstructive fiction (the practice of taking language or works apart "to discover their unacknowledged inner workings"). He gives plenty of examples from ancient to modern times as well as from his own fiction of metafictional and deconstructive impulses and techniques. Gardner, however, wants to avoid what Lentricchia, in *Criticism and Social Change,* calls the "quietism of deconstruction," the very image of our humanist intellectuals feeling "vaguely out of it, desiring change, but crushed," playing into the hands of established power. "The first question before us," Lentricchia adds, "is not whether we are going to be Marxists, but whether or not, and on what ground, the examined life is worth living" (151–52).

With Gardner's fictional principles of process and purpose in mind, and with his definition of moral fiction clarified, our main interest will be to consider how his principles of character development and dialectical narrative relate to other structural devices and to the theme of ethical revelation through the agency of the magus in *The Sunlight Dialogues.*

We need to understand first the enormous significance of character to Gardner as expressed in this novel. Eccentrics and grotesques, these many characters' physical and moral deformities make even the minor characters all the more suffering and limited creatures that we humans are. Moreover, it is through the varied consciousness of a number of important characters that Gardner structures his plot, not by chronology. In nearly seven hundred pages of the novel only a few days pass. As in a Faulkner novel, the reader goes over and over the same recent events from a variety of points of view, each mind openly and convincingly presenting his or her version of present action, its relation to a richly remembered past, and its meaning. As Tony Tanner notes in his review, Gardner's density of detail in each point of view expresses the unique inner life of each character, and such density not only makes each vision plausible but also makes it difficult for readers to easily "capitulate to any one pattern of speculation."[11]

Like Fowles', Gardner's strategy is to use secondary characters to complicate the ethical choices before us. Many secondary characters act as foils to the Sunlight Man and Fred Clumly. That is to say, they act as alternatives—sometimes as commonplace alternatives—to the ethic developed out of the conflict between the magician's vision and that of his novitiate, an ethic which eventually expresses the possibilities for human dignity and freedom. To the extent that characters act as foils, they once again help us define the kinds of anarchism and consciousness the magician and his hero do *not* represent.

There are, to suggest a few examples, several minor outlaws in the novel: Nick, a mentally and morally defective killer; Kleppmann, a money-obsessed con man; Dr. Buzz Marchant, a debauchee; and Ollie Nuper, a self-righteous socialist and sexual opportunist who advocates racial violence. Their commonplace outlawry or anarchism is obviously unacceptable as an alternative to cold legalism or hypocrisy, but like the more complicated outlaws, these minor criminals tend to be either solipsistic hedonists or self-righteous theorists. The hippie Freeman is more like the magician, Tag Hodge, a wanderer who sees contemporary civilization as built on "two thousand years of the wrong information." Yet Freeman is a foil to the magician, a "nonreferential" anarchist who believes that change of consciousness trapped by bad civilization is impossible.

More fully developed than these other outlaws, the petty thief Benson-Boyle is, like the Sunlight Man, a shapeshifter. But Benson-Boyle is a dual personality of increasingly irreconcilable polarities. Freakish and alienated at fifty-six, he sees that "his whole life was a waste," or as Tag puts it to him, "Asleep since the day he was born."[12]

Another response to our historical circumstances is romantic alienation from society, represented by Tag's nephew, Luke Hodge. "So much revolution in you," as Tag describes him, "so much hatred for order, so much hatred for anarchy—and so much love. How terrible! Where can you run to? I tremble for your soul" (617). Luke, ever the victim of his own romantic dream, turns his understanding earned in the magician's ordeal against himself. He carries self-sacrifice to its extreme reduction in suicide, the grand gesture of driving his trailer truck into a deep gorge.

Millie Hodge, Luke's mother, is another significant outlaw-foil struggling against the oppressive authority of legalism and social system. Beautiful, intelligent, a monster of egotism and manipulation, Millie believes and acts according to her motto: "I exist. No one else." She is the devouring bitch goddess who revels in her self-creation as a cold temptress beyond mother-love, hate, and time: "Bitchiness was her strength and beauty and hope of salvation" (180). Insinuating her way into the Hodge family, she is at least partly responsible for its dissolution, "planning the destruction of Stony Hill years before she knew she was going to get it from the Hodges and sell it for trash" (182), just as she is more clearly responsible for the disarray of her well-meaning but bungling husband Will and for her son's incapacity to pull his life together and express his love. Millie's belief that "God is physical" not only sums up her approach to others as a beautiful and manipulative whore, but sums up the representativeness of her vision and its distance from the vision expressed in Tag's four dialogues.

Against Tag, her husband, her son, and saintly Ben Hodge, Millie confuses her own will with the order of the universe: "A natural force, unconstrained, and not merely ignorant. They were the cosmic outlaws, not she. . . . Her lines and life were free" (432). Millie demonstrates the familiar confusion between original *ideas* (whether prophetic, revolutionary, religious, or political) and corrupted *ideologies:* "For centuries people with stupid theories have been murdering people who try to just live, enjoy life, seize the day and make the most of it. Priests, politicians. Truth is mostly in the sewer" (438).

But even Millie, like Luke and, as we will see, like Chief of Police Fred Clumly, learns from her experiences in the magician's mills.

> And so at last they were face to face. He made her a foul old witch for her crimes, and how he was chief victim of her witchcraft. Or she'd been a witch before and he had exorcized her demon, had brought her gaze down from grand visions of sex and subtle wit to the bare earth where he stood. Either way, she had seen him clear, "as if scales had fallen from her eyes"— the brittle scales of her theory on how to "be"—and she knew him, and knew herself, so that he too suddenly knew. (625)

Perhaps Millie's greatest incompleteness as a human being is her incapacity for love, her denial of it, a denial which Tag also reveals to her: "She was ugly, and the father-in-law she had admired too much was dead, his house in ruins. The war was over. She had underestimated love" (624).

These examples of characters who act as outlaw-foils to the Sunlight Man are only part of the characterization technique Gardner uses to clarify the kind of revelation the magician bears to his community. Rather than representing varieties of outlawry, another group of characters represents varieties of defeat by capitulation to or by mindless acceptance of a system, code, or larger force. The caricature of old Miss Woodworth, for example, is reminiscent of Fowles' caricature of Mrs. Poultney in *The French Lieutenant's Woman* as the embodiment of the hermetic genteel morality of class mannerism and received ideas— that autocracy of convention which turns petty and vicious.

More significant as a defeated character, more complexly human and fully presented is Will, Jr., Tag's other nephew. A collector of debts in a large Buffalo legal firm, an escapee from the rural values of Genessee County, he represents the conscious-but-helpless capitulation to legalism and urban values: "he had grown up, had finally broken free of the myth . . . broken out of Eden . . . it was a transition place, an evolutionary stage he and his kind had broken out of for the world coming in: the city" (333). Once Will had discovered moral disorder, he responded with thoroughgoing relativism.

> But the world the Old Man had created at Stony Hill was different from the world where he worked, doggedly honest but out of place, in the end. Stony Hill farm . . . was as self-contained and self-perpetuating, even as serene . . . as Heaven itself. It was a garden for idealism. . . . It made you want to be a minister.
> All mere illusion, he knew now. Mere entertainment. But if there was no God, there was no Devil either. So much for absolutes, then. So much for politics. (338–39)

He is, then, easily sucked into the rat race, as he calls it, and "perdu," as are so many other characters in the novel.

Will, Sr., is in a way an equally defeated man: often ineffectual, uncertain of his values, not cut out to follow in his father's path either, beaten by his marriage to the sexual adventurer and witty destroyer Millie, "his whole life . . . an ingenious toggle, a belated but painstaking shoring up against last year's ruin, destructions in no way his own but his to repair" (126). Unlike his son, however, Will, Sr., will be disturbed by the events the magician sets in motion. And by watching Clumly, knowing of Tag's return, and seeing the aftermath of his son Luke's suicide, Will, Sr., gains a certain wisdom by the story's end. Indeed, he will finally act as a kind of choric figure whose thoughts, as he contemplates Luke's death and his brother Tag, prepare the reader for Clumly's closing speech—the central revelation of the novel: "His son's sacrifice, however impure it may have been, had purified Will Hodge. He was indifferent to the hunt, whether the crimes of cops or robbers: it was necessary, merely, that order prevail for those who were left, when the deadly process had run itself down; necessary to rebuild" (644). Grief, as Will sees and Clumly comes to see, is perhaps the best response to humanity's tragic condition. For grief might finally lead one to act, not merely watch, to rebuild and go on against the dissolutions of legal order and illegal disorder. Grief is the basis of compassion.

One quality that nearly all of these characters share—whether as outlaws or as people defeated by the various codes they receive or develop—is self-righteousness, a danger Tag himself struggles to overcome. And it is not only most of these characters I have discussed here at some length, but other figures as well who share this failing: whether it be the prostitute Clumly tries to bust, the young cop Kozlowski with his righteousness of youth, old man Paxton who spouts clichés in his monstrous righteousness, or (to take a major character) Clumly himself with "that tiresome leer of self-righteousness," most of the people in this book are good examples of the dangers of self-righteousness, for Gardner as for Fowles, the stuff of moralism, not of moral vision.

Ben Hodge, a foil of a different sort, is one of the few people free of that curse throughout the novel. Based on Gardner's father, Ben represents one positive alternative to Tag by his lack of egotism, his efforts to take in wayward youths, his passive mysticism, and his pastoral life. Living in a kind of timeless moment where all things are an instance of the eternal holy, Ben, unlike Tag, requires nothing of you, is "no more demanding or self-conscious than the land, or a bird, or somebody else's cow." There is, of course, a passive, unconscious nobility in his way.

The Sunlight Man is neither so passive nor so transcendental. His behavior is of a more bumptious, unsettling sort. Moreover, the Sunlight Man's outlawry, as Police Chief Clumly realizes after the final dialogue, is "irregular." Another magician who shrouds himself in mystery and whose antics seem inexplicable and irrational, Gardner's "lunatic magician" also initiates larger consciousness in those whom he turns in his mill. He is another figure from contemporary fiction of archetypal proportions and purposes. Like a banished scapegoat, he returns to Batavia, New York, "about my father's business," bearing his message to people in a world seemingly "rotten beyond hope of redemption." Gregory Morris has compared Taggert Hodge to Enkidu the cosmic scapegoat of *Gilgamesh* who is sacrificed to the demands of order and the discipline of the gods. Clumly, he compares to Gilgamesh, who through struggle and sorrow is driven to epiphany and heroic understanding. *Gilgamesh* is a source Gardner alludes to in the novel, and he acknowledges A. Leo Oppenheim's *Ancient Mesopotamia: Portrait of a Dead Civilization* (1964). Gardner's lunatic, Morris further points out, is also parallel to Oppenheim's description of ancient "prophetic ecstasies" wherein willfulness and self-consciousness dissolve to allow the expression to divine madness through the holy fool. And David Cowart reminds us that for Gardner "lunatic" frequently means one who is "healthily determined not to be content with certain of the more deleterious aspects of reality."[13]

Like an "exorcist going to the house of a patient," Tag Hodge promises only an intolerable struggle for anyone who would keep his or her human dignity amidst the oppressions of social order, on one hand, and the chaos of social disintegration, on the other. Into the chaotic world of the 1960s, the Sunlight Man comes not as solemn teacher, nor as warrior-hero, but as trickster and fool—spouting apparent nonsense, arcane learning, and the patter of a master stage magician. When he recalls how Jung described the evolution of the trickster into an "approximation . . . of a savior," Cowart suggests the mythic role of this central figure, and traces the ways Tag is symbolically compared to Jesus throughout the novel.[14]

Compared to Houdini, the Great Deceiver, and a stinking ghoul returned from the dead, Tag's ancient literary lineage as shapeshifter, con-man, and fool is as clear as his talismanic marks of the hero—his Cain-scarred face, his white divining stones.

> He came to be known as the Sunlight Man. . . . In the depths where his turbulent broodings moved, the solemn judgments of psychiatry, sociology and the like, however sound, were frail sticks beating a subterranean sea. . . .
> You could not tell whether he was speaking to you or scoffing at you for your immersion in the false; whether he was wrestling with a problem of immense significance to him or indifferently displaying his hodge-podge of maniac learning. (59–60)

Gardner is of course aware of the archetype; indeed his sense of the fiction writer's work, like Fowles', is fundamentally archetypal, as he explains in *On Moral Fiction*. Literature is "exhausted," he explains, in the sense that it does not tell new stories, but literature is always renewed because it tells "archetypal stories in an attempt to understand once more their truth" (66).

This magician's literary heritage includes not only the trickster/fool heroes before him, but the literary artist himself. Like Fowles' creator of metadramas, Gardner's is likewise armed with his reading, his "magical" techniques, his stock of lore and tricks. Here again the magician is the metaphor for the artist, the creator of a dramatic reality and enlightening art form. "Art," Gardner puts it in *On Moral Fiction*, is "the only true magic" (146). Like any artist incapable of embracing and uniting humanity in common cause against stupidity, cruelty, folly, and the forces of dissolution, the magician-artist must turn instead to his magic show, his art, in order to dazzle, entertain, and carry the message of his vision, and in order to awaken our potential to reduce our disproportions of egoism, greed, and harshness toward one another. Tag perfectly expresses the necessary frustration of the artist who would engage the moral world in a moment of self-revelation before Millie:

> He had suddenly a terrible urge to embrace her and sob, ask for help, but he said, "I have terrible urges to embrace someone, cry out for help." He laughed, "My whole nature howls

'Stop! Why can't we start over, fresh?' In the graveyard, for instance, when I knew for sure
. . . that my sons were dead. 'This can't go on. . . . We're human beings, a common cause!
We ought to present a united front against the wolves and the trolls and the World-snake!' . . .
I thought better of it. I decided to turn instead to a life of art." (521)

If the Sunlight Man is a representative, one might even say traditional,
literary figure, Gardner does not oversimplify. He makes Taggert Hodge something more than a hollow figure in a simple allegory or fable by giving us a full
sense of his particularity, of his past and his inner life. When the novel turns to
Tag's point of view, he reveals himself as a complicated, purposeful, yet harried
human being, a person with private suffering and self-doubt. And Gardner
establishes the family roots and the personal history that make Tag the one
chosen, or fated, to bear his message. Tag is the one to whom the town's Great
Man, his father Congressman Hodge, passed on occult and metaphysical inter-
ests along with the talismanic diviner's stones. A lawyer acting outside the legal
system to save his insane wife, Tag, once the hope of his declining family, is a
suitable spokesman for the gap between the legal and the ethical orders, just as
he will become the spokesman for the gap between the human and the cosmic
orders.

The knowledge this hero-fool will bear upon returning to his home, the
potential "boon of greater consciousness" for personal "transformation" (to borrow Joseph Campbell's terminology) that this self-announced anarchist, student,
and magician will bring into the world of lost men and women, is best traced
through the dialogues themselves. Like Police Chief Clumly, each reader is
probably at first tempted to see the magician-prophet's words as the automatic
ramblings of an empty machine who mimics the rise of old prophets. But that
view, Clumly discovers after his labors and lessons, will not hold.

Like Fowles, Gardner takes delight in tempting his readers as well as his
characters to hold such a view of narrative meaninglessness, here as elsewhere
in the book, when he mocks us with the mask of the metafictionist. At such
times the third-person narrator or one of the characters will intrude and comment
on how dry the novelist's presentation is (135), or how bored the reader would
be if this were a novel (462), or how the characters feel themselves "trapped in
an allegory" (470) or trapped "in an endless, meaningless novel" (621), or how
foolish the reader is to be trying to make sense of "all this rubbish" (622), or
how the novel might implicitly parallel other fiction, like Melville's *Pierre*: "it
was a stupid novel, it was a brilliant novel" (639). Of course, such are the
temptations of fiction readers today; it is hard now to be innocent of all the
metafictional questions, tricks, and narrative subversions. But a careful reading
of *The Sunlight Dialogues* as well as Gardner's other fiction and nonfiction
makes succumbing to these temptations more difficult.

Like both Fowles and Mailer, it takes Gardner on the order of seven hundred pages to express the vision his magician brings to this world. That vision is complex, even problematic, and requires suffering initiates to act upon and develop it to make it useful and healthy. Tag expresses his message in two ways that parallel Maurice Conchis' techniques. First, it is expressed through object lessons, or physical parables, that the magician imposes upon characters, and, second, it is expressed through a series of dialogues, or verbal parables, delivered to a single initiate, Chief Fred Clumly. All the people he brings his message to are in varying ways the "living dead," to borrow Clumly's phrase, whom Tag tries to inspire to transformation.

What I have called his "physical parables" are indeed object lessons in self-revelation through suffering. Tag's purpose is always to hold the human eye and mind closer to reality. The variation of Plato's allegory that Tag tells Clumly about a young Black thief held in a cellar, for example, is to a lesser extent acted out on Luke and Millie. Likewise, their imprisonment emphasizes that one must be removed from the world before one can return to accurately perceive it.

As a result of their sufferings in "real parables," so to speak, both Luke and Millie move out of themselves and closer to external reality. But both respond in starkly different ways: one with suicide-as-self-sacrifice and the other with altered consciousness and self-knowledge. The magician always leaves each person free to respond to the ordeal and the resulting perceptions in his or her own way.

The magician's second vehicle of revelation is a series of four dialogues with Chief Clumly—the principal initiate and the recorder of the magician's words. The dialogues do not begin until three hundred pages into the novel, but they are prefaced by a series of initial interviews and confrontations between Clumly and the Sunlight Man that, like the imprisoned magician's wild statements, are intended to confuse, unsettle, attract, and prepare the Chief (and probably the reader) for, as Tag puts it, the "Metaphysics" to come. Clumly's side of the dialogue stretches intermittently throughout the novel, and both the prefatory confrontations and the dialogues themselves provide the structural foundation of this complex story. This foundation, as Gregory Morris suggests, has roots in Mesopotamian religious literature. Oppenheim described that ancient dialogue form: "a skeptic and a pious man alternately present their views in a polite and ceremonious fashion, complete with learned abstrusities and far-fetched expressions."[15] But as I've suggested, Gardner is drawing on a larger literary tradition too, as do both Fowles and Mailer. The dialectical structure of the classical and medieval debate or dialogue between the hero and the guide is a sort of psychodrama (or "psychomachia") in the visionary tradition of literature.[16]

Through repetition and development, each dialogue builds toward the essential reality Tag hopes to express. The first dialogue, "On Wood and Stone," suggests the forgotten but helpful wisdom ancient Mesopotamia might offer the modern world, that is, the necessity of realizing the connection between mind and matter in opposition to our tendencies to separate consciousness from matter and from historical process.

During the dialogues Clumly represents America's Judeo-Christian (and Cartesian) foundation. Tag lays down his theme in the initial dialogue: the separation of "substance" or essence from the matter that creates an irreconcilable dualism of spirit and flesh develops from both the Buddhist and Judeo-Christian lines. Such separation leads inevitably to misperceptions of reality and creates confusion and guilt, as for example our separation of spirit and flesh creates guilt in our relationship to our sexuality. Out of the torments of our varieties of guilt come our obsessions with individual salvation, obsessions leading in turn to a kind of egoism, solipsism, relativism, and other worldliness of vision.

Tag, sounding more than a little like Conchis, will clarify to Millie near the end of the novel that egoism and solipsism blind us, for example, to the real interrelationships between human beings, interrelationships that make up a kind of huge social-religious organism. "What we are, instant by instant, is part of a system of relationships. As in classical ballet. I stand in such and such a relationship to you; that is my meaning, my significance. If I go over there and stand by your son, my significance must change. . . . Insofar as there are common elements in all these situations, there is continuity, which is to say, I begin to embody values. . . . It's very moving, in a way, to be part of the common core. That's what religion is" (621).

In this first dialogue, the Sunlight Man charges that the contemporary results of our philosophical lineage are a life-denying solipsism, on one hand, and an obsession with "law and order," on the other. Such an approach to reality is necessarily out of tune with it. We seek to escape external reality by our denial of it. We are, therefore, in danger of fulfilling the fate of the young thief trapped in Tag's allegorical cellar: "He'd misunderstood reality, and so he died." It is, in short, dangerous to both individual and species to be cut off from reality, not to be synchronized with the order of the cosmos, but to be marooned in the self listening to a solipsistic drone.

The fault in Tag is not so much his vision's inaccuracy as his tendency to accept the vision as the basis for a belief in the futility of any effort to change and create. "You ask me what my answer is to America's problems," Tag says to Clumly, "—psychological, social, political. I have none. I do not deny that we ought, theoretically, to continue fighting, labor on, struggle for improvement. But I doubt that anything in all our system is in tune with, keyed to, reality. . . . I mean your laws are irrelevant, stupid, inhuman. . . . There is good and evil in the world, but they have nothing to do with your courts" (327–28).

But the ancient wisdom of Mesopotamia might also play a fundamental role in readjusting our self-conception to be more consistent with reality. Were the Mesopotamians not one of the greatest mercantile and spiritual civilizations ever? Tag asks. "Their alchemy and astrology was religious to the core, a celebration of the essential holiness of matter itself. . . . With everything they did they asserted the fundamental co-existence, without conflict, of body and spirit, both of which were of ultimate worth. And as for the connection between the body and spirit, they ignored it. It was by its very essence mysterious. They cared only that the health of one depended upon the health of the other, God knew how" (318).

The Babylonian approach to the individual that resulted from such a religion, Tag argues finally, is that each individual lives life as fully as possible as "merely a part of a physical and spiritual system." All Tag asks Clumly to consider at this point is the possibility that the Mesopotamian approach may redress the present imbalance between matter and spirit, self and others, self and cosmos. That approach did, after all, survive "for a thousand years, it was embraced by some of the greatest generals . . . and some of the greatest poets, magicians, statesmen, artists, and, above all, architects. Were they all doubters? Were they all fools . . . ?" (317).

The second "Dialogue of Houses" (the astrological houses) builds on the first by considering the method and purpose of ancient divination. If the orders of the modern conscious mind and the cosmos are dissimilar, how do we discover the nonhuman order? The volumes of statistics amassed in the ancient anthologies, Tag argues, are not for prediction, and still less for the magical or scientific manipulation of gods or nature. Their purpose is to discover the "profound patterns" of the cosmos and their relationships to humanity. The ancient books of Mesopotamia, Egypt, and India seek to discover "what the universe is doing," what the patterns of reality really are, so that one's practical and spiritual lives act within the patterns. Through divination you discover which way things are flowing, then "you swim in the same direction."

Individual freedom thereby is defined not as self-assertion against cosmos or others, still less as the creation of alternative realities, but as the "radical freedom" of being "in shape to act with the universe when the universe says 'Now!'" And personal responsibility becomes not the Jewish responsibility of "obeying laws, performing . . . duties," but the Mesopotamian responsibility of "stubbornly maintaining one's freedom to act . . . jumping when the Spirit says, 'Jump!'" (420). Freedom is thus defined as discovering, and then remaining free to act in accord with, the patterns of the real.

The magician ends the second dialogue, significantly, on another note of scepticism, a scepticism that will render Tag's vision useless for his own salvation. It is doubtful, he argues, that humans possess the ability to discover those patterns and to act bravely within them. The human susceptibility to self-righteousness and egoism is too great, as the regular decay of civilizations demonstrates: "in the valleys at the bottom of the sea, layer on layer, sunken treasure ships. *Istaru!* [i.e., the pattern of existence for Time and Space, as opposed to *sintu* or personal fate] Food of the gods!" Hence, further, the futility of social causes, psychotherapy, and professional educationists. Only an impossible revolution in consciousness can counteract our heritage and our egoism. As for himself, well, as Tag says not quite accurately since he is teaching Clumly, he has chosen passive anarchism—silence, exile, cunning—waiting to act as far as possible within universal, not human, law (422–25).

The third dialogue, "Of the Dead," recapitulates the points argued in the first two and emphasizes, as Fowles does, the wrong-headedness of the struggle for merely "personal fulfillment." Like Melville's Pierre, whose name and quest echo throughout Gardner's novel, Tag's self-examination and experience lead to the essentially modern question:

> Shall I act within the cultural order I do not believe in but with which I am engaged by ties of love or anyway ties of fellowfeeling, or shall I act within the cosmic order I *do* believe in, at least in principle, an order indifferent to man? And then again, shall I act by standing indecisive between the two orders—not striking out for the cosmic order because of my human commitment, not striking out for the cultural order because of my divine commitment? Which shall I renounce, my body—of which ethical intellect is a function—or my soul? (533)

At this point we can see that Tag's real fault is his inability to rekindle for himself the Mesopotamian union of the two. He is victim of the very dualism he has deprecated, the product of his own culture's myths.

The final dialogue, "Of Towers," is apocalyptic and nihilistic. It argues that humanity will fail to discover and then to act within the order of the reality, the cosmic organism, within which it lives. Even the magnificent towers of Babylon might represent the human being's inner mystery—the knowledge that one is born for death, the destructive principle, entropy, which stimulates humanity to build ascending towers that speak of its desire to be one with the universe. But the towers always fall, Tag argues, and will fall again in the coming final age of man, foreshadowed everywhere by increase of bondage, disgust, ennui, guilt, violence, chaos. Vietnam is perhaps the beginning. The error is inherent in civilization, and "the error . . . is man." We do not know, or learn to know, reality; and so we die. Tag's final vision, as he calls it, is like something out of Blake, as the epigraph to chapter 19 might remind us:

> The Caverns of the Grave I've seen,
> And these I show'd to England's Queen,
> But now the Caves of Hell I view,
> Who shall I dare to show them to?

Hell's jaws yawn and cities sink as blind people speak in a babble of tongues and "total chaos" reclaims all order.

This final dialogue is significant to our understanding of Tag's nihilism, for, like Grendel, he has looked into the abyss and is paralyzed by his vision of it. He is reminiscent of the dramatic Renaissance magician that Barbara Traister described—a man of good intentions and power who is also proud and fallible.

If the Mesopotamian vision of reality renders an order based on human relationships that are all important *because* there is nothing beyond them but void, Tag can act on only half the perception. He sees the void, and rather than turning to the order of human community as significant and potentially creative, he despairs. He sees only the apocalyptic destruction of all human order and effort. Whether it is limited by the Christian dualism of matter and spirit passed on from the Congressman's Eden, or whether he is victim of his romantic heritage, Tag descends to a nihilism the Babylonians avoided. If he discovers that love is creative, it is too late by the time he does, and he is unable to act upon that discovery. It will be, therefore, up to his apprentice Clumly to carry the logic of Tag's Babylonian vision toward a viable synthesis for present life—a faith in community and a compassionate, selfless relationship to it.

Tag's role in the novel, then, is as the representative, the revealer, of the nonhuman, indifferent order. This is particularly true as he is seen through others' eyes. He is the one whose own eyes, Luke and Millie notice, are not quite human. Tag's return to New York gives frightful premonitions to officer Miller (85). Clumly feels the same thing: "the creature waking up, or anyway . . . moving toward him, coming from darkness outside the city limits. . . . It's like a creature waking up from the center of the earth, scratching and scratching" (89, 91). Like the "antique serpent . . . Time," the hidden dragon of destruction and revolutionary change, Tag brings into the world of the novel a single large truth about humanity's circumstances. Like the scarred and bearded sailor of Clumly's dreams, Tag takes one out on the stormy sea of metaphysics. His purpose is to register in other people the gap between the human and the cosmic orders. If the view of that gap might lead to nihilism, it might also serve as the basis for a new humanism, for if we were to act from such a perspective, surely our acts would radically alter. How could the inflations of ego survive such knowledge? If it is left to Clumly to "humanize the whole," as Fowles has put it, if Clumly will have the last and hopeful word in the novel, it is still worth recalling that in Gardner's "Prologue" Tag's truth appears to have renewed itself over time. For Clumly is no longer held by his neighbors to be the hero of the day, the effective spokesman for responsibility and compassion, but is now forgotten: "opinion was divided, in fact, over whether he'd gone away or died."

The human constructions over the abyss, against entropy, are no less valuable and necessary, but they are ever-shifting and tenuous, ever in need of renewal.

In Gardner's novel, as we have seen, it is not a young man who becomes the heroic object of the magician's mill. The one to be transformed and to bear the message of his experience is an older man about to retire. Police Chief Fred Clumly's journey and trials shape, as do Urfe's, the central narrative. From the beginning Clumly, like Tag, is a marked man, another of Gardner's grotesques. His entire body is "creased and white and completely hairless" from a disease contracted in the Navy long ago. His only remarkable feature is his large mole-like nose. Though he may otherwise seem an unlikely hero, Gardner's narrator tells us that Clumly looks like "a philosopher pale from too much reading, or a man who has slept three nights in the belly of a whale" (8). Clumly is indeed on a quest that will work a sea-change, and his early intuitions about the bearded prisoner portend that this magician will be the instrument of such change.

The change Clumly undergoes is all the more striking because he seems to be such a representative, ordinary man. He is deeply unsettled by the convulsions in contemporary life, and expresses his unease through the usual clichés. For a long time he approaches the Sunlight Man's parables as literal truths: "Were his stories true? Has the man really kept a Negro boy locked in his cellar all that time?" (313). He exemplifies the modern keeper of the law, the schizophrenic cop that Tag's journal article identifies—a man whose body must be separated from his soul, who eventually approaches madness, who must regularly "deny to himself—far below the level of conscious assertion—that the voice with which he speaks is his own." He becomes "the Law," constantly sliding away from the humanity he shares with others (209–12). And like all of us, he has his share of suffering, his lifetime of self-denials, political compromises, failures, errors, and bad luck. As his blind wife Esther says, contemplating their dead life together: "they must live out their lives like two people in a dungeon, and for her the dungeon was blindness. . . . But just the same she was his dungeon" (276).

Clumly is representative in a more abstract sense, and that too is why Tag chooses him: "He [Tag] had meant to go to Ben, had instead gone to Clumly. . . . It was, he could only explain, necessary. What he must say he could not say to a brother; it must be to the coldly reasonable unreason of officialdom" (305). Clumly had not learned sorrow: "There was only order, lifted against the world like rusty chickenwire to keep out a smell of cows. . . . There were only Clumly's ancient codes, the torturous cravings on his tablets" (249–51).

Gardner's concept of the traditional hero from Homer to Tolstoy is that the hero represents a noble image for humanity. If, as Gardner explains in *On Moral Fiction,* the traditional hero's standards come from the gods or God, are enacted by the hero, and are recorded by the poet, the modern hero, like Clumly, must be a representative of human potential whose standards, recorded by the artist, come from "an impression of what might be, an ardent wish," in short, an affirmation (28–29, 36). If Clumly is to succeed in any degree, however, to change and bear the message of his transformation, he, like any hero whether prophet or fool, will have to extricate himself from the prevailing order, move outside the community, violate its standards and suffer its ostracisms, dive down into that anti-civilized self and discover some other domain and order within.

Clumly's obsession with the Sunlight Man leads him on his journey. The obsession begins with a mere desire to exonerate himself in the eyes of his community: "He'd beat them yet. What could they do to the Police Chief who'd brought down the Sunlight Man?" (226). But his obsession does not remain so self-interested. Halfway through the novel he becomes more concerned for the community: "I've tried your way. . . . I'm responsible for this town. . . . It's *like* a king. If a king's laws get tangled up and his knights fail him, he's got to do the job himself. They're *his* people" (378). And later still his obsession develops into a personal quest—at the expense of job, social position—for the knowledge and change this magician's strange rant somehow seems to promise. Having taken up Tag's talismanic stones, his monomania finally is the magician himself and his metaphysics, as if he were playing Ahab to Tag's Moby Dick.

Shortly before the final dialogue the external symbolic changes suggest how completely Clumly's interior life has changed, a transformation that will be expressed in his closing speech to the Dairyman's league:

> He would meet the Sunlight Man, tonight as Fred Clumly, Citizen. Or less. As Fred Clumly, merely mortal, nothing more than—without any grandiose overtones—a man. . . . He could not endure it without, at least, the black coat handed down to him by his father. . . .
>
> He doubted that he had been a good husband. . . . He doubted that he had been honest with himself or honest with his wife either. . . . The unrealized life lurched and groped inside him like some primeval creature in an ancient jungle, and its presence inside him mocked and poisoned the life he had lived. . . . Any life a man chooses, Clumly mused, betrays the life he failed to choose. . . . He would be gone, dressed as an ordinary man, and whatever he learned or failed to learn would have nothing to do with law and order in the common sense. He had promoted himself. He was now Chief Investigator of the Dead. (606)

Clumly's growth in understanding and compassion, a change revealed in his final speech, is further indicated when he lets the Sunlight Man go free, after the final dialogue when Clumly has the opportunity to capture him.

The content of Clumly's last speech is ironically contrasted to its title,

"Law and Order," just as with equal irony Tag's death certificate describes his death as caused by "police action in pursuit of order." One thing Clumly has learned by now is that there is more than one kind of order; he speaks not, therefore, of order "in the common sense." Because he has heard that the Sunlight Man is dead, Clumly departs from his prepared remarks. He speaks from his heart as if he were reading words cut into the wall "like runes from a stylus" by an angel's hand "in order to communicate with you all here tonight, this crowd of friends and neighbors I've known all my life."

Clumly argues that order in the common sense—the order of law-abiding lives, of our ceremonies—is good, but it should not be mistaken for justice. Tag chose to live outside our order, so we cannot honor him with "the kind of order we give those others." Yet, Clumly says, he had the "finest mind" and knowledge and magician's ability he had ever seen. What the Sunlight Man came to teach, then, requires our attention.

Recapitulating the magician's argument himself, Clumly tells the people that even though the world seems to be falling apart and we need so often to depend on the order created by the "Watchdogs of Society," we also need at other times to reach beyond such order and beyond our fears to reaffirm our humanity, to live as if the dissolution all around us were not so. "It's a little like the Einstein universe, as I understand it," Clumly explains, "which is reaching outwards and outwards at terrific speed, and the danger is . . . it can get cold. Turn ice" (672).

Clumly, through Tag Hodge, becomes finally connected not so much to the simple outlaws in the story—Nick, Millie, Benson-Boyle—but to such visionary artists as Melville and Blake whose echoes resound throughout the novel. As the Sunlight Man once phrased it to Millie and Luke: "There are no laws . . . only the laws of man, which are easily beaten, and the laws you make up yourself, which may be obeyed, once they're made up, but only then" (521). Later Clumly will sarcastically say much the same thing to the Mayor's investigating committee that will require him to step down. Clumly thereby provides a transition between the Sunlight Man's anarchism and the humanity of his own final speech: "I enforce the law . . . I pull you in, I leave it to the court. And they don't have to think about it either, right? The lawyers can look up their precedents, they can hang you because they hung some poor devil in 1866. And . . . I can go on making speeches about law and order . . . and nobody has to think. Nobody! That's democracy, you follow me. Like a huge aluminum dome made out of a million beams, and not a single beam is responsible" (590).

Looked at from the eyes of history, Clumly tells his audience at the novel's end, "we may be wrong about the whole thing." Though a little confused himself and not entirely sure he has said what he means, Clumly ultimately suggests that the best approach for them all to take before the awesome strangeness of events, change, impending catastrophe, and legalistic coldness of heart is simply humility. Humility reduces cold arrogance and looks for forgiveness; it is born of our suffering, our grief, our muddled efforts to remain human. "Blessed are the meek, by which I mean all of us, including the Sunlight Man." The audience responds to this affirmation with "floor shivering" applause that lifts Clumly "like some powerful, terrible, wave of sound and things in their motions hurtling him up to where the light was brighter than sun-filled clouds, disanimated and holy." "Powerful sermon!" cries the Fire Chief, "God forgive us." To which Clumly—"shocked to wisdom"—cries, "Correct!" (672–73).

He has arrived at a point not far from where his wife, in her own way, has long been—selfless, suffering, blind, lovingly devoted to another even once physical love has waned. As Gardner suggests in his interview with Joe David Bellamy: "Mrs. Clumly is the Beatrice of *The Sunlight Dialogues*. She guides everybody because she loves. This is the kind of imagination which holds the world together." Both the Clumlys possess the greatest potential because they have the "most imagination" or imaginative empathy. They "see into other people's minds. . . . At least he has compassion, which is a kind of imagination."[17] Against the reality of entropy and the coldness of legalism, Clumly holds humility, forgiveness, and sorrow. These are the virtues that lead to a responsible sympathy by which we, like Fowles, generally mean love. This is what Gardner meant when asked what principle one should base one's decisions on to "be like the hero," he replied: "Love. Whatever is the most loving thing to do." This "love" as he describes it arises from "principled ethics which are based on a deep understanding of human nature and human need" that is fundamentally "intuitive." [18] If this understanding is something the Sunlight Man comes to feel as he paints "love" on the street, it is something he is unable to turn to positive effect, a discovery too late in his own life. It is the human coherence that is missing from his vision. And that is the reason why he must turn his vision, as a failed hero, over to another, to one who can humanize it, turn it into a workable, flexible, and uncodified ethic for human community. "True art's divine madness is shot through with love," Gardner says in *On Moral Fiction:* "love of the good, a love proved not by some airy and abstract high-mindedness but by active celebration of whatever good or trace of good can be found by a quick and compassionate eye in this always corrupt and corruptible but god-freighted world" (204).

It is, we have seen, in the process of the constructive dialectic of oppositions that the transformation takes place *despite* the abyss. Perhaps such a process is Tag's hope when he tells Clumly: "I respect you, you see. But I'm in fundamental disagreement with your philosophy of life. I thought if our two stands were clearer, perhaps" (315). Out of their opposition is born synthesis—a forgiving and loving potential for human life in the face of an inhuman, entropic reality. It is the same discovery Nicholas Urfe makes in the face of "Hazard" and inhuman cruelty.

Gardner's body of work is of course uneven, and I do not want to argue that structural and thematic unities save all. Though I am indicating what I take to be certain weaknesses here and there in each author under consideration, I am more interested in establishing the intentions, risk-takings, and unities of, and between, each author. I want to make them more clearly understood as counter-hermetic and counter-hegemonic forces in Anglo-American letters.

Gardner once argued that *The Sunlight Dialogues* represents his discovery of "a governing metaphysical system that I believe" and that he has been "pursuing small aspects of the governing system" ever since.[19] Gardner did not write his novels in the order of their publication, however, and our sense of *The Sunlight Dialogues* as prototypical increases when we understand that, again like Fowles' *Magus,* it is one of Gardner's earliest manuscripts finally published, as Gardner explains in a discussion of the backlog he collected over fifteen years.[20]

Taking Gardner's lead, Bruce Allen, among others, has speculated on the consistency of pattern and theme (or "system") in Gardner's work. Allen perceptively identifies Gardner's theme a "man's need to know that the world he inhabits makes sense and that his own actions matter." This theme, Allen continues, is depicted through the conflict between social order and individual freedom. More to the point still, Allen sees that Gardner's stories concern themselves with the "initiatory journeys toward knowledge" of a succession of seeker-heroes. Yet Allen otherwise reads too quickly and summarizes too much. He glibly calls Gardner's vision "existential," as if seeing only half of Gardner's dialectical oppositions and taking, thereby, the nihilism for the whole. To Allen, and such later critics as Robert Frederickson, Gardner ultimately argues for a "universe which asserts their [the heroes] irrelevance and ignores them." It surely misrepresents Gardner to see his work as "chronicles of wreckage and waste."[21]

I have been arguing that the magician and his confrontation with the hero is a device adapted from a literary tradition and used in inceptive, prototypical texts to get at the ethical and "secular" themes of three contemporary authors. Though each author plays variations on a traditional device and on his ethical themes, both the device (in the prototypical novel) and the themes (extended throughout each author's canon) coincide sufficiently to unite all three authors as a kind of progressive counterforce to the more hermetic impulses and manifestos of post-modernism. The commonalities of texts in each author's canon are of course not limited to the device of the magician. Certain other novels of each author do include magicians, magicianlike figures, or characters that take on similar redemptive roles, but the magicians of the prototypical texts announce or discover (or in Mailer's case consolidate) the dialectical and thematic patterns, as well as the metafictional techniques, of each author's larger body of work. Gardner is an exemplary case.

Though its labyrinths may be more intricate, its subplots more developed than those of Gardner's other novels, *The Sunlight Dialogues,* through the conflict of the magician and his initiate, does epitomize Gardner's major patterns and themes. The central pattern is the hero's journey toward affirmation, his discovery of life's possibilities against its real dangers. Whether Gardner focuses his narrative through an old or modern heroic quest (especially in *The Wreckage of Agathon, The Sunlight Dialogues, Nickel Mountain, Freddy's Book,* and *Mickelsson's Ghosts,*) or through an aesthetic debate between competing visions of art and life (especially in *The Resurrection, October Light,* and *Grendel*) the narrative energy combines elements of the pastoral and heroic traditions and tends toward the affirmation of love and imagination. Such affirmation is typically characterized by the hero's resurrection or redemption in a universe of death, irrationality, absurdity, and chance. Although each of Gardner's other novels would serve well, I will suggest through four particular examples, in the interest of space, the nature of that continuity which, emphatically established in *The Sunlight Dialogues,* runs throughout Gardner's novels. If there is not always a magician figure at the very center of the conflict, magicians, seers, prophets, and fools do keep reappearing. And the central continuity always lies in the dialectical nature of the quest structure and affirmation theme.

In *The Wreckage of Agathon,* to take my first example, another ragged, odoriferous fool is imprisoned for his anarchism. The Seer Agathon represents one side of, at the least, a three-way debate. On the merely political level the debate has many more participants, but the central question is, again, about the best ethic to guide and order human lives and communities. Agathon, the revolutionary Helots, and Lykourgos carry the debate forward. Again the Seer-Fool comes to stand for one sort of nihilism, a vision of the abyss summarized by the ditty:

> Agathon is sinking fast
> While standing still.
> The travel of the Universe
> Is all downhill.[22]

Such entropy is the "deadly inevitability, both in myself and in the world." It is this "skull behind Zeus's mask" that, for Agathon, levels all human effort and hope to deterministic valuelessness.

Agathon argues his position at length—his long diary of events is juxtaposed throughout to Peeker's briefer diary—but his position in the face of entropy is that of the relativist who confuses law with ethics: "Ethics is some theory a man imposes on the world. A man makes up a set of rules, or some fool priest makes up the rules." Hence Agathon can raise his cry: "I say No to the universe. 'Fuck it!' saith angry Agathon," just as he can now argue that the best way to live is to deny the gods and "be satisfied with substance" only. An opposite, yet equally life-denying approach, Agathon hears from old Thaletes: only mind and ideal exist; all else, including torture, prison, oppression, is "mere facticity" and irrelevant (47, 54, 78, 140–41, 185, 209). Agathon is, further, the "half-cracked" gadfly of Lykourgos and his "impossible ideal." Lykourgos is the second principal voice in the debate. He is the one whose oppressions drive the plot as well as the fear and the courage in the novel's characters. He is the ultimate lawgiver, the fascist who would squeeze his city "tight into one man's image" (4, 9, 209). Though he is a shadow figure, presented indirectly through Agathon, he is a formidable presence in the novel.

But the truly opposing vision to Agathon's is the third voice in the debate— the Helots, especially Iona and her husband Dorkis. Here lies the contradictory position in the dialectic: those who would fight oppression through a knowledge of evil, an underground civilization, and revolutionary action. If Agathon is shocked and impressed by Iona's belief that "people can *change* reality" and creatively participate in their history, her belief is a principle by which he cannot live. Indeed, Agathon's relativism renders him capable of betraying those he loves (Konan and his wife, Iona and Dorkis, his adopted people the Helots). As Dorkis puts it: "You care more for knowledge than for people." Against Iona's argument that bigotry and despotism are absolute evils and against Dorkis' acceptance of evil as a "necessary principle of the world," Agathon the relativist views death merely as "a broken machine." Such an approach to life and humanity Peeker (the Seer's disciple) describes as "that thing [which] comes over him, that deadly, heatless clarity of Apollo's light" (100, 134, 141, 167, 188).

The Helot Dorkis presents the true opposition to Agathon's vision. Dorkis' prayer to Zeus near the end summarizes his development through grief and suffering as the most responsibly human voice:

> Forgive us our stupidity and hate. Tease us to kindness and forgiveness of our enemies and, hardest of all, ourselves. Teach us to live with contradiction, and lead us . . . away from the dark pits of meaninglessness and despair. And as we feed our restless, willful bodies, teach us to learn to love them and all their kind. (228)

Grendel (1971), to take my second example, is Gardner's fiction about fiction. It is possible, if little rewarding, to read the novel on the simplest allegorical level; Gardner encouraged such a reading when he identified modern philosophers with some of his characters, most notably Grendel with Jean Paul Sartre.[23] In fact, much of the good press *Grendel* received was because the novel was mistaken to be one more timely issue of nihilistic black humor. The unreliable narrator is so convincing and such a likeable monster that he was taken at his word. But as Cowart recognizes, this is a novel about the triumph of good art over bad.[24] Here again we find the dialectic of the existential nihilist (Grendel and the Dragon) and the poet and the hero (the Shaper and Beowulf). It is most rewarding to read the book as a tale *and* a debate on aesthetics. This debate develops ideas in earlier novels and helps clarify the dialectic in subsequently published work, *The Sunlight Dialogues* included. Though he is tempted to the opposing position, Grendel is the arch nihilist of the tale, the very type of contemporary solipsism: "I understood that the world was nothing: a mechanical chaos of casual, brute enmity on which we stupidly impose our hopes and fears. I understood that, finally and absolutely, I alone exist. . . . I create the whole universe, blink by blink. . . ."[25] Grendel's cynical view of the worst attributes of humanity—its petty, pretentious, bloody little battles; its ravishment of one another and the forest—is a view anyone can appreciate and share at times. But Gardner introduces an artist—the Shaper or *scop*—who not only points out that a Grendellike cynicism is only partial vision, but who creates the noble, purposeful vision of humanity that, in our best moments, we might still aspire to. Grendel, briefly, is shocked, impressed, obsessed by this "king of the Shapers" in Hrothgar's Hall. The creative ecstasy and imaginative fire in the Shaper is obvious even to the monster: "It went on and on, a fire more dread than any visible fire. . . . What was he? The man had changed the world. . . ." (36). By the power of song the Shaper has built Hart Hall through Hrothgar, has brought Thanes together in peace, has recorded models for heroism which first Unferth, with small success, and then Beowulf will fulfill. Realizing that Shapers create a new reality alien to him—"a vision without seams, an image of himself yet not himself, beyond the need of any shaggy old gold-friend's pay: the projected possible"—troubled Grendel descends to the Dragon, a kind of cosmic nihilist, Satan, and voice of the abyss to ask about the Shaper, his art, its effect on mankind.

"Illusion," answers the Satanic Dragon from his perspective of all time and space, mere "games" and "crackpot theories." All is relative, fleeting, meaningless. There is no Truth beyond petty solipsistic truths. Rather than try to improve the world, advises the Dragon, or alter the future, better to seek and count gold (53, 63). But as a representative of the void, the chaos, the abyss and the Dragon himself, Grendel does have one function reminiscent of Tag's, and a bleakly amusing function at that from the Dragon's scope of the timeless void: "You improve them, my boy! . . . You stimulate them! You make them think and scheme. You drive them to poetry, science, religion. . . . You are, so to speak, the brute existent by which they learn to define themselves. The exile, captivity, death they shrink from—the blunt facts of their mortality, their abandonment. . . . You *are* mankind, or mankind's condition. . . ." (62).

The tale inevitably leads to the battle between the heroes and the monstrous void. If Grendel is able to humiliate Unferth, Unferth nevertheless expresses an opposing heroism, which even in defeat "sees values beyond what's possible. . . . It kills him, of course, ultimately. But it makes the whole struggle of humanity worthwhile" (77). If Grendel is able to humiliate Queen Wealtheow by his brutish violation of her in the hall—"I would begin by holding her over the fire and cooking the ugly hole between her legs . . . would squeeze out her feces between my fists" (94)—he is awed by her beauty and unsettled by her self-sacrifice and quiet endurance on behalf of peace between her people and Hrothgar's. Her beauty exists, as does the reality of her spirit, as do the high models and ideals of human shapers in song. But the ultimate battle, of course, is with Beowulf, "the fish," the opposing Dragon to the Satanic Dragon, the redeemer, the human ideal incarnate in the hero and in Christ. As Gardner explains, the two great dragons always at war in medieval art are Christ and Satan.[26] Like the magical *scop,* the "good artist," Beowulf is the Christlike transformer. Against Grendel's modern theory that "all order . . . is theoretical, unreal—a harmless, sensible smiling mask men slide between two great, dark realities, the self and the world," Beowulf places his "magician-power that could blast stone cliffs to ashes as lightning blasts trees." This power, the force of regenerative order, Grendel intimates when the body of "the stranger" seems to him "a ruse, a disguise for something infinitely more terrible" (135–38).

The message that Beowulf whispers to Grendel in his defeat is the message of regeneration: "where the water was rigid there will be fish. . . . It is coming my brother. . . . Though you murder the world, turn plains to stone, transmogrify life into I and it, strong searching roots will crack your cave and rain will cleanse it: The world will burn green, sperm build again . . . the hand that makes (fingers on harpstrings, heroswords, the acts, the eyes of queens). By that I kill you" (149–50). That there is a world outside the self capable of order and regeneration through the processes of nature, imagination, hero, and act is Beowulf's final word as he slams Grendel's head against a very real wall. "Feel the wall: is it not hard. . . . Hard yes! Observe the hardness, write it down in careful runes. Now sing of walls! Sing!" (150).

Gregory Morris, in piecing together Gardner's medievalist scholarship, suggests an interesting parallel here.

> In Gardner's own fictional design . . . Beowulf emerges as the hero, as the embodiment of the unified medieval soul. . . . In contrast stand the three configurations of corrupted virtue. There is the fouled primus or concupiscence of the dragon. . . . And there is the blighted *virum* or irrationality of Grendel, whose anger and bloody purposefulness are the results of a flawed intellectual system. Grendel's defect is the most important because it is rationality that rules the other two faculties (as Plato tells us), and it is this "wrong reason" that has misled twentieth-century man so drastically. Grendel's distress is our distress, his embarrassment our embarrassment.[27]

Gardner continues the dialectic between nihilism and faith, aloofness and heroic commitment, in *Freddy's Book* (1980). This novel, with its incomplete frame story and its total absorption of one narrative by a second, clogs and stumbles; however, it is a consistent contribution to his work. As in so many of Gardner's novels, the action is set in a period of profound change or the transformation of social orders, in this case the transition from the Middle Ages to the Renaissance, the Protestant Reformation, and the revolutionary shocks in sixteenth-century Sweden when the Stures family rebelled against the Danish crown. As he does in *Grendel,* Gardner creates an imagined medieval warrior-hero, here Lars-Goren Bergquist, who defeats the Satanic Dragon and debates through his acts and beliefs the arch nihilist, Bishop Brask. Brask is the brilliant churchman who turns wit and energy to the games of money-grubbing, politics, and war once he comes to believe that there is no connection between language and world and that neither God nor Devil exists. He is a bishop cut off "from heaven by boredom and despair, a man who no longer had feeling for anything except, perhaps style."[28] Not a totally lost soul, however, Brask has his moments of wistful remembrance and even suffers a sort of "death-bed" regeneration. But throughout most of the tale, he is the consummate unnatural man, an aloof stylist cut off from the earth as well as from human community and compassion. Juxtaposed to Brask throughout is Lars-Goren who, unlike Brask, sees no unreal power games in, for instance, the Stockholm massacre, but real human suffering, real public tortures and deaths.

Lars-Goren's quest to beat the Devil is both inward and outward. It begins in his character itself—his compassion, his faith, his strength of body and heart. Whether the Devil be real or in himself, he must pursue and defeat the Adversary: "my wife was right as usual," he muses, "It was rage that made me tremble; fear that the chaos is in myself, as in everything around me" (231). Yet he continues his quest for the Devil, not merely because King Gustav finally sends him and Brask on such a mission, but because the Devil must be conquered to make the world safe for his loved ones. That has been his first impetus and remains so throughout Freddy's tale: "He did not like Gustav's strange cooperation with the Devil, but he did not waste time over annoyance at what Gustav was doing . . . to say nothing of the somewhat larger matter of understanding all human beings who take favors from the Devil. . . . The Devil had entered the scene, and where the Devil was involved, Lars-Goren had no choice, as a knight, and a father of small children, but to involve himself also" (91).

So as his cousin and friend Gustav concerns himself with establishing a new government and turns gradually insane, Lars-Goren grows more and more toward understanding and outwitting the Devil. Like Clumly, it is Lars-Goren's plodding persistence and his growing compassion for humanity that lead to his success. Lars-Goren's adversary is continually described as chaos itself. Having neither the power of control nor a focused goal, the Devil's method is simply to keep everything in confusion, baffle and madden, and to hope things will get ever more chaotic; humankind, in such circumstances, will do the rest. What action does one take when history turns insane, chaotic, uncontrollable? Lars-Goren faces the choice before all of Gardner's heroes, just as he faces the choice before all Mailer's and Fowles'.

Part of Lars-Goren's successful heroism, his strength and potential, is the result of his roots in pastoral life and values, as is so often the case with Gardner's pastoral heroes, especially Henry Soames and James Page. Brask unwittingly emphasizes this aspect of the heroic theme: "You have a good life here in Halsingland, Lars-Goren. I see how your peasants look up to you, and I'm filled with amazement, exactly as a man might be if he visited Eden" (215). But of course to Brask this Eden is not a source of strength, but an "unreal" world too far from the real centers of ambition—Paris, Vienna, Rome, Stockholm. Yet the far north is where the Devil makes his retreat as well, the Serpent in the Garden, though he be blinded by the world of light blazing off sun and snow all around him.

It is apt for the pastoral dimension of Gardner's theme that the Lapplanders will aid and guide the hero in the last stage of his quest. These simple people are so unified with nature and the deer that they have "second sight," are unconcerned about the Devil, and live in a magical universe rather than in a rational, disputatious one. Though, as Lars-Goren's son Erick has seen, it is not possible for civilized man to be like the Lapps anymore, it is nonetheless "good to know the Lapps existed, not dreams or illusions, real people, living at the extreme" (238). If it is the Lapp headman who leads Lars-Goren to the Devil's mountain, it is the Lapp magician, with the child beside him, who brings all the mighty forces into balance at the climax. Tapping his drum with his fingers, the magician dances the three divining stones from the deer's belly (even more symbolic of the action than Tag's stones) on his drumhead and records the final battle in the drum's thud as it reverberates like thunder through the Lappland silence. After Lars-Goren has scaled the Giant and slit his throat, the magician tells the child not to bother telling anyone of the Devil's death because for centuries no one will believe it, "and then all at once it will be so obvious that only a fool would take the trouble to write it down" (246).

The Devil is dead, yet history continues insane. Even as the Devil dies, mad kings like the Tsar of Russia declare war on other countries out of egoism. But no longer is the responsibility the Devil's. Whatever evil we make in our lives and history, like whatever order and good, is our own creation now and our own responsibility. Humanity, indeed, is in a more difficult, uncertain position than ever. In the finest analysis of the novel yet, Walter Cummins reads *Freddy's Book* as "a mythic imagining of a turning point in Western civilization, an ironic exploration into the history of ideas" wherein Gardner broods "over the consequences of a shift in our conception of evil" and the "moral implications" of this historical process "for the future of civilization." The birth of the modern world leaves humanity without "any authority that provides control and meaning," a center that will hold psychologically.[29]

Like Freddy, the reclusive giant of the introductory story who has imprisoned himself in his father's house to create an imaginary world of his own, Gardner himself, through the device of the tale within the tale, creates and records fabulistic models of heroic action and virtue. The artist's ancient role is affirmed, as it was in *Grendel,* in Gardner's interior tale by Bernt Nothe's wood statue of St. George and the Dragon. Here too an ideal is captured: the knight seeming to say, "I am humanity, living and dead"; while the dragon "was evil itself; death, oblivion, every conceivable form of human loss" (147).

In his last completed fiction *Mickelsson's Ghosts* (1982), Gardner seemingly returns to where his published novels began. As in *The Resurrection,* a philosophy professor moves to a rural retreat and searches for redemption while going mad and gaining second sight along the way. These similarities are relatively superficial, however, for in its underlying structure and theme, *Ghosts* reiterates the larger conflicts and patterns of all Gardner's novels. In this sense it is a fitting culmination of a distinguished career, even though most critics seemed to agree that *Ghosts* is not one of Gardner's better novels. Here the dialectic between denial and faith, flesh and spirit, reality and ideal, death and life, evil and good continues. Yet the familiar conflict resumes *within* the troubled and flawed hero. Carried forth by an interior dialogue, the dialectic is, however, shown forth by opposing character qualities or by opposing metaphors: Jessica as unapproachably virtuous love and beauty, Donnie as eminently approachable lust; shabby rural Susquehanna and effete, cosmopolitan Binghamton; academic colleagues and rural folk; cynical positivists and ethicists; Finney and Nugent; and so on.

Never has a Gardner novel set in the modern world been so occult, so anagogical; psychic and mystic powers and experiences drive the action and the moral dilemmas forward. As Morris has pointed out, this is an "acutely autobiographical" novel; however, neither Gardner nor his hero Peter Mickelsson has ever before stepped into a sentient cosmos so like Norman Mailer's. Mickelsson becomes his own magician. Here are witches and mysteries, here second sight is common, here psychic powers and battles are part of the inner machinery of plot and character, here sexual intercourse symbolically suggests the macrocosmic dualisms and the dialectic so common to complex allegory. Characters can be seen as metaphoric projections of the struggles within the hero, of the dialogue of body and soul and of the soul with itself. Like Mailer's heroes, Gardner's more and more (Lars-Goren, Mickelsson) live life at the extreme edge of violence, temptation, despair, and mystical relationships. Here is a world where people and totems come to life as if we were witnessing some archaic ritual or drama of purification. Gardner's last hero lives in that extreme and dangerous state of consciousness worthy of the transformed and transforming hero. "He knew the theory," Mickelsson muses, "Nietzsche, Sorel, Karl Jaspers . . . that the human spirit comes alive in the proximity of danger, or perhaps one might better say, with Sartre, the presence of temptation—the temptation to sink back into Nature: bestiality and death."[30]

From the moment we meet Mickelsson, we meet a man for whom the slide into the abyss is well underway. His personal and professional relationships "out of control," he grows more isolated and self-conscious every day. As he turns physically more monstrous and bestial, his mind grows more chaotic and uncertain, and his private ghosts and demons—especially Nietzsche, Luther, and Wittgenstein—grow more real. He is attaining the condition MacIntyre describes in *After Virtue* (which Gardner reviewed and admired): "To cut oneself off from shared activity . . . to isolate oneself from the communities which find their point and purpose in such activities, will be to debar oneself from finding any good outside oneself. It will be to condemn oneself to that moral solipsism which constitutes Nietzschean greatness" (240). Mickelsson is an ethicist turned amoral, and turning immoral. His journey, like the journey of Mailer's heroes, will take him all the way into the pit—fornication, thievery, manslaughter, the betrayal of friends and lovers—before he will begin his ascent back to life and to any degree of redemption. This dissolution, this journey through loneliness and despair to nihilism, is foretold at the very outset of the story. Events in his personal life and in our national life in the late 1970s call into question the basis of his lifework, his ethical theory that life is "presumed-until-proven otherwise to be noble and worthwhile." This presumption becomes more and more difficult to maintain as the ethicist grows "increasingly cynical, increasingly impressed by accident. . . . He did not doubt that human beings had the equipment to make relatively unbestial choices, but he doubted more and more that they would ever get around to it or that, in the final analysis, it mattered" (7)

As we follow Mickelsson through his process of disintegration, even the least likeable characters come to seem more positive and sympathetic than Mickelsson. One example of this is the misshapen, nagging Department Chairman Geoffrey Tillson. For all his shortcomings and pettiness he seems at times more humane and well-meaning than the protagonist himself. "Now, in his bed, his mood more complex . . . he saw Tillson in a new way, as a pitiful man, no fool, fighting for the department, giving slack to his rainbowed youthful ideals, compromising, feinting, fighting by every means at his disposal to save whatever might be saved in these foundering times; and fighting heroically though no doubt futilely for Jessie as well, not because she was his lover but because what she stood for was right—while he Mickelsson stood aloof from it all . . . too self-absorbed and disdainful of the trivial task to risk getting pigshit on his soft, pink hands" (473).

As his musings "groping toward revelation" continue (counterpointed by lines from Nietzsche on the *Übermensch* and from Wittgenstein on the impossibility of the ethical, the God-revealed world) Mickelsson becomes gradually aware of true modern heroism in the sense that Gardner always presents it, as the ordinary people who struggle and create and endure against every conceivable form of human loss—decay, death, destruction: His mother, for example, accomplishing so much for her family on so little; his carpenter father working a "surprising transformation" of his house. "He, not Nietzsche's Prussian officer—much less the artist, philosopher, or saint—was the Übermensch" (475). It is during such thoughts from the bottom of the pit, and quite late in the novel, that Mickelsson begins to realize that he has been trying to reconstruct a regenerate self all along, but that so far he has only labored to construct a projection or metaphor for the renewed self through his extensive renovations of the old farm house: "His first quasimystical feeling about the place had been right: it had become his expression, a projection of the self he meant to be, visible evidence that what he hoped for in his life and character might perhaps be attainable" (477). All that he needs is conscious "infallible faith and love" (476).

Faith and love do not come simply or immediately, but only after a close brush with suicide, after facing death honestly as Ed Lawler works him at gunpoint, and after the return of his son Mark. But it is, like Clumly, with an understanding of faith and love and a new humility that Mickelsson returns to the spurned Jessica, dressed in a scarlet huntsman's coat, Liberty tie, feathered fisherman's cap, black gloves, and silver-headed cane—like the humble fool he is. "Jessie . . . it's true that the get-up is a fraud. But the craziness is real. You have to help me. If had my way, I'd come to you as the perfect lover, flawless golden lion" (587). As in Fowles' *Daniel Martin*, Gardner too has come to ignore the modern necessity of the unhappy ending in serious art. To be sure the positive conclusion—full of renewed communion and love—is tenuous until the last moment and even then vaguely open-ended (there is no happy marriage or feast). But self-knowledge, courage, selflessness, and love are all values renewed as Mickelsson and Jessica—her party guests just beyond the door—make love again despite her more rational and understandable impulses to avoid him. Their love-making is the story's ultimate affirmation of life against all the possibilities of destruction and death in the world: "Now the bedroom was packed tight with ghosts, not just people but also animals . . . more than Mickelsson and Jessie could name, and there were still more at the windows, oblivious to the tumbling, roaring bones and blood, the rumbling at the door . . . pitiful, empty-headed nothings complaining to be born" (590).

I have been examining the largest continuities of theme and structure in Gardner's novels. I want to mention briefly, moreover, the relationship between the novels and Gardner's two collections of short fiction. In his own chapters on the short fiction, Morris increases our sense of the unity throughout all of Gardner's work. Morris demonstrates that *The King's Indian: Stories and Tales* (1974) is no collection of chance bits of writing but a complex and coherent construction with the force of a novel. Here Gardner at his most fabulistic explores the themes I have been discussing so far in the novels.

Morris sees two central concerns in *Indian*. First, it is an aesthetic examination of Gardner's artistic theory and practice, rife with all the metafictional techniques and musings such a fictional examination entails. Art, the tales say to Morris, is the only human creation that eludes the limits of time and space and manages to endure.

Second, the book is centrally concerned with the opposition of anarchy and order, with the synthesis or balance of the two that allows for human freedom without senseless destruction and pain. To be sure, especially in tales like "Pastoral Care," "The Temptation of St. Ivo," "The Warden," and "The King's Indian," anarchists and magicians terrorize and tease the heroes toward some new consciousness of human limits and possibilities within the magical, perplexing, and threatening universe.[31] But perhaps Gardner's own observations on this collection suggest as much as Morris about the role of this collection in Gardner's larger body of work:

> The way I think the collection works generally is that the opening stories are fairly dark and each one up to the last one in the first section presents a kind of miraculous or "absurd" resurrection. . . . "John Napper Sailing Through the Universe" is my fundamental theory of art, which I'm spelling out in a different, more discursive way in a book . . . called *On Moral Fiction*. . . . The artist can't just describe the world, "bitter reality"; the artist has to create new and wonderful possibilities. . . . "The King's Indian" uses the Yankee Melville, the Southerner Poe, and the middleman Twain as a sort of basis, and Coleridge as a sort of background. It's an attempt to create a new world—a vision—which at the same time is a story of American democracy, a people's self-expression in their ship of state, "The New Jerusalem."[32]

Gardner's second collection of short fiction, *The Art of Living and Other Stories* (1981), focuses a little more on Gardner's own past and works out, as Morris puts it, "at least a temporary truce with private emotional bogies" in such stories as "Redemption" (about the death of Gardner's younger brother Gilbert) and "Come on Back." Yet the most consistent theme to emerge in *The Art of Living*, Morris demonstrates, is the "relation of the artist to his art and to his life." In both the personal and aesthetic themes, the message is the same: art is a vital, redemptive force in life, just as love is. And as often as not one depends upon the other.

Throughout this collection cynicism, nihilism, and despair are opposed again to hope, faith, beauty, and masterful shaping or artistry. Usually the artists in these stories—whether painters, musicians, or chefs—pass down through the stages of nihilism and despair, like Mickelsson, and through love or commitment to the celebratory, magical, and redemptive power of art, emerge as people with resurrected faith, purpose, and vitality. "Reality and matter and the world are transmogrified by the lunacies of love and art," Morris explains. "Darkness gives way to light . . . the sort of light that blinds the Devil in *Freddy's Book* and illuminates the hero's eyes, the sort of light that turns the Vermont landscape mystical in *October Light,* the sort of light that pierces the blackness of John Napper's painting and bursts upon Queen Louisa's kingdom. It is the same redemptive and transformative light that shines through all of Gardner's fiction" (201). One might add it is the shocking "sunlight" the magician holds on reality in *The Sunlight Dialogues* as in *The Magus.*

If, as Morris says, John Gardner made himself the Jeremiah his time seemed to require, Gardner is in this sense also closer to Mailer than he may have thought. For as Gardner, particularly in *On Moral Fiction,* stands as our Jeremiah of the contemporary novel, Norman Mailer (equally self-appointed) stands as our Jeremiah of the contemporary world. Both are "philosophical novelists," novelists who excoriate our fictional and real lapses of moral seriousness and courage, artists as capable of using the ancient and classical traditions as they are of using the fabulistic and metafictional. For both authors the central issue that humanity faces is the confrontation of Life against Death in the modern world, the confrontation which gives their novels their strikingly dialectical quality.

By endeavoring to revitalize the textual power of narrative through connecting story-telling to human life and to life-enhancing dissent or change, both authors reach to become heroes for their time. Such fiction writers and critics are, as MacIntyre points out in *After Virtue,* the real heretics in our culture:

> Literary historians from Auerbach to John Gardner have traced the way in which the cultural place of narrative has been diminished and the modes of interpretation of narrative have been transformed until it has become possible for modern theorists as different as Sartre . . . and William Gass to understand the form of narrative, *not* as that which connects story-telling with the form of human life, but precisely as that which segregates narrative from life, which confines it to what is taken to be a separate and distinctive realm of art.
>
> The contrast, indeed the opposition, between life and art . . . provides a way of exempting art . . . from its moral tasks. And the relegation of art by modernity to the status of an essentially minority activity and interest further helps to protect us from any narrative understanding of ourselves. . . . To think of a human life as a narrative unity is to think in a way alien to the dominant individualist and bureaucratic modes of modern culture. (210–11)

As Gardner once put it in terms similar to Mailer's; the heroic novelist "becomes an affirmer of life instead of a whiner against it. He takes responsibility and recognizes responsibility in other writers and in other people. He sees through complacency and righteousness. No hero is ever righteous: a hero makes mistakes, recognizes them . . . and tries to do something about it. He affirms the goodness of life and the badness of thinking you've got the whole answer."[33]

For Gardner the fight for life against death, through art, is both heroic and tragic, for ultimately the cosmic dragon entropy, and the trolls who serve it, are destined to win. "Art is essentially serious and beneficial, a game played against chaos and death, against entropy," Gardner writes in *On Moral Fiction*. "It is a tragic game for those who have the wit to take it seriously, because our side must lose; a comic game—or so a troll might say, because only a clown with sawdust brains would take our side and eagerly join in" (6).

It is this tragic game (to humanity) and this comic game (to the dragon) that Gardner, Mailer, and their prototypical magicians and heroes have so eagerly joined. Both authors, like Fowles, seek to renew the mystery and vitality of life against the machine, against the trolls, and against the worst potential in ourselves. Though late in his career Mailer will go directly to ancient texts and peoples in search of the archaic vitalism and magic, both Gardner and Mailer aspire to be artists of living in a dead or dying world. They seem to have caught the old fire from D. H. Lawrence, among others, who says in *Mornings in Mexico:* "We have lost the art of living; and in the most important science of all, the science of daily life, the science of behaviour, we are complete ignora-muses."[34] To Lawrence, ancient and primitive peoples are closer to the art of life and to the flame of vitality than we (exiles from the garden, masters of the machine) will ever be. He speaks for both Gardner and Mailer as well as for himself:

> The Hopi sought the conquest by means of the mystic, living will that is in man, pitted against the living will of the dragon-cosmos. The Egyptians long ago made a partial conquest by the same means. We have made a partial conquest by other means. Our corn doesn't fail us: we have no seven years' famine, and apparently need never have. But the other thing fails us, the strange inward sun of life; the pellucid monster of the rain never shows us his stripes. To us, heaven switches on daylight, or turns on the shower bath. We little gods are gods of the machine only. It is our highest. Our cosmos is a great engine. And we die of *ennui*. A subtle dragon stings us in the midst of plenty. *Quos vult perdere Deus, dementat prius.* (77)

4

Norman Mailer:
The Magician as Tragic Hero

To whom do I speak today?
Brothers are evil,
Friends of today are not of love.

To whom do I speak today?
Hearts are thievish,
Every man seizes his neighbor's goods.

To whom do I speak today?
The gentle man perishes,
The bold-faced goes everywhere.

To whom do I speak today?
He of the peaceful face is wretched,
The good is disregarded in every place.

To whom do I speak today?
When a man should arouse wrath by his evil conduct,
He stirs all men to mirth, although his
iniquity is wicked.

. . . .

To whom do I speak today?
The pest is faithful,
But the brother who comes with it becomes an enemy.

To whom do I speak today?
There are no righteous,
The land is left to those who do iniquity.
                    "The Corruption of Men" (ca. 2000 B.C.)
                              as rendered by J. H. Breasted

With the publication of *Ancient Evenings* it became clear that a serious reassessment of Norman Mailer's career was due. Any such reassessment, it seems to me, must take into consideration the degree to which Mailer's self-proclaimed magnum opus is a culmination of his themes, especially the fantastic and magical themes. The novel also represents a culmination of his heroes' struggles to gain independent moral stature, even amidst failure. Perhaps because it was published so late in this author's career, *Ancient Evenings* even more than Fowles' or Gardner's magical narratives is prototypical of the author's body of work. We have now a novel that gives significant order and emphasis to the narrative qualities and the ethical issues developed throughout Mailer's fiction and nonfiction career. Chief among these qualities and issues is the dialectic between vitality and entropy. Those opposing forces create the conflict behind all the other conflicts in the narrative, just as, in turn, each specific conflict helps to characterize the nature of the hero's task and the connections between his life and death.

We are reminded of Gardner's dialectic of art and chaos, of artists/heroes and the abyss, of opposing philosophies (or constructive oppositions) that test values and seek synthesis or personal transformation. He and Mailer are both seeking consciousness rather than codes. Mailer's underlying conflict between vitality and entropy is in Egypt mythologically reflected in Ra's nightly descent into darkness to battle the great serpent of entropy and in Osiris' role not only as Lord of Resurrection and Mind (consciousness). Similarly, that dialectic is symbolized by the conflicts between the gods and their opposing qualities. And ultimately it is symbolized by "the balance of Maat," which holds in creative equipoise the dialectical polarities of existence—barbarism and civilization, bestiality and nobility, death and life, waste and generation, Set and Osiris. Entropy to Mailer is that which destroys the balance, the devouring of life principle by death principle.

Yet in Mailer's case the initial critical reaction to *Ancient Evenings* has been as curious and exorbitant as the novel itself. A few have thought it brilliant, some have thought it execrable, others have thought it both. More than a few have been unable to make up their minds. On the best and worst lists of 1983, *Ancient Evenings,* as Mailer predicted, bewildered everybody. Nearly all the reviewers were willing to grant Mailer power and significance as a major force on the American literary scene. But what to do with this new artifact? Indeed, the book, as Mailer had promised, is "out of category." Vance Bourjaily was stunned by it: "The longest damn *tour de force* I ever read," Bourjaily wrote in *Esquire,* "a monument like no other . . . a strange eminence." It may be a masterpiece, he went on, but it is "also totally beyond judgment." Any writer in his sixties, Bourjaily suggested, has nothing to lose; he or she can cut loose from all of us and, if nothing else, show us how "wide the final swings may be."[1] In a similar, though less sympathetic and more reductive vein, Leslie Fiedler wrote of the novel as a "deep-sleep nightmare" and "outlaw of the underground," as perhaps even that mythical "longest ball ever to go up into the air . . . of our American letters," which Mailer had promised back in the 1950s.[2]

Almost every reviewer has had his or her difficulties (and fatigues) with the novel. It is difficult, perhaps irresponsible, to consider this novel without first assessing this cacophony of critical reaction. Those who are generally favorable seem to have been able to suspend disbelief and prejudgment enough to confront this strange work on its own terms. They frequently offer worthy insights into the possibilities and meanings of the work. Those who are unfavorable either have been unable to sufficiently suspend disbelief or have been overwhelmed by the flaws apparent from the perspective of either traditional or current fictional conventions.

At their worst, some negative critics seem to have been saving up their anti-Mailer bile for just such an opportunity. Reading the more spiteful reviews, one conjures an image of Mailer toppling into the waiting arms (or jaws) of, for example, Margaret Manning of the *Boston Globe* or Sey Chassler of *Ms. Magazine.* Manning calls the book "oceanic, unstoppable, and mad"; she attributes Mailer's interest in reincarnation to egoism and wonders why he chose to write about "this period of degeneration," necrophilia, and artistic decline. According to Manning, Mailer is also "one of the world's great literary snobs" because many of his characters are high-born Egyptians. Moreover, she would have him treat the Greek pantheon because she likes Greek gods better than the "boring and structured" Egyptian gods. Since Manning doesn't get her facts straight (the hero does not learn reincarnation from a woman, to take just one example), and since she lets her prejudices get in the way of her critical reading, it is no wonder she dismisses the book as claustrophobic "rubbish." Mailer fares even worse in *Ms.* Chassler stops suddenly in the middle of her brief review to complain about the tone in which a Boston newspaper reported a gang rape, refers to the tone finally as "typically Mailerian, ordinarily masculine," and ends with a howling non sequitur. *Ancient Evenings,* Chassler announces, "turns out to be about gang rape after all."[3]

This is not to suggest that all the negative reviews are simply spite. A few are. Others are thoughtful, raise serious questions, and emphatically stipulate what events and ideas in the novel were not to the reviewer's tastes, nor, by extension, to the tastes of civilized adults in America today. Robert Gorham

Davis, Mailer's writing teacher and friend from Harvard days, focuses on two issues—the execrable subject matter and certain stylistic-formal qualities of the novel. Though Davis grants Mailer the creation of "states of awareness that go beyond anything ever attempted in literature before," he finds dominance through homosexual rape, ancient violence, "polymorphous and inexhaustible sex," and "regressively unscientific ideas about the body" all things that "simply do not bear thinking about." They are "the stock in trade of fakirs and mass cultists," and, furthermore, embarrassing to read. On this point he echoes Joseph Epstein's and James Wolcott's witty repugnance with Mailer's "obsessions."[4] Though Davis' criticism of style—"there is hardly a distinctive phrase or metaphor, an unexpected choice of words"—has been debated even among the negative critics, his second criticism of the novel's form indeed raises a central question about the impact and effectiveness of the novel, and Davis seems to be alone in raising it clearly. Does the "transcendence" expressed in the final pages of the novel excuse, give purpose to, or clarify the preceding seven hundred pages of "betrayal, gloating cruelty, and the immediate gratification of every impulse at whatever cost to others?" Davis asks. "Is it more than an easy out, a rhetorical flourish . . . when there has been heretofore not a hint of what a noble purpose might be or how it is achieved . . . ?"

Although Davis misses a few "hints," his question is an important one. The question is complicated because Mailer writes from the unprivileged position of one who is—like all of us and his characters—at times consumed by his passions, confusions, obsessions, and eccentricities. He imaginatively participates with such narrative energy in all the carnality and egoism he describes that he is always in danger of undercutting the ethical issues he raises. One could argue that in his tireless heaping of betrayal, cruelty, and self-gratification Mailer fails his sympathetic readers—those who might see the ethical undercurrents, purposes, and (in the end) subversions of his gruesome tale.

Yet if transcendence and purpose are expressed only from the perspective of five failed lives and a future time when Greek and Roman classical civilization reign, as is the case at the novel's end, and if one of Mailer's greatest efforts in writing the novel was to expunge from his mind later (i.e., Greco-Roman and Judeo-Christian) definitions of the spiritual and ethical nature of humanity, as he suggested in his *Harvard Magazine* interview, then Mailer may have left himself no formal choice but a final, brief retrospective section from which vantage alone we, like Menenhetet his hero, see the value, or lack of it, in the lives these characters have led. Be that as it may, placing such a burden on his ending is among the greatest risks Mailer takes in this audacious novel. Whether the final revelation of the novel works or not, however, may ultimately be more a matter of taste than of aesthetic law or necessity. And it will be taste in turn which leads a reader to decide whether the quotation Davis cites from Mailer's old *Paris Review* interview (repeated in *Cannibals and Christians* and elsewhere) helps us to read the book as registering a positive or negative potential for the evolution of humanity and spirit: "violence, cannibalism, loneliness, insanity, libidinousness, hell, perversion and mess . . . [are] states which must in some way be passed through, digested, transcended, if one is to make one's way back to life."[5]

Benjamin DeMott's intelligent review emphasizes the familiar distaste with the subject matter; it is all, finally, a little too kinky and embarrassing. But DeMott adds a further dimension to the criticisms already noted. Though he was surprised and prepared for a masterpiece from reading the opening chapters, though pulled "inside a consciousness different from any hitherto met in fiction," the novel finally is a "disaster" for DeMott. It is the social drama of books 3 through 6 that sinks Mailer's ship. The failure amounts to replacing that opening, magical consciousness of the dynastic world with the obsessions of a twentieth-century mind—Mailer's. In dramatizing these obsessions, Mailer too successfully represses his own sense of the ridiculous, but few readers will be able to do so.

These are telling criticisms that raise questions once again of taste as well as questions of a reader's own preconceptions of life in 1200–1000 b.c. Egypt. It is a very good line, but is it accurate to say that all the characters are a ludicrous blend of Mel Brooks and the Marquis de Sade? Especially if to support that quip DeMott can only summarize out of context the King-as-Fool's pranks and obscenities on the Night of the Pig—a night, like no other, when foolery, role reversal, and obscenity are *supposed* to reign. Such festivals are, further, not anomalous; rather, they are cyclical historical events that ring down the centuries from Egypt through Rome to Medieval Europe, right into the carnivals and Mardis Gras of our own time. They are intentional and sanctioned days and nights of excess with cathartic social and religious purposes. DeMott may be right about flawed moments of "unintended hilarity," but surely much of Mailer's material is not presented as if "it were without comic dimension," and just as surely Mailer does not always fail in presenting Eastern sensuality.[6]

Writing in *The American Spectator*, Peter Shaw offers a sobering assessment of the critics. Shaw reminds us, first, that Mailer is using Egyptian mythology in such a way that the incestuous and anal passions of the gods "are enacted by their human counterparts for whom these profane matters become the objects of religious and metaphysical speculation." If with an "unprecedented, easy condescension . . . the reviewers were vastly amused . . . to report that *Ancient Evenings* came down to a treatise on ca ca," they may have forgotten, first of all, that the scarab or dung beetle was a hieroglyph for creation and the commemorative symbol of pharaohs. And if the reviewers have expressed their distaste for such subjects as excrement and sex and the violent Eastern mythologies presented throughout the novel, they have been, secondly, expressing a distaste for D. H. Lawrence, Norman O. Brown, and James Frazer (not to mention, I might add, Eliot, Pound, Yeats, Freud, Graves, and Jung, among others). They have, in short, denied Mailer a similar context and materials; they have admitted a "self-confessed philistinism" which is one "measure of the present revolt against high modernism."[7]

Among the positive critics like Shaw we find those who are, as Henry James admonished, willing to grant Mailer his subject, idea, and starting point. Having done so, they offer the most insight into the novel. And, like James, they are also willing to "estimate quality" by applying the only possible test, finally—"the test of execution." Execution, James argues in "The Art of Fiction," belongs "to the author alone; it is what is most personal to him, and we measure him by that. The advantage, the luxury, as well as the torment and responsibility of the novelist, is that there is no limit to his possible experiments, efforts, discoveries, successes."

As Shaw intimates, it is Mailer's starting point that seems to offend so many. Just as Mailer had to "keep making certain that there wasn't a single Judeo-Christian idea" in his head as he wrote *Ancient Evenings,* so too did he never avoid the violence of the pagan world and myth, nor the ambitions of gods and humans. He is searching for the pagan, he would say "karmic," roots of human life. And there is nothing like war and sex for stripping off the surface and revealing the roots. "I think people are going to be immensely confused by the book" Mailer said. "They are going to say . . . What is he saying that means something to him. . . . What is in this."[8] Mailer may have been strategically naive by being repetitious and heavy-handed. But his exposé of the connections between war and eroticism—the erections of warriors in battle, the brutalities of "carnal ownership" of victor over vanquished—and between sexuality and politics, power, wealth, and state violence, if offensive, are at least honest by his own lights. "Maybe it is in war that you come to the place where the rainbow touches the earth, and much that has been hidden is simple," Mailer's hero Menenhetet says. Wouldn't it be nice if it weren't so? we want to say with the reviewers.

It is this audacious honesty as much as anything that gets Mailer into trouble with the reviewers. We see just one example of audacity in the long and brutal description of the night after the Battle of Kadesh. Here is not only Ramses' nobility and bestiality, but the worst horrors of the Nazis, the Pol Pot regime, and all the government-sanctioned massacres and famines of the modern world. It is a description of the eternal human descent into Hell.

> Over it all was the smell of sweat. I could smell the buttocks of half an army. A fit husband
> was that odor to blood and smoke. I would speak of these acts as abominations but it was less
> than what was yet to come. Besides, I will offer no judgment. . . . I can only say I was part
> of it, and much stimulated. I swear, if it were not the Night of the Pig, you would not know
> so much of this. . . . Sometimes you could not tell the oaths of pleasure from the wails of the

doomed. Through such cries did Hera-Ra and I walk, among the flames. . . . I have never seen women [camp whores] so insatiable, so brutal, so superior in pure joy—it is their art, not a man's. . . . It must have been all the blood and burning flesh. Maybe Maat approaches with love when all are choking with smoke. You have to wonder how many generals are conceived on campgrounds such as this. . . . Before the night was over, I, too, indulged the meat of a limb, burned it in the fire, took a taste, and knew the pleasures of a cannibal. . . . Suffice it that the first step in what is considered the filth of my habits was taken. It has led me through many a wonder and many a wisdom.[9]

"None of us," Mailer remarked in an unpublished portion of an interview, "has been able to explain the concentration camps, and in fact we step away from it in horror because the most logical answer is that those horrors are in all of us, and there to be tapped. We draw back from that as a conclusion about human nature. So the question is unsettled. Because it is unsettled, no one is rewarded for approaching that question. We don't really want to know the answer to it." We are reminded here of George Steiner's argument that the Holocaust cannot be separated from the psychology of religion, from the vengeance of some deep polytheistic and animistic need, or from the "egotistical failure of common, instinctual behavior" set against the ideal. The bloodlust, barbaric warfare, and orgiastic pain of ancient Egypt erupts in Mailer's novel, as Steiner points out it did in the 1850s in *Salammbô,* like some "metaphysical provocation" or sadistic dream of violence against the "interminable Sunday and suet of a bourgeois life-form."[10]

Those critics like Richard Poirier, who can stand the audacious honesty, grant Mailer his chaff but seek the kernel. Poirier finds it not remarkable that American reviewers have found things to make fun of. Any work of "sustained visionary ambition" (e.g., *Paradise Lost, Moby Dick*) is bound "to have stretches of tiresome exposition, phrasings that are ludicrous, whole scenes that, as Dr. Johnson remarked, 'should have been not only difficult but impossible.'" What is remarkable to Poirier is that so many of Mailer's risks pay off in "moments of subliminal ecstasy, visionary descriptions." Seeing *Ancient Evenings* as a work of magnitude, Poirier also sees it as a work that retrospectively orders Mailer's entire body of work: "Mailer has imagined a culture that gives formal, and not merely anthropological sanction to what in his other works often seems eccentric or plaintively metaphysical, like his obsessions with 'psychic darts' and mind-reading, with immortality, with battles of the gods . . . with villainous homosexuality, with magic and sorcery, and with excrement as an encoding of psychic failure or success."[11]

Harold Bloom similarly focuses on the losses and payoffs of Mailer's risks, and he sounds the same note as Bourjaily: "Our most conspicuous literary energy has generated its weirdest text, a book that defies usual aesthetic standards, even as it is beyond conventional ideas of good and evil." Despite working his own hobbyhorse of literary influences, Bloom does suggest (and in two cases develops) four useful approaches to Mailer's novel. First, *Evenings* can be seen as a culmination of Mailer's metaphorical vision. By an "outrageous literalism," Mailer makes the metaphorical seem literal, thereby granting a "reality" Mailer has always attributed to metaphor. In this primitive, magical world literal perceptions are meaningless without their metaphorical, intuitive dimensions and energies. Second, Mailer's connections to a literary heritage of "religious vitalism" require readers to take him seriously or not at all. Like D. H. Lawrence, Mailer is a writer who would both "save our souls" and "renew our original relationship both to the sun and to a visionary origin beyond the natural sun." Bloom is, third, one of the few reviewers to suggest, at least, a real connection between Mailer's ancient world and contemporary America. And, finally, Bloom develops Mailer's connection to the nineteenth-century American Literary Renaissance. Like his forebears, Mailer finds in ancient Egypt a vision of resurrection that not only gives flesh and history to his long-held obsessions about life, death, power, courage, and the relationship between the human and the divine, but is an analogue of resurrection or personal survival through works of art.[12]

George Stade, to take one final example, carried further the many reviewers' references to the novel's fantasy and nightmare qualities. Stade sees ancient Egypt as Mailer's "metaphor for the unconscious." Indeed, it is with dream logic and energy that Mailer has worked since *The Naked and the Dead,* I might add. Such logic and energy are simply carried to their furthest, most risky, use here. And, of course, the images arising are often as rationally inexplicable, alien, surprising, magical, and distasteful to rational consciousness as they can be in our nightly dreams. For Stade, we are witness to a form of consciousness both alien and familiar that makes other novels of ancient magic, like Robert Graves' novels, psychologically shallow by comparison and without formal distinction. Stade describes the design of Mailer's novel as a kind of spiral interweaving two narrative strands around each other and sustaining a series of narrative parallels between gods and humans.

It was Mailer himself who first suggested in *Harvard Magazine,* incidentally, the spiral image, but this spiral has really three, rather than two, narrative strands or parallels: the reign of Ramses II, the reign of Ramses IX, and the eternal realm of the gods. The gods and their carnal possessions, ambitions, intrigues, battles, and gifts are mirrored by human counterparts. As Stade notes, the gods are metaphors for the permanent energies of the human psyche and the character types they produce. What Stade means by Mailer's "somber excavations of our aboriginal and buried human nature," is what Bernard Dick means by Mailer's continuing creation of "a holograph of the psyche." Mailer himself prescribed such excavations and holographs in 1966 when he called for "robust art": a "hearty" quest for that which is fundamental and primitive in our nature, a "savage" antidote to all the "dissolution" and "entropy" in our world. Such art would above all be characterized by the dream (or dream novel), for the dream and the novel are "country cousins."[13]

What Stade and Dick, and even Bloom, remind us of, then, is that Mailer is not merely showing us powerful, affecting elements in human racial history through national and heroic events (i.e., a traditional historical novel); he is trying more to create a history of the dynamic and collective human psyche, which, as Jung among others argues, we can never sever without catastrophic loss and self-destruction. It is probably on that basis—as part of the history of the human psyche and its dynamic energies (including what James Breasted calls "the dawn of conscience")—that *Ancient Evenings* will have to rest its claim for meaningfulness.

To understand and to begin to assess *Ancient Evenings,* I think we need first to grant the novel its chunks of ponderous, turgid writing and static ceremony. Then, beyond that admission, we need to discover whether anything of value, and how much, remains to us as readers. Joyce Carol Oates, in her chapter "The Teleology of the Unconscious," reminds us how easy it is to go wrong with Mailer. "Norman Mailer's efforts to dramatize the terror of the disintegrating identity have largely been mistaken as self-display, and his highly stylized, poetic, image-making structures of language have often been mistaken as willful and perverse hallucinations, instead of countermagic." It is largely because Mailer's literary countermagic is melodramatic that he has met with so much resistance from critics. His lurid texts, founded on the void left by our loss of the sacred, do indeed, as Peter Brooks has argued of melodrama generally, "depend for their validity on a kind of visionary leap," on a suspension of our disbelief.

The desire to express all, to utter the unspeakable and dramatize deepest feelings through heightened and polarized gestures; the underlying Manichaeism and its accompanying hyperbole and extravagance; the "super-signification" of a world of charged interconnections, correspondences, and meanings—all are essential qualities of the melodramatic mode of expression that, as Brooks argues, seeks "a victory over the repression and censorship of the social reality principle, a release of psychic energy by the articulation of the unsayable." The goal of this victory and release is to suggest that what is being played out in the realm of manners or the quotidian is charged with meaning, value, and "significance from the realm of the moral occult," a domain of "spiritual values" or deeper sources of being where the stakes are life and death. We are always, of course, perilously close as readers to feeling that "the represented world won't bear the weight of the significances placed on it." The metaphorical relationship between the represented world and the occult world—or in Mailer's case the stark immediacy of the occult *in* the represented—is what makes the fictive world barely supportable to the reader. Yet it is just this metaphorical nature of the text that creates "an expanded moral context" and "ethical consciousness." Indeed, Brooks speculates that it is just this search to bring into the drama of manners and quotidian existence "the higher drama of moral forces" that is "one of the large quests of the modern imagination" since Romanticism; our "most Promethean writers" insist that the realm of the moral occult exists; they "write their fiction to make it exist" and to show "its primacy in life."[14]

If, as Brooks says, melodrama is the only form of the tragic left to a world where there is "no longer a tenable idea of the sacred," Mailer balances precariously on the edge of the tragic and the melodramatic because he balances so precariously on the edge of the sacred and the profane. Such balancing acts place enormous demands on us as readers.

The suspension of disbelief Mailer requires of us in this novel has proven too much for some readers, even in these post-modern times when the irreal becomes common. When we add to that demand Mailer's long-standing idea that the first ethic required of us is courage—the courage and strength to take risks and to rebel against anything that would diminish us—we can see why Mailer would be bound for heavy weather indeed in, if Mailer is right, an epoch of adjustment, compromise, and homogeneity.

The connections between courage and power, magic and power, and sexuality and power suggested repeatedly in this novel are not unlike Mailer's own connection between risk or courage and power in writing as well. Like so many of his characters, Mailer is valuable as a writer in part because of his ability and endurance in risk-taking. He pursues, now more than ever, his questions and instincts through whatever slimes and sublimities he discovers along the way. He may outrage most of his critics, but he could least of all be accused of writing, in Donald Hall's apt phrase, mere "letters to Stockholm." He seems willing, not unlike Melville, to put everything on the line in a book, literary establishments and taste-makers be damned! He may arguably (as many have argued) fail. But there may be as much nobility as ludicrousness in his failures, if that they are. In his interview for *Harvard Magazine,* Mailer phrased it this way:

> If I had tried to write the book in a year, the fear would have been so great it couldn't have been written. But over ten years, you can carry the fear. *Writing* a book is the fear. . . . Most people take pride in the fears they can endure. It's obvious that you can't be a professional writer for as many years as I have been without taking a certain pride that I can endure those fears. I would say that writing is like all occupations that have some real element of risk. . . . And I will say I've taken more risks with the Egyptian novel than any book I've ever written. It's the most, dare I say it, audacious of the books I've done. (48)

Two questions need to be addressed before we can make sense of Mailer's strangest novel. First, what is the central relationship between *Ancient Evenings* and Mailer's previous work? Second, what is it about ancient Egypt that drew Mailer to that subject in the first place?

Mailer's previous work stands, like Fowles', emphatically antagonistic to a common element of post-war literature—the absurd or anti-hero. Above all, Mailer's rebel heroes glory in their search for the power to advance their own lives and visions, even when they fail. Whether as "Life," "Vision," "God," or "It," the power Mailer's heroes seek is unconscious, divine, regenerative. With this power the hero gains the only effective force available to struggle against a deadening, homogenizing, and totalitarian world. This power, this Vital Life Source, is a principle in the order of creation that stands in opposition to entropy, whether the entropy of violent personal defeat, or totalitarianism, or of chaotic force. Chaos and order, Devil and God, now Osiris and Set battle in human as in supernal realms. Each hero pursues and repeats the archetypal act of regeneration. What to Mailer keeps our condition from being absurd merely is just this universal dialectic. The God of Life is not all-powerful but at war, suffering—even as ourselves—defeats as well as victories.

This search for the rebellious, divine energy within is exactly what connects Mailer's heroes to the mythological heroes of the past, to the ancient heroic adventure, to the archetypal return to the life-source within. The hero then returns to the world with expanded consciousness or nourishment for himself and others. In a previous book, I argued in detail how each of Mailer's heroes makes such a journey and how, taken as a composite, they express a regenerative synthesis of both conscious and unconscious psyche (or "heroic consciousness") characterized by five main qualities. The first two qualities are metaphorical perception (or the capacity to see interrelationships and telepathies between things) and divine or instinctual energy, the basis for courageous self-potency with which the hero opposes whatever would deaden or defeat him. These first two qualities especially are the sources of the hero's deeper vision into life and his moral force. The third quality of heroic consciousness is a revolutionary attitude toward the status quo. Such an attitude is the basis of that violence which precedes personal and social transformation. The fourth quality of heroic consciousness is the impulse to restore "wholeness" or balance to self and society whenever there is disproportion and imbalance. The final quality is extraordinary individualism, which best expresses Mailer's own faith in the intensity, power, and truth of the subjective perceptions of heroic or tested individuals. These last three qualities especially define the relationship of the hero to his society or culture. Through all of these qualities Mailer is reacting to what he sees as two shortcomings in contemporary novelists. First, they create heroes (or anti-heroes) who are "passive, timid, other-directed, pathetic, up to their nostrils in anguish." Second, their work shows great felicity (Fowles' rococo) but little other significance: "There seem to be more and more felicity all the time. Each year there seem to be more people who can really write stunning prose. And technique gets more and more elaborated. But I can't think offhand of any young writers who are philosophically disturbing at this point."[15]

These attributes of the Mailer hero connect the author to a literary and mythological tradition (including Fowles and Gardner) that seeks a larger foundation, a greater potential, for human aspirations than that of most anti-heroic twentieth-century existentialists. In American literature alone, this tradition of human transcendence, with its roots in Puritanism, ranges through Emerson and Thoreau, Melville, Twain, Fitzgerald, and Faulkner. This is a lineage of artists who have sought to awaken the moral consciousness of their culture by, often, depicting the journey of the individual soul as somehow connected to the journey of America itself. In British literature a similar lineage continues at least from Blake through D. H. Lawrence. These writers have continually warned humanity of the dangers of the drift toward spiritual impoverishment, loss of unconscious life or soul, mechanization, and what Mailer more inclusively has called "totalitarianism." By that term Mailer means the human impulse to defeat nature, to avoid risk and chance, to homogenize all diversity and opposition, and to destroy mystery. When he has defined evil in his fiction and nonfiction, he has defined it as stasis, stereotype, and bland homogeneity.

In light of these attributes of Mailer's mythic heroes, what is it, to address my second question, that drew Mailer to ancient Egypt as the subject of his first massive work of a possible trilogy? This question is all the more likely to arise when we recall that since *Armies of the Night* (1968) Mailer had turned exclusively to nonfiction, including the "nonfiction novel" *The Executioner's Song* (1979). He found in contemporary history itself the same quests, the same archetypal order, the same allegories for social criticism, and the same material for his preoccupations that he had imagined in fiction. Suddenly in 1983 with the publication of the Egyptian novel, Mailer seemed to shift away from the contemporary and the increasingly realistic. In a sense Mailer has reversed direction from his published work; on the other hand, he was writing *Ancient Evenings* off and on throughout the 1970s and early 1980s. He anticipated the issue himself: "the trouble is everybody is going to be saying, 'How the devil does Norman Mailer get himself up to start writing about Egyptian pharaohs? I mean that's really going too far.' "[16]

Mailer had pursued his themes as far as he could in the contemporary and naturalistic *Executioner's Song*. In Egypt Mailer could cut loose and develop his "karmic" concerns in a bold and original way, finally freed as much from the restrictions of fictional realism as from twentieth-century rationalism and scientism. Put simply, Mailer found in Egypt an ancient heroic and primary civilization; he found, in other words, an extremely fertile ground in which to plant and let flourish his fascination with the way extraordinary people have acted out and often failed in the eternal drama of the soul's struggle for "salvation" through the ancient patterns of rebirth. He found in Egypt a primal area in which to stage the conflict basic to all his novels and major nonfiction books—the struggle to balance and control the ageless, conflicting, and dynamic forces in oneself and in the world. It is the struggle for the creative power of life itself. Because Mailer intended to include future and present civilizations in his trilogy of regeneration, it is not surprising that he wished to begin that drama at its root, at one of the places in the Ancient Near East where civilization and recorded history began. In scope and ambition, this proposed trilogy is as audacious as anything ever written by an American. Whether Mailer succeeds or fails, literary history will determine.

There are, moreover, some generally acknowledged principles of Egyptian civilization that might further explain Mailer's attraction to Egypt and help clarify my later discussion. The constancy of Egyptian civilization through Old, Middle, and New Kingdoms and through successive dynasties, despite internal and particular changes, is significant. If ancient Egypt could be be said to initiate and repeat the patterns of degeneration and regeneration familiar to us as the briefer cycles of later civilizations, Egypt's continuities are the basis of its survival for three millennia. Chief among these continuities, this cultural identity, is its mythopoeic approach to experience and existence, that is, there is no clear division between the sacred and the secular, no desacralization of the world. Much to the consternation of his realist critics, Mailer has always sought this sacralization of the cosmos and human life. Mircea Eliade, in *The Sacred and the Profane,* suggests the archaic consciousness Mailer would approach:

> The man of the archaic societies tends to live as much as possible *in* the sacred. . . . The tendency is perfectly understandable, because, for primitive as for the man of all pre-modern societies, the *sacred* is equivalent to a *power,* and, in the last analysis, to *reality.* The sacred is saturated with *being. . . .* It should be said at once that the *completely* profane world, the wholly desacralized cosmos, is a recent discovery in the history of the human spirit. . . .
>
> For nonreligious man of the modern societies, this simultaneously *cosmic* and *sacred* dimension of conjugal union is difficult to grasp. But . . . it must not be forgotten that religious man of the archaic societies sees the world as fraught with messages. Sometimes the messages are in cipher, but the myths are there to help man decipher them. . . . What we find as soon as we place ourselves in the perspective of religious man of the archaic societies is that *the world exists because it was created by the gods,* and that the existence of the world itself "means" something, "wants to say" something, that the world is neither mute nor opaque, that it is not a mute thing without purpose or significance. For religious man the cosmos "lives" and "speaks." The mere life of the cosmos is proof of its sanctity. . . . For nonreligious man, all vital experiences—whether sex or eating, work or play—have been desacralized. This means that all these physiological acts are deprived of spiritual significance, hence deprived of their truly human dimension.[17]

As Gardner uses ancient Eastern wisdom in his magician's dialogues as a counterforce to our (i.e, Clumly's) habitual assumptions and perceptions, and as a tentative redirecting of lives out of balance with the cosmos, so does Mailer. But the difference of course is larger than the differences between Mesopotamia and Egypt. Mailer bases his novel completely on an archaic approach to life (as best he can gather it). His disruption (or "defamiliarization") of our assumptions and perceptions is not incidental but total. We enter a magical universe and a psychic condition counter to our own. We find ourselves in an unsettling realm where the sacred and the profane, the metaphorical and the literal, the micro- and macrocosmic are inseparable.

The Egyptian pharaoh is but another example of this archaic view; he is the unifying and life-giving god-king. The king is Lord of Two Lands not only because he unifies Upper and Lower Egypt, but because his role is both histori- cal *and* cosmological, both natural *and* supernatural, both human *and* divine. He represents a unified cosmos in which nature, humanity, and gods all partici- pate in the cosmological order and drama. If he functions as a charismatic hero-god with powers beyond other mortals, his rule is not arbitrary nor, histori- cally, free from the corruptions of disproportion. He, like everything existent, is subject to Maat—truth, justice, order, harmony, and the equilibrium of oppo- sites or "balance," to use Mailer's repeated word. As guardian of Maat, the king is responsible for Egypt's order instead of chaos, truth instead of falsity, har- mony instead of conflict. As sun-king and fertility god, his health and potency must be preserved through magic, ceremony, and celebration as in the Sed Festival, to take one example, commemorating his accession to power.

The king is, furthermore, without equal, and by his wealth and power is divorced from mere mortals in his social relationships. His identity like any god's is, therefore, at once aloof and multiple. Such identity and power entails responsibilities. The king's affirmation of Maat is part of the eternal pattern of recurrence, of death and regeneration, of the cycles of the sun, the Nile, and Osiris.

The gods are especially important in Mailer's novel. They, like those attaining godly powers, express their multiple identities through many names and transformations. The pharaoh embodies two gods—Osiris in death and Horus in life. Particularly after the Old Kingdom, Osiris is at the center of Egyptian religion as well as Mailer's novel. He is the very power and symbol of resurrection, of eternal recurrence. He is bringer of civilization and law- giver. His eternal adversary is Set, his evil brother, the god of opposition, desert, discord, confusion, chaos. (As Osiris-Horus, of course, the pharaoh himself would typically hold himself in opposition to the Set-principle.) Osiris is also god of the vitality of vegetation, soil, and Nile, life-giver as well as law-giver. In supernal realms he is equally important, identified with Orion and the ever-changing moon. In the Underworld he is King of the Dead. In his suffering, death, mutilation, and resurrection, the Egyptians saw their own life after death.

So at the very source of Egyptian civilization is a principle Mailer has argued for years: death and life are a continuum, and not merely absurd. Death is risky and adventurous, a state in which the debts and wastes of one's life carry significance beyond earthly existence. Mailer calls his version of this idea loosely "American existentialism" and "Karma," and by such terms he hopes to expand the meaning of existentialism to a sense of one's responsibility to others, to one's "soul," even to the "gods," as well as to oneself. As Mircea Eliade describes this approach, "For religious man, the appearance of life is the central mystery of the world. Human life is not felt as a brief appearance in time, between one nothingness and another; it is preceded by a pre-existence and continued in a postexistence. . . . Hence, for religious man, death does not put a final end to life. Death is but another modality of human existence."[18]

Osiris is at the center of the judgment of one's life in one's death, for he presides in the dramatic ritual of the Judgment of the Dead. Here, in the presence of gods, the dead make their "negative confession," denying commission of forty-two sins while their hearts are weighed against the feather of Maat in the balance of Anubis. Beginning in the Old Kingdom, and developing in the Middle Kingdom, even as nobles and nomarchs (provincial rulers) gain more power through decentralization, the possibility of salvation and regeneration passes down through the nobility to everyone, though only the wealthy can afford elaborate rites. By the New Kingdom (1570–1090 B.C.), the setting of *Ancient Evenings,* the cult of Osiris and democratization of regenerative power has spread, in principle, throughout society. In times of social responsibility (between cycles of social decay) one's judgment in death depends on having lived an ethical life.

James Henry Breasted's *The Dawn of Conscience* is the classic study of the evolution of this ethical dimension in ancient Egyptian life. Mailer could hardly have overlooked such a book. Breasted's thesis is that in Egypt we find the first social prophets who ultimately develop "a standard of morals far superior to that of the Decalogue over a thousand years before the Decalogue was written." Breasted traces the processes of that struggle—its growths and recessions from a Memphite drama dating back to the fourth millennium B.C. It is with the Pyramid Texts, after 3000 B.C., that the first sophistication begins. The sun-god remains the original source of approved and disapproved conduct, but in the Pyramid Texts the pharaoh embarks on an epic journey after life to test the power of his courage and magic, to become the lord of the gods themselves, a hunter of gods, a devourer whose cannibalism appropriates godly power. Yet even here, justice and righteousness are mightier than the king. It is at this time that Maat rises as the highest principle of existence, and a cosmic and national moral order becomes clear [in the "Maxims of Ptahhotep"]. In the collapse of the Old Kingdom, Breasted finds a disillusionment with the failure of the ideal before the corruptions of humanity and government, so eloquently expressed in "The Dialogue of a Misanthrope with His Own Soul."

With the social regeneration of the Middle Kingdom arises a series of moral sages who contrast ideals to be striven for with society as it is, as in the "Admonitions of Ipuwer," and in the teachings of Neferrohu and the Messianists (who call for a righteous king). In the Coffin Texts the possibility of afterlife extends to common people, as does the power of magic, which therefore includes everyone in the moral imperative of righteousness and justice (as opposed the merely the powerful and the wealthy). The afterlife is by now (after 2000 B.C.) an ethical ordeal, a drama of justification.

Breasted points out that with the rise of the New Kingdom and Egyptian Empire after 1600 B.C., the "sense of [one's] own personal responsibility for the quality of his character" grows even larger. By now the Egyptians have "pondered deeply" their own nature and place "each man's moral responsibility squarely on his own understanding." The growing conception of judgment now expressed in the *Book of the Dead* emphasizes the claim to innocence. And later in the period, the "Wisdom of Amenemope" not only establishes conscience as the voice of god within; that wisdom is the single most influential body of Egyptian moral teaching, reaching far beyond the Nile and ultimately to Palestine as the source of much Old Testament moral teaching.

Of equal importance during the Empire is the rise of a counterforce to ethical conscience—magic. In the *Book of the Dead* magic becomes an agent for moral ends and priestly profit. The negative confession is purchased as a charm, not unlike a Christian indulgence, to *profess* an innocence in the afterlife that did not exist in life. The magical potency of the scarab beetle, to take another example, is that it prevents the heart of the dead from betraying one's true character. This manipulation of one's ultimate judgment and ethical ordeal, Breasted argues, suddenly arrests the early moral evolution of humanity. The use of magic itself becomes a disproportion, for the good of magic holds many protections against destruction, evil, and disease in everyday life, and Isis the greatest of magicians uses her magic in Osiris' resurrection. But once magic becomes a commodity sold to deceive the dreaded Judge, to obscure the scrutiny of one's transgressions and the moral quality of one's life, it becomes a corruption. Ethical decadence parallels social decadence. And Egyptian civilization heads into a decline rapidly in the last century of Empire from which it never recovers.

We are witness, nevertheless, through Breasted's history of ancient Egypt, to that process by which the forms of state "pass over into the world of the gods" and the "relations of social life" deeply influence religion. We see the birth of the dialectic between external organized power and the internal power of the moral imperative.

Man's ancient love of power is enormously older than The Age of Character and it has thus far been so dangerously victorious over new-born conscience and character that we are faced with the grave question of the survival of civilization. . . . Man's growing eagerness for power as national organization advanced, until the machinery of human government became the organized expression of the thirst for power—the appetite for the exercise of force.

In wandering for years through the ancient lands of the Near East I have been impressed with this outstanding fact: the insistent monuments now surviving in all those distant lands have been primarily expressions of man's *power*. It is as if his struggles with the forces of nature, a struggle which has now been going on for perhaps a million years, had imbued him with a defiant consciousness. . . . Today you may enter one of the lonely valleys of the Sinai. . . . There he [a pharaoh's statue] has been standing since the Thirty-fourth Century before Christ, the oldest historical monument in the world. With uplifted weapon he is about to crush the skull of an Asiatic captive whom he has thrust down upon his knees before him. A monument of brutal force, it was a declaration of possession by right of conquest. . . . It strikes the note of force which has dominated human history ever since.[19]

The particular setting for Mailer's novel is a period of international empires and power struggles in the Near East—from the reign of Ramses II to the end of the Egyptian Empire (1290–1090 B.C.). Egypt was the greatest empire, rivaled in the late 1200s by the Hittites over Syrian lands. Egypt was then an enormous, centralized state. When imagining a hierarchical, bureaucratic society combined with the power of a divine king who rules an international empire by decree, one imagines a totalitarianism indeed, complete with monolithic government and personality cult. One of Mailer's most enduring obsessions is the nature of power-establishments and totalitarianisms, whether of East or West. And he believes that writing about Egypt taught him much about the nature of wealth and power in all times: "I think I've come to an understanding of the wealthy I've never had before, dealing with Egypt, its gold, and its pharaohs. . . . Fitzgerald was trying to say something, and Hemingway was trying to keep him from saying it. The very rich are not like you and me. Just as movie stars are not like you and me. . . . They no longer have a trustworthy relation to the society around them."[20] It is possible that Mailer's understanding of wealth and power engenders the deepest structural principle of the novel. For if indeed his narrative is a series of embedded tales, if it has the episodic and comic elements of the picaresque, and if it can even be described, as it has been, as an epic, *Ancient Evenings* is, to the extent that it concerns humanity in *this* life, a tragic epic in prose.

In the novel, as in Egyptian mythology, an enormous principle of death, degeneration, and evil exists in the cosmos and humanity with a counter-potential for life, regeneration, and righteousness. Jeffrey Burton Russell, in *The Devil: Perceptions of Evil from Antiquity to Primitive Christianity,* explains the Egyptian merging and differentiation of the two principles:

> No deity ever becomes the principle of evil, but in one god, Seth, the destructive and inharmonious element is more evident than in others. . . . That Seth is in conflict with his "good" doublet [Osiris] means that he himself has to be to some extent "evil." He therefore sets about to do the opposite of what is needed. . . . Horus [son of Osiris] castrates Seth, so depriving him of his power, but Seth in turn mutilates Horus: in the form of a black pig, he tears out Horus' eye and buries it.
>
> Both gods suffer from their bloody fray. That each loses a vital organ is a sign that their battle was a divine error. What is needed is not a struggle between the two parts of the divine nature but rather an effort at harmony, centering, union. Seth's attempt at union with Horus by sodomizing him fails because it is the wrong kind of effort—an effort at union by force and by transgression of *ma'at*. Only through . . . a coincidence of opposites that again renders the divine nature whole and one, can the entity Horus/Seth (or Osiris/Seth) be restored. Unhappily, the myth does not relate their reconciliation.

True dualism does not arise until the Zarathushtrian prophecies after 600 B.C. The Egyptian opposites are manifestations of the One, lending an ambiguity to divinity and evil that is perhaps more in keeping with the human experience of them and with Mailer's themes. Yet for Egyptians the destructive, evil principle arises and exists most commonly in the form of Set.[21]

Egyptian mythology therefore provides a view of human earthly life in its full tragic (entropic) potential. In some accounts, for example, Ra himself creates mankind, then sees that his creation is not good, but evil and rebellious. He sends Hathor to destroy humanity but, relenting, causes Hathor to become drunk on blood-red beer; hence, she lets some humans escape to carry on.

Mailer's previous novels, as well as *Ancient Evenings,* are saturated with tragic defeats, often the defeat of considerable potential. Those few heroes who succeed somewhat in their struggles to gain life, vitality, and creative force (Sergius and Rojack, for example) make only tentative gains. Here too in *Ancient Evenings* a heroic king goes down in corruption and defeat. Likewise the hero-commoner—a peasant of extraordinary physical and psychic power—tells his story of ambitions and capitulations through four lives. Only in death, in the journey through the Land of the Dead, is there vague hope of regeneration to a creative and purposeful life. And only if Mailer completes the trilogy may we know whether the quest for regeneration and nobility is to Mailer ultimately a living quest or a tragic one.

Indeed, Menenhetet I's adventures—the largest and most significant series of embedded tales—and the brief life of Meni II both make sense, it seems to me, only if we understand how bleak a vision of human vanity, waste, and degeneration most of Mailer's Egyptian tale is. If one has to make it to the final "Book of Secrets," and even to the final two chapters, to realize this tragic perspective, such nonetheless is the angle of Mailer's vision in this gargantuan, sometimes tedious book. This is not so say that the story is without many moments of humor, or, like its predecessors in ancient Eastern and Western literatures, its moments of human and godly triumph, heroism, epic fornications and death. Yet it is to say that humans are so confused by their Faustian lusts for power, wealth, and the "divine" royalty at the top that they cannot know whether their motivations and purposes are noble or base.

The ambiguous morality of our actions, the difficulty—even impossibility—of knowing, finally, whether we act for noble or base purposes, whether we are more fundamentally guilty and evil or innocent and good—this is a theme Mailer has been tracking for years, most emphatically in such previous works as *Armies of the Night* and *The Executioner's Song*. And after *Ancient Evenings*, in *Tough Guys Don't Dance* (1984), Mailer emphasizes that theme at even greater pitch, this time again in the late twentieth century; and he is reshaping still another genre, the mystery novel, for his own purposes. Tim Madden, the protagonist, is a man solving the mystery of his own guilt or innocence in the murder of his wife and an acquaintance. Uncertain of his motivations and actions on a previous evening, he must learn to act courageously, for he had no ethical north or boundary, as did the Pilgrims who first landed in Provincetown where Tim now lives.

This concept of good is repeated throughout Mailer's work: you can't cheat life, nor exploit death. Physical courage may be the basis, as well as the type and symbol, of spiritual and moral courage, especially in what Mailer likes to call "apocalyptic times"; that is to say, especially in periods of chaos, degeneration, or totalitarianism.

Like the gods themselves, we can only hope that our courageous efforts will be noble (or even righteous) in the end. But of course most likely our efforts will not be noble, and such a condition we might recognize only from the perspective of our deaths. The history of humanity might be viewed, as much as anything, as a tragic history of rising arcs of aspirations and ideals that are doomed to bend down and away from promise toward base results, toward eventual decay. Whether that is the result of some canker in the very nature of men and women, or some kink in the very order of things (even "the gods") would be an unanswerable question, although Mailer seems to suggest both the canker and the kink.

From the perspective of death, near the end of the novel, Meni II (to adapt Mailer's designations for differentiating the grandson from the grandfather) sees the suffering of others in the Land of the Dead and comes to recognize the tragic waste and worthlessness of his own life, just as he comes to see the failures of his grandfather's four lives. Here is an Underworld worthy of Dante where the unjust, the liars, the wealthy who would buy their way past the gatekeepers and soul-weighers, all suffer their appropriate agonies. Woe to the "enemies of Ra" whose misdeeds outweigh their virtues! For in the final bend of the Duad, Anubis awaits to judge the dead by weighing "the moral worth of the heart," as Menenhetet puts it at the outset of the tale (53), against Maat's feather of truth, that feather of justice and proportion in all things.

Meni II fears in the end that his heart is "heavy as a Canopic jar," though "when the heart was without evil, it weighed no more than a feather." Now he knows how he died and "could count the waste of my life," and that was "suffering enough" (703). The waste and evil in one's life *is* the revelation in death. The magician's tale on the Night of the Pig is a gift to his grandson. It is a revelation during the boy's lifetime of the ways of the world and the gods; it is also a revelation (intended or not) of the continuity of aspiration and waste throughout the tale-teller's four lives. The young Meni, assassinated in a bar-room brawl, was, however, as unable to use the wisdom and revelation to change his life as Ramses IX ultimately is. "I was dead. All that had lived in the little boy who was six, all of his tenderness, his wisdom, his pleasure, all that spoke of his days to come, and the promise of it was gone. There had been no more purpose than in the squashing of a beetle. I could have wept for myself as if lamenting another. In all the debauchery of these last few years, I had never thought that I would not emerge with some—at least—of the expectations of my earliest years redeemed. Now I would not. . . . A young life and a wasted one!" (700).

Even given the opportunity and wisdom of four lives, the failure of the great-grandfather's enormous potential is as great or greater.

> Upon me came the weight of the failure of my great-grandfather in his four lives. I could feel how the magnitude of his desire remained as large as the pain of his defeats. . . . My great-grandfather must live near the sorrow that dwelt in the heart of the Lord of the Dead. Who but Osiris hoped to discover what would yet come forth from gods unborn? . . . He was the God Who longed to create the works and the marvels of the future. So he suffered the most from every high purpose that failed. He would know how bitter it had been for my great-grandfather to be so defeated that the taste of his seed was foul? (706)

Given the choice to die a "second time" or return through "the fundament of pain" to rebirth, Meni II hesitates because of his now-understood unworthiness: "I was worthless, and my grandfather was damned and worthless, and we were beset by mighty curses." When, however, he finally chooses rebirth it is because he realizes his grandfather's whole tale had been told to gain his trust, to prepare to join their souls (Kas) together in a regenerative effort for new strength and purpose. "His body had reeked of the Land of the Dead . . . and now I perceived that in his loneliness, he wished for me to join him. The tales he had told the Pharaoh, had been told for me as well. It was I whom he had wanted to trust. And I did. Here in the Duad, in this hour, I would trust him" (708).

Their souls fused, Meni I and II ascend, gazing "like Osiris upon the portents of all that is ahead, and to try to turn the storm before it breaks." That storm, that apocalypse of gods and men, lies so close by that even as Meni feels that neither he nor his grandfather is "pure enough for such a task . . . [for]

neither of us could offer a feather to lie upon the heart as nicely as a sense of right and wrong," he also comes to believe that things have reached such a desperate pitch in the realms of gods and humans and in the struggles between Osiris and Set that now "purity and goodness were worth less to Osiris than strength." At whatever cost, defeating his adversaries is Osiris' first task; only then might he turn to creation. "Indeed, the Lord Osiris might be as desperate as ourselves when it came to choosing his troops" (708–9).

The novel ends nearly a thousand years after Menenhetet's death, about 322 B.C., which is the farthest point in the outer frame of the narrative. Egypt has fallen, Greece and Rome are now in possession of the gods and of the Duad (where "death is more treacherous than life") itself. Now humanity knows even "less of the differences between gods and men" or "despise[s] such differences." Gone is the understanding that when the Gods threw Set on the ground and Osiris sat on his face, there was "the victory of righteousness over evil," and a true throne (705–6). The gods usurped and misunderstood, the Duad a mere dream—that is the world into which Menenhetet is about to be reborn and to renew his struggles in the heroic round. "May my hope of heaven now prove equal to my ignorance of where I go. . . . I do not know if I will labor in greed forever among the demonic or serve some noble purpose I cannot name" (709). Whether he is doomed to failure through endless cycles of reincarnation, or whether there is some alternative avenue of human courage and endurance, Mailer has yet to discover.

To express this vision of bold effort and failure, Mailer chooses two narrators. In a spirit of outrageous experimentation Mailer grants his six-year-old first narrator a first-person omniscient point of view. Having the lineage and gifts of pharaohs, as Mailer depicts them, Meni II sees others' minds. Through this first narrator, the grandfather in turn tells the stories of his four lives for most of the novel. The grandfather guides the young Meni through the World of the Dead as well as the world of the living, as Conchis and Tag Hodge guide their initiates, by the use of a series of parabolic tales about human nature and history. Like the archetypal guides of ancient and modern literature, and again like Fowles' and Gardner's, Mailer's guide figure is at once magus, odoriferous old man, shapeshifter, and obscene fool. Like the artist himself, the guide may even lie to get at the truth: "The traveler from distant places is an everlasting liar" (65). Previously a student of magic, medicine, and religion, and the High Priest of Thebes, Menenhetet I has the lore to negotiate the Land of the Dead and mediate between the worlds of gods and humans. "I will offer a story far better then any father ever gave a son, . . . and I would like my granddaughter to listen as well," Menenhetet tells the pharaoh. "They are now nearest my flesh of all four lives" (232).

The three interior books of the novel (4 through 6) are devoted to Meni I's story of his first life and all the embedded tales, digressions, and commentaries within that story. This is the heart of the novel, the repository of all the lore, folly, and wisdom revealed to Meni II, his family, and Ramses IX. Appropriately, "Menehetet" means "foundation of speech," and such a name itself associates him with magical powers, for the word to Egyptians is basic to magic, to affecting actuality. The spoken/written word is believed to have a significance, therefore, that any modern writer would envy.[22]

This magician, tale-teller, and guide, like Gardner's heroic models from Clumly to Lars-Goren, is not known so much for his quickness of wit as for his peasantlike persistence, truth-seeking, and courage despite all his foibles and failures. These qualities of endurance and risk-taking are what first endeared him to the youthful Ramses II. Above all, Meni I's tale is one of personal courage, ambition, and folly, and each of these qualities of his tale are in turn reflected by the desires, maneuverings, and comments of his three interlocutors—Ramses IX, Hathfertiti (little Meni's mother), Meni's father Nef-khep-aukhem. All of the characters at both levels of the narrative are caught in a web of conflicting ambitions and historical contexts—a context extended by comparison even as far back to such earlier pharaohs as Kufhu, for example. If by the end of the novel, the historical context extends forward to Greece and Rome, then by appropriate comparisons each reader may extrapolate to modern history as well. Such themes as the value of courage and strength, the necessity of balance or proportion, the brutal and disconnected nature of social and political establishments, and the psychic underworld of ambition, greed, and lust are emphatic themes in the novel with ethical ramifications in many historical contexts.

Mailer's theme of the ethical connections between life and death is sounded early in the novel. Realizing he is dead, the ghost-narrator Meni II suddenly feels happiness beside his fear because now:

> I would be free at last to know all the ways I had failed to live my life, all the boredom I had swallowed, and each foul sentiment of wasted flesh. It was as if I had spent my days beneath a curse, and the sign of it—despite every lively pandemonium of gambling and debauch—was the state of immutable monotony that dwelt in my heart. The sense of being dead while alive . . . I had an inkling then of the force of the desire to die when that is the only way to encounter one's demon. . . . If, in these curious intoxications of knowing I was dead, I had begun to feel as splendid as a hero, still I could not remember my heroism. Nonetheless, I had hardly doubted that my purposes (if I could ever find them) would be noble. (36–37)

The connected journeys through life and death are the subject of the novel. Both journeys are filled with dangers, temptations, and huge risks. What one can endure and overcome depends at each point in the continuum on what one has endured and overcome. The commodities most required are courage and strength. Mailer has long approached, and in Egypt apparently found, this archaic attitude toward life and death described in *The Sacred and the Profane:* "the man of the primitive societies has sought to conquer death by transforming it into a *rite of passage.* . . . In short, death comes to be regarded as the supreme initiation, that is, as the beginning of a new spiritual existence. Nor is this all. Generation, death, and regeneration (= rebirth) were understood as three moments in a single mystery, and the entire spiritual effort of archaic man was exerted to show that there must be no interval between these moments" (196).

In death, the ultimate question is what use has one made of one's life force. That is the question raised at the outset of the novel. The Sekhem (the gift from the sun, the "Power" in oneself) asks the dead person "its dire question": "Some succeed in using me well. Can you make that claim?" How well the hero has used his vitality, his life force, is the question constantly before him, his auditors, and the reader as Menenhetet tells his tale. His vital force is finally all the hero has to oppose the personal, social, and historical forces of entropy. And that is the real conflict in the novel (much as it is in Mailer's life, or in Ali's, the hero of Mailer's *The Fight*)—how to use one's force and all the forces one can attach to oneself against internal and external forces of entropy.

Of course, one may confuse destructive with vital forces, one cannot be certain he or she is not the instrument rather than the destroyer of, for example, totalitarianism, and one may misread one's own intentions and actions. If it is only from the perspective of death that one begins to see the nobility or baseness of one's actions and desires, one has little choice but to act at least, to assert one's life and force against every form of dissolution. It may indeed take something on the order of four lives and deaths, Mailer seems to be suggesting, before one is prepared for nobility of purpose and prepared to effectively channel rather than squander one's spirit and power. "I'm a great believer in karma," Mailer has said. "I do believe that we're not here just one time, and I don't have any highly organized theology behind that. . . . Karma tends to make more sense than a world conceived without it, because when you think of the incredible elaborations that go into any one human being, it does seem wasteful of the cosmos to send us out just once to learn all those things, and then molder in the weeds. It doesn't make as much sense as the idea that we are part of some continual process that uses us over and over again. . . . There is some sort of divine collaboration going on."[23]

Each would-be hero, whether pharaoh or peasant, repeats the battle of vitality against entropy and wins or loses according to how much folly, vanity, and bestiality overcome his life-affirming powers. If the vitalist-hero has to pass through waste, mess, disease, greed, and murder to recast the self, he must also pass beyond such experiences to rebuild a heroic personality. An examination of the three seekers of truth and divine force—Ramses IX, Ramses II, and Menenhetet I—will suggest how much this tragic conflict between vitality and entropy is the deepest structural principle of the novel. Such an examination will also suggest to what extent Mailer's unusual ethic is contained and expressed by the conflict. Just as each potential hero's vitality is arrayed (in each case unsuccessfully) against internal and external forces of entropy, so is it in the nature of existence that the conflict is repeated endlessly, ever in need of renewal. As Eliade put it in *Sacred and Profane,* "If religious man feels the need of indefinitely reproducing the same paradigmatic acts and gestures, *this is because he desires and attempts to live close to his gods*" (91).

Ramses IX, to take our first example, is the weakest of the three seekers, but it is from the perspective of the seventh year of his reign that old Menenhetet's story is told. Ramses IX's condition and story are told by the young narrator, Meni II. What he, and we, discover is revealed, therefore, by the frame-narrator or story; that story reaffirms, as a kind of object lesson in human nature and degeneration, much of what Menenhetet I has to teach through his own tale (that interior series of narratives). What the pharaoh seeks through the old man is the knowledge and heart of his greatest ancestor Ramses II (Usermare). "If He had chosen to become my Father, I was in no doubt of the reason. He was, by now, by way of my mother, nearer indeed now to all that Menenhetet might know, nearer, therefore, to what He desired the most—which was to dwell in the heart of Usermare" (538). That, as Meni II tells us, is one of only two means available to him to gain necessary knowledge and power: to learn from the life of Ramses II, and to receive the favor of the gods. Thereby might he gain "the godly power to rule Egypt" (539).

The reasons why Ramses IX is desperate for such power are emphasized through one of the most common refrains expressed by many of the characters—the historical processes of social and political degeneration. "Do I never hear talk of victory?" asks Ramses IX of his General. By the king's own testimony he danced naked at age ten when other pharaohs led troops; he has never led an army into battle, whereas Ramses II tamed a lion and won at Kadesh; he does not even visit his harem, whereas Ramses II mated with or sired children by "every beauty in Memphi and Thebes." Neither a daring leader of nations nor men, Ptah-nem-hotep (Ramses IX) is merely a sort of witty and enduring bureaucrat (157–58).

It is as if historical processes were ever playing regenerative powers against entropic powers. In such times of degeneration, as Menenhetet puts it, "we are not close to the gods"; or as Ramses IX says: "These are the years when no one in Egypt can be trusted. . . . There are more tomb robberies than ever before. . . . The grain accounts are calculated by corrupt officials. Theft in high places is frequent. . . . The Overseer of the Golden Bowl was stealing from my Person. It convinced Me more than any raids on our frontiers that the Two-Lands are weak. I have not gained the respect of the Gods. Not at least as other Pharaohs. They have been able to speak to Them better than I" (223). Here is a pharaoh (Ramses IX) who ends up as a man desperate for the knowledge that Menenhetet

I might have given him, and a ruthless and uncourageous parent and leader (690). We are seeing a three-millenia civilization well into its ultimate decline; the times, as Mailer would put it, are indeed apocalyptic for Egypt.

Yet even Ramses the Great, to take our second example, must struggle to maintain his favor and power. If Ra himself must battle entropy in each daily round, if Osiris must counter Set, what king or hero, indeed what human being, can be free of such tasks? The long, central account of the reign of Ramses II is itself a story of the bold rise to godly heights (in terms that the ancient, heroic world understood) and the descent to personal and political degradation. One has only to compare the "King of Kings" in the elder Menenhetet's interior tale before and after the Battle of Kadesh to see the pattern.

Well over two hundred pages into the novel when we are introduced to Ramses the Great, we see him, as Menenhetet the young charioteer did, as a heroic model of the ancient world. In the glory of his youth, Ramses is taller, more able, more courageous than any other—a charioteer's charioteer, a king's king. Loved by his loyal legions and his queen Nefertiri, his body bathed in the reddish glow that would associate him with the powers of Set too, Ramses is also marked as the divinely inspired and charismatic hero-king, a son of Ra. His hair is wild and golden, his eyes are unearthly blue.

In the earlier period of his reign Ramses' daily religious devotions are profound and humble before greater gods than he. Just as his inferiors grovel before him, so he grovels in his secret prayers to Amon. His goal, now, is righteousness in his power, so that he may rule the lands of Egypt as the parts of his body, as did Osiris the first king. "All that is evil in me, I throw on the ground," the attending priest says. The oracle promises him victory and increased strength if he remains loyal to Amon (270–71).

The battle of Kadesh is the culmination of his heroism, a heroism as alive with the assumptions of the ancient world as the battle scenes of the *Iliad*. In this epic set piece, gods and men exchange favors and devotions, and victory comes through courage, risk, and acts of desperation. The battle, its aftermath, and Menenhetet's journey before the battle through ancient Lebanon and Syria as a scout are among Mailer's most impressive descriptive achievements in the book. Perhaps one of Ramses' most magnificent moments is when he receives the hands of the enemy dead as trophies to his victory, standing immovable, miraculously restored from his wounds and fatigues, aloof from the carnage and rape of the Hittite warriors like an unseeing god above the Hellish glare of human brutality.

> All through the night, our fires burned, and through the same night, Usermare-Setpenere stood in His Chariot under a full moon and received the severed hands of the slain Hittites one by one. . . . I realized once again how to be near Him was to gain all knowledge of how a God might act when He is in the form of a man. He looks so much like a man and yet reveals

divinity by even the smallest of His Moves. In this case, it was that He did not move His feet
. . . an exhibition of such poise that one saw the mark of a God. (356)

No less than the gods, the king too must battle the serpent of entropy, and even less than Ra or Osiris is there certainty of his success. Even as he begins his tale, Menenhetet prepares us for the other potential in Ramses—the degeneration of the kingship, his marriage, his court, and his kingdom. How much his reign cost him, Menenhetet tells us, is in part suggested by the changes in his physical stature and in the color of his hair and eyes over the years. Indeed, what we do see in this novel is Mailer's chronicle of the king's failures after his finest victory at Kadesh. Ramses II fails to maintain his earlier power as an Osirian king of fertility and civilization whose lands, people, and political systems all depend on him for continuous productivity and harmony. At the heart of his failure lies the insurmountable serpent within: egoism, totalitarian lusts for carnal ownership, and fear—fear of diminished potency and of one's social inferiors. Mailer's portrait of Ramses' hubris is not unlike Barbara Mertz's more impatient description of the pharaoh as "probably the most monumental egotist of all time."[24]

Although there are earlier intimations of future deficiencies in the king, his worst impulses fully emerge by book 4, chapter 13. The novel seems to divide in two after chapter 12 as dissolution sets in. As in Mailer's metaphysic since the 1960s the hero is as embattled as the gods and in danger of defeat and disproportion. From early in Menenhetet's tale of his first life we learned that even those the king loves and who love him he must debase and own, make instruments of his will, as when he first has Menenhetet "by the asshole" and thereby ignites the young charioteer's life-long impulse for revenge. Likewise, immediately following Kadesh, Ramses denies the labors and wounds of his men and generals (even of his right arm Menenhetet) in the king's behalf by taking sole credit for victory over the Hittite armies. His future monuments to himself repeat that claim and, quite likely, sow seeds of later betrayal. "Some had fought, and some had even fought a lot. Many were bloody with their wounds. Yet they listened in shame . . . and when the Generals of the Division of Ptah came forward . . . he did not thank them for saving the day, nor reward His son Amen-Khep-shu-ef for the rigors of that ride, but only remarked, 'What will Amon say when He hears that Ptah left Me alone on this great day? . . . I, and I alone, was the tempest against their chiefs.'" Menenhetet responds: "I wondered if His mind had not taken a wrench from the screams of that Asiatic God who roared out of His throat" (354).

But it is after his return from fourteen years of exile in Eshuranib that Menenhetet notices the most dramatic change in his king. Ramses has become a liar, increasingly selfish and vain, and filled with petty vices. He has built a monumental cult of personality, and by accepting the Hittite princess Rama

Nefru as his favorite he has taken in strange gods to help him stand against whatever sedition—divine, magical, or political—may be afoot. As his paranoia enlarges, his fear of death becomes great as well (see especially 381–88, 501). A vicious circle of fear and plots now blind the king, and he spends the rest of his days looking back to his moment at Kadesh, hoping somehow to regain the power to rule Egypt wholly again. "Usermare lived so much in fear that He was like a man who looks at a field glistening in the sun and thinks it is a river" (396). And once he learns that the Hittite King Metella had not even participated in the Battle of Kadesh, even that great memory is corrupted "like vines that would grow into His pride" (607).

Of course Ramses will seek to renew strength and courage during his period of decline. He will even on occasion find such strength and courage, albeit more momentary and attenuated than in his youth. The focus of such efforts is his "Third Festival" in celebration of his thirty-fifth year of reign (i.e., the subject of book 5, "The Book of the Pharaoh"). He will, to take one example, reaffirm his potency as a god of earthly fertility from whom all abundance and generation flow.[25] But such scenes of godlike potency reveal their underside as well. As in Mailer's scenes of the cheering populace, the attentive and obsequious priests, the retinues and protocol, the mass and frenzied worship of the great man, one sees the ancient roots of those modern spectacles of totalitarian worship—that mutual, frenzied species of orgiastic rituals and sexual longing for the master power.

Later in the Festival, to suggest a second example of Ramses' search for renewed potency, the king will publicly hide his fear and choose Rama-Nefru over Nefertiri: "There is no magic whose terror is more powerful than the fear of a Pharaoh before the strength of his Son. To choose Nefertiri would calm every force that might rise against Him. With Rama-Nefru, He would only possess the radiance that is in the light of far off lands. Yet His pride that He was the One was great, and He hated to bow before His fear of Amen-Khep-shu-ef. . . . I see Him, and understand that He could never make His choice from fear, or He would be no longer divine" (649).

Despite such kingly efforts and momentary successes, it becomes clearer that the last years of Ramses II's reign in Egypt are a period of failing kingship, official and priestly corruption and wealth, tomb-robbery, and general dissolution. And in the successive reigns of further Ramseses the corruption worsens and is reflected in Menenhetet's own lives. Without the balance of Maat, entropy turns the wheel toward a cycle of degeneration.

If Ramses IX is a diminished and bureaucratic monarch, and Ramses II is a heroic man who loses control of the forces that inhabit and surround him, then the narrator-hero Menenhetet I is a portrait of a prodigious power that is, once again, enervated and wasted. The battles between his own vitality and entropy during four lives are the second center of interest in the elder Menenhetet's tale.

Favored by the gods and associated with Osiris in particular—Lord of the Dead, of the mind, of order, and regeneration—Menenhetet is a Mailer hero of truly mythic proportions. It is Osiris whom he most seeks as a student of magic (215), Osiris who speaks to him at Kadesh (344–45), and Osiris into whose temple the sorceress-queen Honey-Ball initiates him as "First Priest" through their repetition of the Isis-Osiris ritual (446–49).

Menenhetet's rise from peasant to soldier, to charioteer to confidant of Ramses II, to General of the Armies, Governor of the Secluded, Companion to the Queen, and Master of the Secrets in books 4 and 5 is the story of an epic adventure that is the result of great physical strength and courage, persistence and endurance, and finally political, sexual, and magical wisdom. In still another sense he is truly a Mailer hero, for his chief heroic attribute is his sense of rebellion and the force to perpetuate it. For Sergius in *The Deer Park,* Rojack in *An American Dream,* Gilmore in *The Executioner's Song,* and even Mailer's own clownish heroism in *Armies of the Night,* it is just this principle of rebellion—as rebel artist, hipster, criminal, or citizen—that defines heroism for Mailer. Menenhetet pits his rebellion against perhaps the most powerful authoritarian force in history—one of the greatest absolute rulers of the Ancient Near East. To build the structure of a heroic self, Menenhetet, like his predecessors in Mailer's pantheon, will not only have to use his best impulses and qualities, but he will also have to descend into the maw of the beast, live in its filth, steal its powers and receive its gifts. What judgment is to be offered comes only in the Land of the Dead. But while alive he participates in all the human joys and depravities, all that is admirably and disgustingly human. Like the excesses of the gods, like the opposing principles of Osiris and Set, each human and each epoch repeat the drama of embattled oppositions. Heroic success is the balancing of all these forces one comes to know and use; it is the defeat of disproportion and entropy through balance. Heroic failure is the capitulation to state and ruler as much as to waste, ambition, greed, pettiness, and vanity. And only in death does Menenhetet begin to realize that there may be conceivably more noble if mysterious purposes of our rebellion than avenging personal shame.

The initial source of Menenhetet's heroic rebellion, a source that creates the channel that will direct his great vitality and knowledge, is Ramses' "carnal ownership" (i.e., anal rape) of Menenhetet when Ramses shows him the king's secret tomb. When the rape is repeated, it only strengthens Menenhetet's resolve. Mailer's Egyptians practice such violations to express a kind of sexual chain of being (or hierarchy of power) from gods, to pharaohs, right down to the lowest commoner or prisoner. It is the victory of ownership over another person's body and will, his or her life and death, which each absolute ruler of course holds over all his minions. As Menenhetet describes his violation: "something in the very sanctuary of myself flew open, and the last of my pride was gone. I was no longer myself but His, and loved Him, and knew I would die for

Him, but I also knew I would never forgive Him, not when I ate, not when I drank, not when I defecated. Like an arrow flew one thought through my mind: It was that I must revenge myself" (288). During his long journey, however, Menenhetet is not above stealing the prides and gifts of others in similar fashion. He gains all the "bad habits," all the "strength and bravery and the cheap treacherous shit of this cutthroat" when he rapes a thief in the mountains. "There was a thief in me for the next ten years" (306). As Rojack used Ruta's, Menenhetet will use the thief's treachery to forge his acts of courage and rebellion against others, from the King of Kadesh to Ramses himself.

His rebellion against Ramses will not only include sexual rebellion in the harem with Honey-Ball and Nefertiri the Royal Consort herself, but rebellion through all the forces he can bring to bear against the seemingly insurmountable power of the king. The most important of these forces is magic. Mailer has commented that in Egypt "magic was being converted into social equivalence, in effect used as an exchange," and that because of this common usage "the book has an immense preoccupation with magic as such."[26] Nowhere than in Ancient Egypt, as Frazer reminded us, were the magic arts more carefully cultivated. A drop of one's blood, a clipping of hair or parings of nails, excreta, a strip of garment, a footprint, a name, a portrait—all might be used "to give a sorcerer complete power" over one.[27] Though in his later lives Menenhetet will seek the powers and mysteries of magic as High Priest and master magician, magic will even in his first life become a significant part of his heroic rebellion and revenge, another source of his vital power. With the sorceress Queen Honey-Ball, Menenhetet will learn the power of both foulness and beauty, loyalty and treachery, and through her, he will learn of magic's connection (like every other form of power) to courage and to sexuality. "I decided to seek the courage of madness itself. I would dare what no one else was ready to dare, and put myself in bed with one of the little queens. . . . My shame, carried for so many years, was now inflamed" (426–27). Against all the powers of the king and state worship on Ramses' side, Menenhetet and Honey-Ball, who has her own shame and vengefulness, will do magical battle, causing such a stir of anxieties and mishaps that the king and his new Hittite queen will mount counterattacks and protections.

As with any risk-taking for Mailer, magic requires the courage to seek out everything and, in seeking, to strike the balance just necessary to stay destruction. That is one of Menenhetet's earliest lessons to his grandson at the outset of their journey through death and life:

"The Gods . . . are capable of anything. They do everything." And in sudden wrath, he added, "That is why They have real need of Maat. If not for Maat, there would be no end to the destruction They cause. Nor the wild passions They strew when They turn into animals. The abominable situation is that Their transformations depend on shit, blood-sacrifice, and fucking, and They respect none of it. They do not appreciate how magic is obedient to the deepest principle [i.e., "the balance of Maat"]. . . .

"In its [magic's] true exchange, one cannot gain a great deal unless one is willing to dare losing all. . . . You do dot buy a few words of power. . . . One has to pay a price for magic. . . . That is the obligation. Look for the risk. We must obey it every time. There is no credit to be drawn from the virtue of one's past." (65–66)

Courage (in this case the courage of risk-taking) is of course, as MacIntyre reminds us in *After Virtue,* one of the great heroic virtues or excellences of the ancient world. MacIntyre develops the point at length: physical courage and strength are universally admired in heroic societies not only as the basis of a healthy social order but as a necessity of life under the pressure of one's *worldly* fate—ultimately defeat, not victory. To face "the patterns of harms and dangers," the personal and the god-inspired passions, and the accountability to others that shapes one's identity out of an "interlocking set of . . . narratable lives," one needs courage. "We are," MacIntyre writes, "whether we acknowledge it or not, what the past has made us and we cannot eradicate from ourselves, even in America, those parts of ourselves which are formed by our relationship to each formative stage in our history. . . . Even heroic society is still inescapably a part of us all, and we are narrating a history that is peculiarly *our own history* when we recount its past in the formation of our moral culture." History forces us, among other things, to ask whether human life can be viewed as a victory or a defeat.[28] The heroic ethic of courage Mailer adapts in all his work to modern men and women, since he believes that courage is what we most lack yet most need, and is the only sign of the "good" left to us.

Magic most requires courage because the magician stands to lose as much as gain, to debilitate as much as augment her own force. Nowhere is this clearer than in Honey-Ball's exchange with Heqat—sorceress of primordial energy and chaos, of the entropic lizard, of a host of demons and the eight mothers and fathers of the slime who precede the gods themselves (557, 566).

Hence, we begin to see in this novel an idea that has long been part of Mailer's existential metaphysic, to borrow his own terminology. When the gods fail in virtue, courage, or balance it is because we humans fail. Just as in the fantasy of *Why Are We in Vietnam?,* to take but one example, whether some bestial or some enlightened, civilizing god emerges to shape human life and passion depends on the quality of our conscious and unconscious life, so in *Ancient Evenings* does the virtue and harmony, or bestiality and disorder of the gods depend on our deepest passions, desires, and dreams. "The Gods listen to mean thought," Menenhetet explains to Ramses IX. "None of us is without magic when we speak to the Gods in a dream" (215).

If the war of magic between the Isis and Seti-Ka powers of Honey-Ball and all the state's magical powers and Hittite gods of Ramses II did succeed in breaking the pharaoh's ring of protection, it did not "turn his head" and defeat him. Menenhetet, as a result, is once again reduced to being carnally owned by Ramses and to, quite literally, kissing the king's arse. Raising the ante further, Ramses II, now believing he has regained ownership of him, dispatches Menenhetet to watch over the now-mistrusted Nefertiri. And of course like every ruler before or since, whether metaphorically or literally, the king promises Menenhetet a place in his golden boat in the afterlife if he remains a loyal servant.

But Menenhetet's heroic proportions have not yet been fully tested. He will take even greater risks with the Consort herself. The sexual betrayal increases and the magical war renews, this time through the power of the pharaoh's leavings, which Menenhetet steals from the Golden Bowl. "I hated my Pharaoh, but such hatred was worthless since I wished to be able to love Him, and it was hopeless. He would only love me less. How I wished to destroy Him" (505).

If the queen and her guardian fail by their magical rebellion to destroy the king this time too, their magic is more effective, with the help of Honey-Ball again, and nearly leads to Ramses' death. More successful is Nefertiri's and Menenhetet's sexual rebellion. Short of assassination, their greatest revenge is for the Queen to violate her sexual fidelity with a peasant and with him to break every taboo. In this revenge they both revel—she claiming the power and being of the pharaoh, and he traveling through the Land of the Dead and rising to the celestial city and Amon at the climax. Knowing at once "a change as great as death itself" and the full fury of Ramses in the queen's orgasm, Menenhetet can say as he did on first beginning their lovemaking, "my buttocks were my own again"; he has retaken ownership of his carnality.

Yet for both, the revenge seems incomplete, and they dare even more— further fornications and agreeing to assassinate the king. That is how Menenhetet ends his first life and (through Nefertiri's womb) begins his second. Yet each life will be less noble than the last, though each confirms the lessons of human existence gained in the first. "If I failed in my first life, and betrayed much in my second, fouled every nest in my third, so must I see my fourth life as the one where I sought to use what I learned in order to learn much more" (681). That is a way of expressing the dialectic of courage and entropy, of the efforts and failures of his lives. For if even in his fourth life as a physician, general, nobleman, notable, and magician, Menenhetet had sought the knowledge finally to restore Egypt to her former harmonies and powers, "to enrich the marrow of our failing lands," as he puts it (215), his efforts were not without that taint of vain ambition to be a pharaoh himself. Such ambition earns him only the betrayal of his granddaughter Hethfertiti for her own place in the sun, and ostracism at the hands of Ramses IX. "My hopes are extinct," he realizes; his monumental story-telling efforts on the Night of the Pig have failed, at least for his own political and social ambitions (683). This failure to become a pharaoh, the premier social, political, and religious ruler of peoples and lands, the source of life and strength—indeed the failure to become godlike—is the ostensible failure. The real failure is the hero's inability to remain undefeated by ambitions, to remain a heroic vitalist furthering the cause of life against death, balance against disproportion, nobility against baseness of purpose. As he realizes in the moment he decides to dare all with Queen Nefertiri: "for the first time I saw my life without pride. I did not think of my achievements (which were the blood and bone of my good esteem each morning) but saw instead all I had not done, the friends I had never made (for I trusted no man), the family I would never have (for I trusted no woman enough to keep a family) . . . my nostrils full of the puke of others. Just as atrocious seemed the contents of my own heart. I saw then the helplessness of growing into an old man—for me, at least" (614).

Mailer is also working well within the English literary tradition here. Magicians' failures are typically Faustian and symptomatic of their tragic humanity. Their temporal concerns trap them—their aspirations finally unequal to their degeneracy, their sensual moral failures the emblem of spiritual failure. Bacon, Faustus, Prospero (before the island) are the types. These magicians continually fall by their overwhelming desire for power as well as by their inability to balance contemplation and action, humility and vanity, control and excess. In each case Prospero's words about Caliban are apt: "This thing of darkness I / Acknowledge mine."[29]

One is tempted to read much of the elder Menenhetet's tale and musings with autobiographical resonances of the author: Mailer running for mayor or "president," Mailer betrayed by his own ambitions, Mailer whose turbulent family life is the stuff of gossip magazines, Mailer whose "star" status skews his relationships to others and to his society, Mailer the infamous and conceivably the failed artist. But let us leave such speculations to others and say merely that much of what Menenhetet displays of his ambitions, vices, confused moral stature, and risk-takings (to cite but a few parallels) suggests at the least a high degree of imaginative sympathy of the artist for his hero. And it would not be too much to say that, accurate or misinformed, the tale embodies what Mailer has learned of ambition, vanity, violence, and dread in our world.

What we learn of Ramses IX through Meni II, of Ramses II and Menenhetet I through the old magician's tale, then, contains Mailer's principal theme and provides the largest structural principle of the novel—the conflict between entropy and vitality. Each of these noble characters displays the personal hubris of his pride, vanity, and ambition, and each, through these and other faults, is incapable of urging his vital power an potential above the wastes and defeats of his life. Such, it turns out, is also the case with young Meni's brief life, until his journey into Death with his grandfather finally promises, perhaps, something more.

Those external, which is to say social, entropic impulses against which Menen-
het struggles are, as I have only suggested to this point, a form of totalitarianism. The forms of entropic totalitarianism and the pressures of social conformity
and abnegation are both central concerns in all of Mailer's work; *Ancient Evenings* is no exception.

The conflict of self against totalitarian hegemony is for Mailer part of the
continual drama of disintegrating/integrating identity. Mailer has always argued
that one quality of modern hegemony is, as Lentricchia puts it, the transformation of "the Romantic yearning for the new" into an "energetic consumer-
ism." That transformation is effected through, in Mailer's terms, a corporate
totalitarianism and all its "cancerous" plastics, wastes, and rhetorical-symbolic
mechanisms of repression. What Lentricchia identifies as the total absorption
of romantic Utopian impulses by corporate "economic perpetuation" is also one
face of the hegemony both Fowles and Mailer rail against, and against which
they place their counter-rhetoric, symbolism, and myth. It is this very image of
commodity utopia that, Lentricchia argues, turns revolutionary, dissident, antinomian force into the desire to conserve consumer capitalism. With such an
adversary, Fowles and Mailer invest their texts (as Lentricchia and Kenneth
Burke do) with greater significance and urgency. What these contemporary
writers and critics see as a version of Western totalitarianism has made them
reject the currency of textual pleasures in favor of adversarial textual powers.

Even though Mailer has frequently argued (as Burke has) that the normaliz-
ing, disciplinary mechanisms within our bureaucratic institutions do not necessarily apply physical force, the mechanisms do saturate our lives, our sense of
ourselves, and our relations with *their* values. Mailer, however, melodramati-
cally depicts the lusts and mechanisms of totalitarianism in *Ancient Evenings*
as, largely, physical force and repression. The relationship between the ancient
and the modern is not merely "historical," but metaphoric. The melodramatic,
physical oppression is the metaphor for all oppression, including psychic or
spiritual oppression. What matters is the fact of centralized efforts to control
and exploit human beings, to reduce freedom, to codify consciousness. Mailer,
no more then Fowles or Gardner, simply cannot as an artist avoid such historical
issues of oppression or freedom, of flowering or withering of consciousness,
of life or death. All three authors are committed to the terrain of history *and*
fiction; they insist on the combination—the mutual nourishment—rather than
separation of the two. As Lentricchia argues, there is "no privileged mode of
persuasion available" to the radical mind; "there is no morally pure, no episte-
mologically secure, no linguistically uncontaminated route to radical change."
Lentricchia then adds: "To attempt to proceed in purity—to reject the rhetorical
strategies of capitalism and Christianity, *as if such strategies were in themselves
responsible for human oppression*—to proceed with the illusion of purity is to
situate oneself on the margin of history, as the possessor of a unique truth

disengaged from history's flow. It is to exclude oneself from having any chance of making a difference for better or worse."[30] Indeed, it is to exclude oneself from ethical consciousness, choice, and act.

But I have yet to define the nature of those totalitarian concerns in *Ancient Evenings,* or their interrelationships, adequately. There are familiar qualities to totalitarian power in this novel—the tendency toward homogeneity, the reduction of dialectic to static order, and the collaborations of wealth and political power to dominate and shape society for the ends of a few. Whether it be Eitel and Sergius struggling against a witch-hunting American government and a commercial, conforming Hollywood, or D. J. and Mailer-Aquarius caught in the toils of the military-industrial establishment, or Rojack fighting the manipulative wealth of Kelly, or Gilmore fighting the whole liberal establishment for the right to choose his own death and expiation, Mailer's heroes always confront one kind of oppressive social order or another; they express what Samuel Coale calls an "essential romantic anarchism."

Since the Egyptian concept of the pharaoh as life-giving god would not have encouraged Egyptians to see kingship in any modern or objective sense as a cult-of-personality dictatorship, Mailer is more cautious here than elsewhere in presenting the issue. The question becomes, perhaps more accurately from the Egyptian view, to what degree the king represents the principle or the violation of Maat. It is in the violation of Maat that kingly power turns to degenerative tyranny, that personal nobility turns to vanity, pride, and carnal ownership.

One element of totalitarianism in Mailer's novel is the tyranny of pharaonic power, expressed through the themes of carnal ownership and social brutality. The underside of kingly power, its brutal and disconnected nature as it reaches down through all the social classes, is clearest from a number of glimpses Mailer gives us of the conditions of slaves, laborers, poor people, and those upon whom kingly retribution falls. It is as if the very root of civilization—its wealth, power, and economic stability—has been nourished only in such soil from the beginning. One of the best examples of this theme comes in book 3, "The Book of the Child." On his journey with his family to the court of Ramses IX and during the conduct of business at court, six-year-old Meni notices and contemplates the "long cry of that labor" of oarsmen rowing an obelisk upriver, the hovels of the poor in that section of town the rich, like mother Hathfertiti, would prefer to avoid sight of, the withered hands of thieves nailed to posts in a flourishing garden, the "shiny stumps" of many a eunuch slave, Bonesmasher's drunken wanderings in a poor quarter while he recalls his family's impoverishment, a manacled prisoner with stumps of forearms near the palace walls where a woman lashed to another post holds her dead baby, a maid who once had her nipples cut off for stealing the pharaoh's snails, the legions of men who have gone blind from quarry dust and splinters, and a previous pharaoh so obsessed with his wife's fidelity that he ordered everyone in Memphis not to make love without his permission. One of Meni's most revealing intuitions of the nature of absolute power and submission comes when he looks into the eyes of Pharaoh's dog Tet-tut:

> I thought I would laugh—but sorrow seemed to come right out of Tet-tut's heart and into mine. . . . A melancholy . . . so complete as the woe I felt when Eyaseyab told me about her relations who worked in a quarry and had to load great slabs of granite on sledges and pull them up ramps with ropes. Sometimes, while working, they were whipped until they dropped. . . .
>
> The sorrow of Tet-tut's eyes was like the look I had seen in the expression of many an intelligent slave. Worse. It was as if the dog's eyes spoke of something he wanted to accomplish but never would.
>
> So I wept. . . . The dog had managed to tell me of a terrible fright in a far-off place and I was more afraid than I had ever been, as if I might not live like a slave but still knew the fear that sooner or later I, too, would know a life I did not want, and be powerless to go where I wished. . . . Yes, at six had a sight of myself debased in the Land of the Dead when I was twenty one. (139–40)

In old Menenhetet's story Ramses II will use the same dog-master metaphor in his prayers to Amon explaining the divinity-pharaoh-royalty-nobility-commoner-slave chain of power: "I am as Your dog . . . even as the soldiers are My dogs, and the soldiers of the Hittites are My soldiers' dogs" (271). Menenhetet describes the feeling of such power over others just before his ambush of the thieves: "I knew it was the peace that comes when you can choose what to do with another man. You can kill, or let him go. . . . Indeed, my Pharaoh always seemed to live in just such a way" (303).

Such carnal ownership, as I mentioned, is that personal tyranny most often expressed in this novel by anal rape. Mailer is of course aware of the humorous possibilities of the "buggery order," a colloquial metaphor in common usage, after all. Indeed, the book has more intentional humor (much of it scatological) than most reviewers found. Mailer's bawdy may become monotonous, but it has often seemed convenient for reviewers to forget the precedents of Rabelais, Shakespeare, or Swift.

On the other hand, there is a serious, even tragic, side to Mailer's sexual and anal themes. Carnal ownership has become for Mailer the perfect expression of the power held by the victor over the vanquished, or by the ruler over the ruled. It is, therefore, also an expression of the totalitarian impulses of ruler and state. Although nearly everyone in the novel does or has the potential to practice that brutal assertion over another, it is the very wealthy and the entrenched who practice it most.

Mailer makes his theme of anal violence and sexuality resonate with several meanings. The first I have just suggested. Homosexual rape is tantamount to domination, violation, and ownership of another person. The emphasis of such rape is usually political or economic rather than sexual. It is a brutal source of establishing national hierarchy in peace and international hierarchy in war. In a version of the tale of "Horus and Seth" from the era of Ramses V, Set says to the gods: "Let the office of ruler be given to me, for as regards Horus who stands here, I have done a man's deed to him." The Set-power of pederasty is also expressly forbidden, for in the Egyptian Declaration of Innocence and in the accompanying Acknowledgment of the Forty-Two Gods, pederasty is one of the sins one claims innocence of, as are fornication, causing pain, violence, and adultery.[31]

A second thematic resonance is in heterosexual copulation. Here anal sexuality, a deep and repressed drive, becomes rebellious. It is unsanctioned sex, decreative sex, against the laws of gods and humans (which gods and humans will always break). It is, to borrow Richard Poirer's phrase, a "breaking of the vessels," the blackest magic. Hence, it is the violation of sexual taboo Menenhetet engages in with Honey-Ball and, finally, with Nefertiri in their rebellions against the order of king and cosmos.

A third resonance is magical power through excremental ritual. Courtiers work feces magic against the king himself for personal revenge, as we have seen. Here the magical power theme is further connected to the anal-obsessive character of wealth and social status in this novel as in Mailer's earlier novels. Think of the Satanic Kelly and Ruta in *An American Dream,* for example. Menenhetet puts it:

> I brooded much on the nature of such stuff when I lived in the Gardens of the Secluded. . . . I even supposed that dung must be the center of all things . . . that excrement was as much a part of magic as blood or fire, an elixir of dying Gods and rotting spirits desperate to regain the life they were about to lose. Yet when I thought of all the transformation that dung contains . . . I began to think of all those Gods, small and mean as pestilence itself, who dwell next to such great changes. "How dangerous is this excrement," I said. . . . To hold the leavings of another must be equal to owning great gold and wealth.
>
> Was it for such a reason that all who visited the Court would wear as much gold as they possessed? (502–3)

This is in part a rehash of Mailer's "metaphysics of the belly," reaching at least as far back as *An American Dream* (1964–65) and *Cannibals and Christians* (1966). In the latter, Mailer argued that the close relationship of one's being to one's deepest cellular functions explains why people or societies may be obsessed with scatology; waste contains some message from the unconscious that reveals one's (or a society's) state of being and disproportions. By airing one's obsessions, by confronting the messages of disease and waste, and by engaging perversion, death, and dread, one may prepare the disproportionate self or state to grow away from death toward life, from imbalance toward balance.[32] Of course possible defeat by or victory over the shadow self is part of the risk-taking of the embattled hero, that representative of the individual. Mailer's ideas parallel such depth psychologists as Carl Jung and Erich Neumann, for example, who have also suggested a close but mysterious relationship and balance between body and psyche which is basic to our understanding of the unconscious. Awareness of a functional relationship between the body and the psyche is a fundamentally primitive state of consciousness, expressing the functioning of mana (soul or psyche power) in the self and between the self and the external world.[33] By a primitive logic, or metaphor, one would possess the deepest truths of another's self—all the evil and the good—when one possesses another's anus or, in magic, feces. If anal sex is, as it was for Menenhetet and Honey-Ball, "the secret ceremony of marriage" (455), the deepest, rebellious sharing of one another's flesh, anal rape is the absolute control of another for other, often political or economic, purposes.

It is understandable that when Mailer time and again presents such scatological meditations as "literal metaphors," if I may coin a paradoxical phrase, he both fascinates and outrages many critics. His toying with an associational, primitive, subconscious logic is simply not acceptable to them. But like the heroes of his tales, Mailer is not one to blink the most curious secrets and obsessions—as he sees them—of our conscious and unconscious life. The unconscious—that is, obsessive and primitive—roots of sexuality and of totalitarianism are important subjects in this novel.

It is especially in the striving for power over others that yet another element of totalitarianism is depicted in the novel. Ambition for wealth, social status, and privilege becomes a force in itself, perhaps the most degenerative force in the novel; that force becomes a collective energy that seems to make the whole brutal social fabric cohere. The value of wealth, the sources of ambition for it, is that wealth is built on the agony (i.e., carnal ownership) of others. "I was aware suddenly of all that shone of gold," young Meni says, "around my father's chest . . . my mother's head, the gold bracelets of Menenhetet, or . . . the gold in the houses of all the nobles we would visit. It was then I thought I heard, like a faint cry, some echo of the labor that had delivered this wondrous metal, and I saw the Pharaoh nod wisely as though He had also heard such groans and they were part of the curious value of gold" (372–73).

Meni's mother Hathfertiti—insatiably ambitious, a monster of greed and lust—is one of the most fully, and humorously, developed portraits in the novel. Her embraces with Ramses IX are a "joining of His Double-Throne with her insatiable greed" (483); her means of achieving godlike pharaoh-power and wealth are through her son's claims to royal lineage. Of course the culmination of her ambition on the Night of the Pig is to buy her passage on the pharaoh's golden boat on earth and in the Land of the Dead. With her beauty and lust she hopes to buy more wealth, more power, and even eternal life, just as the scribe-priest Pepti will castrate himself to realize his ambitions to power. By the pharaoh's phallus would Hathfertiti "climb the ladder of Heaven" (485). Such false, but such perennially human, ambitions are the true waste in human lives, as Meni realizes only in death. As Mailer argues here and in most of his work, it is not by such ambitions, by wealth or power or lust in high places, that we might purchase any true virtue or merit or peace or even afterlife, but by our courage alone, by always seeking the risk, always placing our individual force against whatever powers would shape, own, or defeat us.

Likewise, Hathfertiti's forerunner Nefertiri dared everything to maintain her own power and wealth amidst a court filled with intrigue, ambition, and greed. And Mailer's depiction of her petty complaints about the upstart family of Honey-Ball is a funny example of the timeless whine of entrenched ambition and privilege against the ambitions of others farther down the social power-chain: "I cannot bear her family. I was entertained by them on my last visit to Sais, and they are common. Very wealthy and common. . . . They have the audacity—oh, they are truly common—to present the names of their forebears as if one were speaking of people of substance. They went on in that manner to Me! . . . She [Honey-Ball] has noble blood, but of the lowest sort. Her family does business with shit-collectors" (514–15).

It is this ambition to power and wealth to the exclusion of other sources or kinds of power, and other sources of merit and virtue, that makes Mailer'snarrative a tragic one in the ancient sense. It is exactly the kind of narrative or catalogue of moral defeat that Breasted's moral prophets of Ancient Egypt have written more briefly. For here is the spectacle of a naturally endowed man and of privileged men and women with their fatal flaws—pride and the blind ambition to wealth and power over the structures of state and the people who populate it. If power in itself is mythically sanctioned in such a society's conception of the god-king and his servants, where is the balance, the truth, the justice, the righteousness (in a word, the Maat) when ambition and pride blind all to everything but greed and lust?

This timeless ambition and pride must have been to some extent what Mailer had in mind in 1983 just before *Ancient Evenings* was published when he spoke of our own manifestations of ego: "On the one hand we, all of us, consciously or unconsciously, contain an adoration of the universe. We also have great animus toward the universe. It's larger than we are and that's intolerable to us. The ego, or the twentieth-century manifestation of it, flames up in us. We have to *score* it. We have to literally score on it, and plastic is a wonderful way to do that because we create something that the universe can't digest."[34] This ancient and modern theme is neatly summed up in the fate of one fat, rich merchant named Fekh-futi ("shit-collector") who had all the proper rituals performed, purchased the all-important "Negative Confession" to show "the Gods, the demons, and the beasts that he was a good man," that, indeed, he "had committed not a single one of the forty-two sins, not one." Yet as

Honey-Ball says, he was so foul he had committed them all. Honey-Ball herself is, however, seduced by the ambitious logic of wealth's purchase on eternity. She dreams that "Fekh-futi thrives in the Land of the Dead, and my little toe beside him" because "the virtue of the papyrus is not to be found in its truth but in the power of the family who purchases it" (451–53).

Yet as we see in the end, Fekh-futi most certainly does not thrive in the Land of the Dead; the power of wealth and status alone is insufficient to outweigh the scales of truth, to cheat life, death, Maat, and Anubis. Likewise does Menenhetet learn through four lives, finally, that ambition is not only insufficient for purposeful and powerful life; ambition can overwhelm, it can tip the balance against even such virtues as great courage and strength.

For modern as for ancient cultures, perhaps the mythic sources of power are not in themselves "evil" or "wrong"; it is, rather, out of abuse, disproportion, and blindness that human evil arises. If the nobles and the highly placed in Mailer's novel seek to buy earthly power and stature as much as to buy eternal life, the ideals and principles of religion in Egyptian Empire suggest that true power and afterlife are not to be bought; they are to be earned through the virtue of Maat, through courage, and through proportion, through, in short, the ever-renewed battle against entropy. Mailer has for thirty years now been writing a similar ethic and seeking a culture and a narrative to embody it.

5

Anxiety and Synthesis

*A doctor can heal, but he can kill as well. A critic can be
like that. He can . . . kill a work, or he can give it new life. But
a writer can do this, too. A writer can be the assassin of his own
text. The world is also littered with works killed by those who
wrote them. . . . They do not take the moral risk or the experimentation. . . . They just lazily continue the tradition without attempt-
ing the creation that makes tradition live.*

Carlos Fuentes

I have tried not to ignore the differences between Fowles, Gardner, and Mailer,
but a study that analyzes how three contemporary authors have acted independ-
ently as counterforces to the hermetic tendencies of post-modernism inevitably
reduces these differences. Most readers probably delight in the eccentricities
and individualities of these three authors, as well as, more importantly, in their
determination *not* to be like other contemporaries. But beyond the more obvious
differences of style and temperament, the largest difference between Fowles and
Gardner, on one hand, and Mailer, on the other, is what I want to emphasize
briefly before turning to the anxieties of post-modernism.

Although all three magicians are metafictionists themselves—the creators
of heuristic masques and tales—and therefore metaphors for the artist, both
Fowles and Gardner avoid the overt mystical associations and occult assumptions in which Mailer revels. If Gardner and Fowles argue for the necessity of
mystery and nonrational processes in the healing of psyche and conscience, they
also take care to leave the reader with a definite sense of the machineries behind
the masque. Mailer, on the other hand, has long assumed, not unlike Yeats, an
intervening realm of the occult and Karmic in the processes of rebirth and in the
sources of identity and history. It is just this outrageous literalness that provokes
his critics most. Mailer risks the most. But he remains now, as before, committed to write *as if* this lurid realm of spiritual influences and confrontations

coexists and is connected with the human microcosm. In writing *Ancient Evenings* Mailer found a hero and assumptions culturally appropriate to his own speculations. It is precisely this disconnection between that ancient culture and our own culture that is, apparently, his point, his strategy, his "defamiliarization" of our world and assumptions. The point and attraction of the novel is, as Mailer puts it: "The lack of connection. I want people to realize, my God, there are wholly different points of view that can be as interesting . . . and as thoroughgoing as our own."[1] Mailer has imagined a culture and consciousness so shockingly alien to our own culture and consciousness that we cannot help but compare the two, we cannot help but see our lives and motives in the strange light this Mailerian consciousness sheds. We may reject it, but we have been exposed and shocked.

If Mailer's "magical" strategy is the most risky, it is endlessly arguable whether it is the most effective. Judging from his contemporary critics, we are led to believe the leap, the contrast, is too great, the gap between this unfamiliar realm and our realm too wide. For that matter, all three authors suffer the many reservations of their critics. We probably do not yet have the distance on their work to judge fully its success, failure, or significance. But we do not need such distance to understand their motives, their art in the world of countervailing hegemonies and impulses, or their deepest differences from so many of their contemporaries. Any future judgments, it seems to me, ought to be founded on such understanding.

As post-war novelists, the elements of their work that connect these three authors are more important than those elements of style, temperament, nation, and belief that separate them. If the enlightening magicians of their prototypical texts connect Fowles, Gardner, and Mailer in the ways we have seen, we also know that there are deeper connections. The most important connection is not the metafictional apparatus nor the epistemological speculations found in their work. The more fundamental connection is their rejection of the post-modern tendency to separate art from life. Each of these novelists has been determined to move the novel into less hermetic, more inclusive definition of our secular responsibilities as artists and as human beings. By their attempt to move beyond the passive acceptances of determinism and hermeticism, beyond the small affirmations of quietism, they have dared—even if they have failed at times—to move themselves and us *through* fiction toward new challenges for consciousness.

Out of their dialectics of varying constructive oppositions, of vitality and entropy, these three authors have sought to create a novel that replenishes experimentation and speculation with life, that replenishes consciousness with history and ethics. They hope, furthermore, to renew the battle against all the erosions of personal identity. They would restore a fictional and philosophical activism against all the controls and mechanisms of totalitarianism, the insanities of history, the disintegrating terrors of the abyss. The magicians' masques, tests, and tales are for both reader and apprentice-hero "therapeutic" structures derived from the heroic quest for enlarged consciousness. The central quality of enlarged consciousness is metaphorical vision—"whole" vision of the relationships between things. This is not simply a rational vision; it is an act of unconscious mind informing and enriching conscious, rational mind, restoring depth to surface, connection to discontinuity, and mystery to life. In Mailer's case, the aim is to restore, moreover, sacredness to life. Hence all three compare fiction to dream, and all three work more in the romance than the realistic tradition. Through their uses of fantasy, experimentation, and speculation, they respond to the hermeticism and attendant anxieties in their time. Through elements of romance and metafiction they seek to lessen, rather than enlarge, the gap between consciousness and cosmos.

Yet it is precisely this gap that has stimulated our anxieties. "It is a proper anxiety to wonder," Malcolm Bradbury writes in *The Contemporary English Novel,* "whether we are making, in art, a world of dehumanization that is not needed, through simple acquiescence in an aesthetic convention." Has our "new baroque," in Bradbury's words, our "post-humanist dehumanization of art," our "foregrounding of style" or techniques served to diminish the human figure not only in art, but in our consciousness and our lives?[2] If Bradbury's collection of essays by various hands is a celebration and analysis of the ways in which the English novel participates in an "international form" and experimentation, the same note of anxiety he expresses sounds in most of the essays by other authors as well. These authors express their concern for, as Bernard Bergonzi puts it, the ease with which a revolt against convention—however initially stimulating and creative—becomes itself a convention (43). There is a general casting about for, in N. H. Reeve's words, "a new synthesis," for some direction or development in the British novel for which the experiments prepared the way.

It also appears that the desire for a new synthesis goes beyond those essayists writing in *The Contemporary English Novel,* beyond the appeals for something greater and more meaningful that we have seen in Scholes, Lentricchia, and Hassan, among others. That anxiety is widespread and arises at times in unexpected quarters. It surfaces among some of the most enthusiastic analysts of post-modern technique, such as Frederick Karl and Patricia Waugh. I'll let three further, but I think telling, examples argue this point.

Karl's massive survey of post-war American fiction begins more optimistically than it ends, lamenting, finally, the lack of synthesis between culture and linguistic/aesthetic strategy. His distaste for Mailer and Gardner leads Karl to ignore their potential to build a foundation for the synthesis he seeks at the outset of *American Fictions:*

> So, Sukenick agrees, the novel *has* died, and one must seek ways to resurrect it. While we should hail Sukenick's defense of the novel, we should be wary of his dismissals. What has kept the novel from dying has not been an awareness of the loss of time, destiny, reality, personality, et al., but a perception that these older ideas exist in a dialectic with their denial; that the old is very much with us, but only as one element of a "reality." What is needed is not a further dismissal of the old . . . but modes in which the dialectic can dissolve, reform, defamiliarize. As this occurs, the novel survives the market place, assimilation, and its critics.[3]

The parallels between what Karl seeks to combine—the old with the subversively new—and the art of Gardner and Mailer in America are, I hope, obvious at this point. But Karl ends up wistfully awaiting such synthesis.

Waugh is less wistful but equally ambiguous, finally, about the real possibility of such synthesis. She looks especially to metafiction, as a mode of writing within the broader cultural movement of post-modernism. Metafiction might convert the "negative values" of outworn literary conventions into "the basis of a potentially constructive social criticism," Waugh tentatively argues, but it is questionable whether our "aleatory writing is going to accomplish all this." Waugh sees greatest potential in Fowles, Coover, Spark, and Lessing.

Her hopes for renewal rather than exhaustion are in the way metafiction defamiliarizes perceptions and thus exposes the habitual and conventional. Few have disagreed on that point. Yet Waugh can offer little by way of examples of "renewed vigor" and "extremely responsible" metafiction "in socio-cultural terms." Moreover, she seems insufficiently aware of the speed by which, as Fowles pointed out, the new becomes conventional, parody degenerates to self-parody, disturbing creative force slides into clever game. And Waugh's parallels between game-theory in economic and political spheres and the endless play of language in fiction are but examples of the problems to be *surmounted* if fiction (like politics and economics) is to be *anything but* a game. To see the seriousness of this issue, we need only think for a moment about the tragic consequences to others (the played) when a privileged few (the players) approach political, economic, or ethical life as if it were a mere game. "History," wrote David Lodge when examining these issues some time ago, "may be, in a philosophical sense, a fiction, but it does not feel like that when we miss a train or somebody starts a war."[4]

Waugh concludes that we cannot now evaluate the "post-Saussurean" critical and fictional revolution or the varying degrees of "post-modernist self-consciousness." Though she agrees that such an evaluation is of "critical importance," it may be possible only "once post-modernism has itself become a 'post' phenomenon." Only then might we judge the *"politically* 'radical' status of *aesthetically* 'radical' texts."

Waugh ultimately enlarges her, and our, sense of uncertainty when she offers her own alternate endings: (1) a quotation from Charles Russell arguing that any closed system of signs is of questionable efficacy, and (2) a quotation from Ihab Hassan arguing that no confrontation with or destruction of the bourgeois ideology is possible, only theft and disguise. These endings are, of course, not precisely alternatives. They are admissions of the ultimate inefficacy in any political, social, or ideological sense of the metafictional project so long as it is defined as a closed system of signs, and so long as its chief strategy is parody and mask.[5]

We have seen analysts of international and American fiction express similar anxieties, at times, moreover, arising from the most unexpected quarters. To take my third example, in the immediate wake of Scholes, Graff, Lentricchia, Hassan, and others who were retrospectively defining the nature and limits of post-modernism, John Barth published "The Literature of Replenishment" in *The Atlantic* (1980). Barth traces post-modernism back through modernism to Sterne and Cervantes, and he provides his own checklist of post-modern attributes based on his reading of Graff, Hassan, and Robert Alter. Barth emphasizes the critics' argument that the self-conscious reflexiveness in so much current literature is rooted in the anarchic desire for cultural subversion *by virtue* of writing less about life, more about art. Barth admits, however, that if Graff and others are right, post-modernism is a kind of sterile and pallid "last-ditch decadence." Any author so willing to reveal his own anxieties captures our trust.

But Barth goes wrong, it seems to me, in forging an eccentric definition of post-modernism to set up his own thesis. For example, he considers Robbe-Grillet, Barthes, Beckett, and Nabokov modernists. Then he presents his thesis: fiction must grow beyond the self-conscious nihilism of such "modernism." Barth then tries to claim for post-modernism a warmth of heart, a seriousness of secular concern, and a transcendence of what critics have identified as its very limits. Yet Barth is unable to exemplify his claim with any Anglo-American "post-modernists."

By conflating some of the most obvious qualities peculiar to modernism and some of the most obvious qualities peculiar (by a long-standing critical analysis) to post-modernism, Barth is prepared to argue that post-modern writers are now creating something better than "modernism." The "worthy program for postmodernist fiction, I believe, is a synthesis or transcension of these antitheses."

Such a synthesis has been on many minds. But Barth's essay leaves important, even obvious, questions unanswered. From what quarter in Anglo-American letters is such replenishment, synthesis, transcension likely to come? Where are our authors "more democratic" than Beckett and Nabokov? Where are examples of our bold experiments that are reaching, delighting, and moving readers; that are rising above the quarrel between "realism and irrealism, formalism and 'contentism,' pure and committed literature"?

Perhaps by implication we need only look to Barth. But Barth actually points to two figures of hope outside Anglo-American letters—Italo Calvino and

Gabriel Garcia Márquez. These are good choices. They suggest that our most likely models for developing a synthesis are practitioners of more international base and scope. Just as Scholes chose Borges and Eco for their potential to connect language and life, Gardner chose Calvino as both a model for certain shorter fictions and an example in such theoretical writings as his *The Art of Fiction*. In that book, to take one example, Gardner argues that through the techniques of voice and convincing, vivid detail Calvino is one writer who causes us to enter irreal worlds and fantastic characters—however unlikely or parodic—in a way that engages us "heart and soul" in the fictional dream *as though* it were real. We engage in a moral, imaginative act because reading Calvino we "sympathize, think, and judge." Mailer likewise points to Borges and Márquez as "two of the most important writers in the world today," largely because of their magical abilities to create compressed yet vivid and convincing fictional worlds. "Borges has this magical ability to take plots and turn them inside out. I sometimes think Borges may do in five pages what Pynchon does in five hundred. Which is he shows us the resources of the novel. He's a magician's magician. . . . Márquez is wonderful. In *One Hundred Years of Solitude* he created not one world but a hundred. . . . In ten pages he'll create a family that has eighteen children and they go through ten years, and you know every one of the children, and all the events that occur in their life."[6]

The testimony of these writers and critics points to a source of vital potential within metafictional, experimental, and "magical" fiction in the international arena. Perhaps Carlos Fuentes has most strikingly addressed this vitality as a joining of effective experimental technique and secular reference when speaking of the future, international role of the novel.

> I do not believe that literature has an immediate partisan role to play, but I do believe that literature is revolutionary and, thus, political in a deeper sense. Literature not only sustains the historical experience and continues a tradition. It also—through moral risk and formal experimentation and verbal humor—transforms the conservative horizon of the readers and helps liberate us all from the determinisms of prejudice, doctrinal rigidity and barren repetition.

Asked to point to a book that has combined these qualities, Fuentes cites *Ulysses*. "It is the moral risk of saying that literature matters, that words matter in a world where they were mattering and have mattered less and less. To make that statement about the value of language, for me, is an extraordinary moral adventure. I think Joyce defined a frontier in aesthetics. He chose to establish the values of art in a world that disregards them completely. . . ."[7]

In part what all these commentators and novelists are seeking is an art, an aesthetic, willing to experiment *and* to return to earth and life enough to get our hands dirty, or, as Gardner's philosopher put it, to get our hands in pigshit. If politics, finance, history, and ethics may get us dirty, the question remains whether we should flee the filth or confront it in our art, enter it, suggest directions beyond it. That is Lentricchia's question to us when he writes of our wish to refuse the "Arnoldian mission," to passionately diffuse throughout society the benefits and wisdom of knowledge and culture, to make them meaningful "outside the clique of the cultivated and the learned." Fowles, Gardner, and Mailer have chosen such a filthy mission through art. They have in that sense come to accept Kenneth Burke's concept of "symbolic action," by which Burke and Lentricchia mean a broad mythic, psychic, *and* representational force that reaches pragmatically (for good or ill, as much through art as through advertising or propaganda) into the structures of society, and thereby into the structures and processes of consciousness and culture and history.[8]

MacIntyre goes so far as to suggest that, indeed, symbolic action is the very ground of battle. For in the social sciences, as in their roles in political and corporate life, "the effects of eighteenth-century prophecy have been to produce *not* scientifically managed social control, but a skillful dramatic imitation of such control." MacIntyre continues: "It is histrionic success which gives power and authority to our culture. The most effective bureaucrat is the best actor" (102). If MacIntyre is right, then the real stakes are played and the real territory (economic, political, moral) is lost or gained through symbolic action. One might envision us all at play for life-and-death stakes in some supertheatre of some super-Conchis. The ageless heuristic mill is narrative. We are, MacIntyre argues, "essentially a story-telling animal" in our actions and practices, just as in our fictions, becoming through our history tellers of "stories that aspire to truth."

> Hence there is no way to give us an understanding of any society, including our own, except through the stock of stories which constitute its initial dramatic resources. Mythology, in its original sense, is at the heart of things. Vico was right and so was Joyce. And so too of course is that moral tradition from heroic society to its medieval heirs according to which the telling of stories has a key part in educating us into the virtues. (201).

We have seen that Fowles, Gardner, and Mailer see symbolic action and their story-telling magicians in this activist, heuristic, and antinomian sense. Symbolic action is, for example, precisely what Fowles means, especially when he describes fiction as "a kind of landscape a reader enters to learn something about life," and, therefore, to become in turn a creative, rather than deadening, force within it.[9]

What Barth did not demonstrate in 1980 has been in large part my purpose to demonstrate here: that there are contemporary Anglo-American novelists who have been engaged in the process of seeking a new synthesis—not a "postmodern art," but a genuinely catholic, "secular" fiction. For while connecting art and life, while using some of the fabulative and technical experiments and moods of post-modernism, and echoing its epistemological concerns, these three novelists in particular have also refused to reject the psychological or spiritual depths as well as the secular commitments of our classical, romantic, and modern literary heritage.

Notes

Chapter 1

1. Elizabeth Bruss, *Beautiful Theories: The Spectacle of Discourse in Contemporary Criticism* (Baltimore: Johns Hopkins University Press, 1982), 9–10, 22; and Alan Wilde, *Horizons of Assent: Modernism, Postmodernism, and the Ironic Imagination* (Baltimore: Johns Hopkins University Press, 1981), 7, 15–16.

2. Vincent Leitch, "The Book of Deconstructive Criticism," *Studies in the Literary Imagination* 12 (1979): 19–40.

3. See Trachtenberg's "Intellectual Background" in *The Harvard Guide to Contemporary American Writing*, ed. Daniel Hoffman (Cambridge: Harvard University Press, 1979), 1–50.

4. *Surfiction: Fiction Now—and Tomorrow* (Chicago: Swallow Press, 1981), 7, 13. See Gass in *The New Republic* 180 (10 March 1979): 25, 28–33.

5. Larry McCaffery's *The Metafictional Muse* (Pittsburgh: University of Pittsburgh Press, 1982) provides a useful summary of metafiction. Such fiction typically examines its own construction as it proceeds, comments on previous fiction, or examines how fictional systems operate *in* fiction. Metafiction is playful, self-conscious, and willfully artificial. Alienated or victimized by a cold, meaningless, fragmented, or entropic social order, the central characters typically create private systems of meaning and may end up controlled by their own systems. Moreover, metafiction reinforces the concept of the radically subjective nature of all systems and perceptions that shape our experience of the world. Rather than interpretive, metafiction is, therefore, self-reflexive, a "mask which points to itself" and whose only reality is that of its own discourse (see esp. 4–5, 7, 16). Several books have focused as much or more on metafictional and larger post-modern impulses in British literature. Patricia Waugh's *Metafiction: The Theory and Practice of Self-Conscious Fiction* (London and New York: Methuen, 1984); Malcolm Bradbury and David Palmer's collection *The Contemporary English Novel* (New York: Holmes & Meier, 1979); and Bradbury's *The Novel Today: Contemporary Writers on Modern Fiction* (Totowa, N.J.: Rowman and Littlefield, 1978) are but a few examples. Some of the authors most often associated, in widely varying degrees, with post-modern practice and theory include Samuel Beckett, Christine Brooke-Rose, Brigid Brophy, Anthony Burgess, Alan Burns, John Fowles, B. S. Johnson, Doris Lessing, David Lodge, Iris Murdoch, Ann Quin, Muriel Spark, David Storey, and Angus Wilson. Waugh expresses a generally acknowledged belief that British experimentation and self-consciousness tend to be more limited and less radical than the more extreme American examples.

6. Gerald Graff, *Literature against Itself* (Chicago: University of Chicago Press, 1979), 64–66; Alasdair MacIntyre, *After Virtue* (Notre Dame: University of Notre Dame Press, 1981), 221.

7. Alasdair MacIntyre, *After Virtue,* 163–64, 204. MacIntyre establishes the "core concept" of virtue as: (1) *practice* (the pursuit of excellence in praxis, including politics), (2) *the narrative order of a single human life,* and (3) *the moral tradition* (especially the classical).

8. Frank Lentricchia, *Criticism and Social Change* (Chicago: University of Chicago Press, 1983), 147–48.

9. Barbara Howard Traister, *Heavenly Necromancers: The Magician in English Renaissance Drama* (Columbia: University of Missouri Press, 1984), 11, 23–30, 67, 179–80.

10. Robert Scholes, *Fabulation and Metafiction* (Urbana: University of Illinois Press, 1979), 206–7. See also Elizabeth Bruss, *Beautiful Theories,* esp. her chapters on Gass and Sontag, for further discussion of theory-artistic practice relationships.

11. *Criticism and Social Change,* 2–6, 10, 38–41, 46–50, 116.

12. Lentricchia, *After the New Criticism* (Chicago: University of Chicago Press, 1980), see esp. 108.

13. Robert Scholes, *Textual Power: Literacy and the Teaching of English* (New Haven: Yale University Press, 1985), 4–7, 49, 74–76, 85–87, 94, 99, 104, 109–10. Alan Wilde's positive look at modernism and post-modernism presents a similar warning about the principal risk of post-modern "suspensive irony," an irony which accepts the world as it is. The risk is "passivity"; see *Horizons,* 155.

14. *After the New Criticism,* 189–207.

15. Graff, 7, 32. Jacques Barzun in "Liberalism and the Religion of Art" and "Biography and Criticism: A Misalliance?" in *Critical Questions: On Music and Letters, Culture and Biography,* ed. Bea Friedland (Chicago: University of Chicago Press, 1982). Similar discussions occur in Anna Balakian, "Relativism in the Arts and the Road to the Absolute," and Hayden White, "The Limits of Relativism in the Arts," in *Relativism in the Arts,* ed. Betty Jean Craige (Athens: University of Georgia Press, 1983). Kroeber's article appears in *PMLA* 99 (May 1984): 326–39. As early as 1969 Fowles had written: "Both academic criticism and weekly reviewing have in the last forty years grown dangerously scientific, or psuedo-scientific, in their general tenor. Analysis and categorization are indispensable scientific tools *in the scientific field;* but the novel, like the poem, is only partly a scientific field. No one wants a return to the kind of bellelettrist and onanistic accounts of new books . . . ; but we could do with something better than we have got." See "Notes on an Unfinished Novel," collected in *The Novel Today,* 149.

16. Ihab Hassan, *The Dismemberment of Orpheus: Toward a Postmodern Literature* (New York: Oxford University Press, 1971), esp. 13–14, 67. Future references are parenthetical.

17. *Fabulation and Metafiction,* 2, 7–10, 13.

18. See "The New Tradition in Fiction," in *Surfiction,* 35, and Klinkowitz's "Literary Disruptions" in the same book, 165–79, where the same argument is repeated.

19. Marcus Klein, "John Hawkes' Experimental Compositions," in *Surfiction,* 204.

Chapter 2

1. In her negative assessment of Fowles' achievement, however, Karen Lever argues that raising such dilemmas is merely confusing, that the reader receives too many "conflicting messages" to make sense of Fowles' didactic purpose. Lever is particularly charging *Daniel Martin* here, but she argues that Fowles' whole career has become a treadmill that has trapped the author, who is even more like an uneducable hero himself than any of his fictional initiates. See "The Education of John Fowles," *Critique* 21 (1979): 85–100. Lever is searching for the pat moral of the tale that Fowles abhors as much as any of his contemporaries. Bernard Bergonzi seems to have had similar difficulties with *The Magus*, charging that it is little more "than a highly inventive series of . . . cruel episodes . . . vitiated by its basic pointlessness." See *The Situation of the Novel* (Pittsburgh: University of Pittsburgh Press, 1971), 75–76. As Barbara Traister pointed out in *Heavenly Necromancers*, the literary tradition of the magician offers no simple answers or absolutes. Indeed, the disguises, character transformations, and ambiguous imagery allow for no simple moral evaluation of character and action. The potentials of magic and magician *are* ambiguous and double. See esp. 68–75. On the other hand, when Fowles is (more and more recently) examined as a metafictionist, his metafictional devices seem to eclipse or exclude his moral concerns in fiction. As William Palmer points out in his introduction to the 1985 special *Modern Fiction Studies* number on Fowles, metafictional studies are the model for the 1980s, especially since Peter Conradi's *John Fowles* (New York: Methuen, 1982), which, Palmer argues, moves Fowles studies beyond the introductory stages and into the theoretical. See Palmer in *Modern Fiction Studies* 31 (Spring 1985): 3–13.

2. John Fowles, *The Aristos: A Self-Portrait in Ideas* (Boston: Little, Brown, 1964/1970), 152–55. Future references are parenthetical.

3. Fowles, *The Ebony Tower* (Boston: Little, Brown, 1982), 111. Future references are parenthetical.

4. See *Mantissa* (Boston: Little, Brown, 1982), 118–20; and Carl M. Barnum, "An Interview with John Fowles," *Modern Fiction Studies* 31 (Spring 1985): 191. Compare further Fowles as quoted in his interview with Carol M. Barnum: "They've [the "French gurus" Barthes and Derrida] been granted altogether too powerful a position on the intellectual side." In the same interview he also speaks of his dislike for a kind of café society pessimism or absurdism (as opposed to the "genuine article"): "various pseudo-intellectual equations, such as serious equals black (or leftwing equals experimentalist), do not impress me. I am not against the *avant-garde* in itself but I think it should be judged by the standards of any other kind of art, not treated as automatically more significant and interesting," see esp. 198–99.

5. *Aristos*, esp. 122–23. Compare William Palmer's analysis of Fowles' two major, interrelated themes: (1) the relationship between art and life, and (2) the quest for personal identity and freedom in a hostile world. Palmer argues that Fowles rejects both obeisance to a literary past and avant-garde definitions of the novel as purely aesthetic. The moral person would rebel against not only convention for its own sake but art for its own sake. *The Fiction of John Fowles* (Columbia: University of Missouri Press, 1974), esp. 2–3, 23, 31–35, 59–64.

6. *After Virtue*, 18, 22, 33, 186.

7. *Literature against Itself*, 5.

8. Fowles, *The Magus* (Boston: Little, Brown, 1977), 57. Future references are parenthetical. I use the revised edition because it represents Fowles' final shaping and clarifying of his vision and because, as Cory Wade and Ernst von Glasersfeld have said, the changes are local and not

significant alterations of mood or theme. See Wade's "Mystery Enough at Noon: John Fowles's Revision of *The Magus,*" *Southern Review* 15 (1979): 716–23; and von Glasersfeld's "Reflections on John Fowles's *The Magus* and the Construction of Reality," *Georgia Review* 33 (Summer 1979): 444–48.

9. Michael O. Bellamy, "John Fowles's Version of the Pastoral: Private Valleys and the Parity of Existence," *Critique* 21 (1979): 72–84.

10. Palmer, 90 ff., suggests how much like ancient mythic characters journeying into interior space the main characters in Fowles' novels are, and Peter Wolfe refers several times to the "birth/motif" and the "Christian . . . cycle of redemption through rebirth" that the Godgame mirrors," in *John Fowles, Magus and Moralist* (Lewisburg, Pa.: Bucknell University Press, 1976), 115–18. Roberta Rubenstein remarked on the general lack of attention to the novel's structure in "Myth, Mystery, and Irony: John Fowles's *The Magus,*" *Contemporary Literature* 16 (Summer 1975): 328–39. But Rubenstein identifies the "underlying structure" as "a labyrinth" in which each line of pursuit leads to a dead end or false corner. Her concern with structure remains a little unclear, however, not only because it is difficult to picture a labyrinth as a clarifying and controlling "structure," but because most of her analysis turns out to be plot summary and theme abstraction, and because she also speaks too generally of the novel's "framework" of myth and mystery. Aware of Urfe's status as a mythological hero, Rubenstein however finds mere ambiguity and confusion when the myths switch around (from Theseus to Orpheus, for example), as if the archetypal pattern must refer only to one mythic hero consistently. Bradbury weakens his own essay on the novel's structure with pages of mere plot summary also. But he does offer important insights about the status of *The Magus* as an effort to "break through contemporary fiction's philosophical or aesthetic impasses." And Bradbury suggests the ways in which the novel can be read as a presentation of art "as psychic revelation," and Conchis' program can be read as a presentation of "a structure for feeling, art, and history" which goes beyond the limitations of twentieth-century rationalism and literal-mindedness. See "John Fowles's *The Magus,*" *Sense and Sensibility in Twentieth-Century Writing,* ed. Brom Weber (Carbondale: Southern Illinois University Press, 1970), 26–38.

11. Susan Strehle Klemtner, "The Counterpoles of John Fowles's *Daniel Martin,*" *Critique* 21 (1979): 59–71.

12. See Lentricchia, *Criticism and Social Change,* 37, 116; and Simon Loveday, *The Romances of John Fowles* (New York: St. Martin's Press, 1985), esp. 5, 7–10, 132, 141, 148. Loveday is particularly thorough and convincing in his critique of the weaknesses of *Daniel Martin,* especially the mimetic claptrap that reduces, finally, the dissident force of the romance (see esp. 116–23). Throughout most of his study, Loveday, justifiably, also faults Fowles for a too-intrusive didacticism. Such didactic intrusions often do not square with the fictional practices (133–34, 138, for example). Loveday's bias, based on Frye, rather too much favors the separation of the so-called "extra-literary" from art—ethics, dissidence to *specific* injustices, praxis generally. As a result he becomes a little too reductive—everything that doesn't fit his definition of romance in Fowles seems unacceptably realistic.

13. It is curious that when the critical fortunes of *The Magus* have waned, they have done so as often as not over confusion about whether Conchis is a positive or negative figure. Rubenstein, for example, finds him to be negative because his identity remains too disturbing and ambiguous for her, his "realistic" function seems unclear, he has no reason to invest so much in "just one man," and he merely puts Urfe through "another version of his own past," disregarding the morality he (Conchis) seems to espouse. On these points her reading of the novel is obviously slack; she asks the same questions Urfe himself does early in the novel but which, with Mrs.

de Seitas' help, Urfe answers more clearly in the end. And it is of course not for one man, but for dozens that Conchis initiates the masques. Ralph Berets' *"The Magus:* A Study in the Creation of a Personal Myth," *Twentieth-Century Literature* 19 (1973): 89–98, answers some of Rubenstein's questions as well, two years before her article appears. As late as the special Fowles edition of *Modern Fiction Studies* 31 (Spring 1985), Conchis still causes critics to read the book as nihilistic. Frank G. Novak, Jr., for example argues that Conchis does not advance any meaningful, transcendent values, that he, on the contrary, is motivated only by his "misshapen purposes and twisted values." Novak also interprets Nicholas to be, even in the end, merely one more narcissistic antihero (see 71–82).

14. See Fowles, *Daniel Martin* (Boston: Little, Brown, 1977), 381, 404, 611.

15. Suzanne Poirier has traced the parallels between the love-ethic theme in Fowles' original source for the tale and his own novel: (1) In both, the magician-priest cajoles, prompts, and pushes the foolish man into "an adulthood worthy . . . of love"; (2) both attack the shallowness of sexual codes whether seventeenth-century courtly romance or twentieth-century loveless sex; (3) both work toward the hero's acknowledgment of physical and spiritual love; (4) both examine human nature in a timeless retreat against the backdrop of current political oppressions and events; (5) both divide the story into separation, mystery, and reunion sequences; (6) both connect "real infidelity" with the lie between lovers; and (7) both assume a certain moral superiority of women and test the hero for some higher purpose than the entertainment of the masque itself. See *"L'Astree* Revisited: A Seventeenth-Century Model for *The Magus," Comparative Literature Studies* 17 (1980): 269–86. As I have been suggesting also, the English literary tradition influences Fowles as well, especially Shakespeare's *The Tempest* with Prospero and his island domain. Shakespeare's magician is also the master of shows, spectacles, and revels (the masque) that serve young love, moral education, and the diversion of the reader/spectator. The play's educational dimensions likewise include the ethical ideals of love and marriage and the necessity of inner transformation before the future can be shaped by free will more than magic. Prospero, like Conchis, is a facilitator of transformation, love, and ethically conscious free will, not the creator of them. Moreover, *The Tempest,* as Traister points out, has long been recognized as a metadramatic play (143); here too, then, is another parallel with Conchis' (and Fowles') metadrama comprising most of the novel.

16. See Roy Newquist, "John Fowles," in *Counterpoint* (Chicago: Rand McNally, 1964), 218–25.

17. See von Glasersfeld's "Reflections" as cited above. Von Glasersfeld admits that Fowles departs from strict constructivism when Fowles adds "the pragmatic and ethical aspects" to his game-novel. This admission, to my mind, leaves von Glasersfeld's whole thesis in doubt, for *The Magus* is thereby not the work, as von Glasersfeld says in his opening, "into which I can read . . . a view of the world and a constructivist theory of knowledge that I have worked at for a good many years." For further reading contrary to my own see Simon Loveday's *Romances,* esp. 35–41. Near the end of his chapter on *The Magus* Loveday investigates a "subversive" or "ironic" interpretation of this novel as opposed to a "naive" reading. In this ironic reading Nicholas would be a static or regressive character. Some of the more convincing reasons Loveday posits for such a reading are, first, that all of the tales of the metadrama and parables are told by Nicholas himself, and the continual subversions of the narrator subvert the narrative itself. I, on the other hand, would see this as Fowles' confrontation with the artificiality of all narrative, including Conchis'—an obvious metafictional concern. Nonetheless, everything in the novel, I have been arguing, points to Fowles' and Conchis' awareness that careful narrative artificiality retains sufficient imaginative power to encourage awakening in the hero or the audience. Secondly, the apparently ambiguous proposals that at one narrative moment freedom and at another love seem to be the supreme values espoused, Loveday adds to the text's

self-subversion. But my point has been that both values are inextricable in the narrative, as in *The Aristos,* and they are perhaps combined in that last historical commandment against pain. Another, more curious, example of an argument for Urfe's stasis rather than growth appears in Bruce Woodcock's *Male Mythologies: John Fowles and Masculinity* (Totowa, N.J.: Barnes & Noble, 1984), 47, 73–79. Woodcock's book has several problems. First, as William Palmer notes in his introduction to the Fowles *Modern Fiction Studies* number (Spring 1985), this critic produces one of the most "inquisitional" and "flagrant 'cricketal' distortions ever published," mistaking Fowles for one of his Bluebeardlike characters. Second, Woodcock admits only to the "social construction" of masculinity and femininity. He is thereby able to argue that any deeper psychic or archetypal male experience of women is *nothing but* a socially created support for political and economic oppression. Denying any mythic level of consciousness for either sex free of social constructions—a level at which Fowles purposely works—Woodcock works with surfaces only, and there finds men wanting. Third, Woodcock argues that no man is capable of examining the issues from the correct feminist perspective, no man is free of his socially constructed male mythos, by virtue of his "privileged . . . inheritance of . . . patriarchal legacy, the penis." One wonders then how Woodcock (a name from the realm of allegory? a witty feminist's pseudonym?) as a male—his penile legacy intact—can maintain pretensions to a correct feminist deconstruction of Fowles' "sexist" texts.

18. See Lever's "Education" cited above, and Richard Poirier's *Norman Mailer* (New York: Viking, 1972), 57, 160.

19. Fowles, *The French Lieutenant's Woman* (Boston: Little, Brown, 1969), 395. Further references are parenthetical.

20. Maurice Beebe, "Reflective and Reflexive Trends in Modern Fiction," *Bucknell Review* 22 (1976): 13–26. Loveday is very good on further self-reflexive aspects of the text, especially the density of self-reference, patterning, and repetition in the design (see esp. 51–53). See also 55–56 on reader manipulation, and 58–59 on the ironic use of conventions of the *noveau roman.*

21. Loveday, 31.

22. Pat Rogers, "Left Lobe and Right," *TLS,* 20 September 1985: 1027.

23. Fowles, *A Maggot* (Boston: Little, Brown, 1985), 499. Further references are parenthetical.

Chapter 3

1. Joe David Bellamy, "The Way We Write Now," *Chicago Review* 25 (1973): 45–49; and John Barth, "How Is Fiction Doing?" *New York Times Book Review,* 14 December 1980: 3.

2. John Gardner, *On Moral Fiction* (New York: Basic Books, 1978), 19, 22, 115–17. Future references are parenthetical.

3. Marshall L. Harvey, "Where Philosophy and Fiction Meet: An Interview with John Gardner," *Chicago Review* 29 (1978): 73, 76. (Future obvious references will be parenthetical). Compare similar comments in Ed Christian's "An Interview with John Gardner," *Prairie Schooner* (Winter, 1980–81): 89: "Moral Art is like an experiment. The artist takes ideas and puts them under stress, in order to determine their validity. . . . I don't want to communicate moral beliefs. I want to explore moral questions, and *come* to moral beliefs." See also Loveday, 138–39.

4. Gardner, "The Art of Fiction LXXIII," *Paris Review* 21 (Spring 1979): 42, 53, 58–59, 63, and Samuel Chase Coale, *In Hawthorne's Shadow: American Romance from Melville to Mailer* (Lexington: University of Kentucky Press, 1985), 148–51.

5. Gardner, *On Becoming a Novelist* (New York: Harper & Row, 1983), 30–31.

6. Christian, *Prairie Schooner,* 72. For a more thorough discussion of the function of dreaming in Gardner's fiction, see Samuel Coale's "The Design of the Dream in John Gardner's Fiction," *Thor's Hammer: Essays on John Gardner,* eds. Jeff Henderson and Robert E. Lowrey (Conway: University of Central Arkansas Press, 1985), 45–46. The dream seeks and makes momentarily possible a unity or wholeness of self and an "intersection of eternity with time," in M. H. Abrams' phrase; it also leads away from mechanical moralities and discursive codes.

7. See Richard Natale, "John Gardner: 'Great Age of the Novel Is Returning,'" *Women's Wear Daily,* 8 December 1972: 16; and David Cowart, *Arches and Light: The Fiction of John Gardner* (Carbondale: Southern Illinois University Press, 1983), 62 esp.

8. *Paris Review:* 46, 48, 67.

9. *On Becoming a Novelist,* 49–51.

10. Gardner, *The Art of Fiction* (New York: Alfred A. Knopf, 1984), 62–63, 79.

11. Tony Tanner, "The Agent of Love and Ruin," *Saturday Review of the Arts,* 6 January 1973: 80.

12. Gardner, *The Sunlight Dialogues* (New York: Alfred A. Knopf, 1973), 549. Future references are parenthetical.

13. See Gregory Morris, "A Babylonian in Batavia: Mesopotamian Literature and Lore in *The Sunlight Dialogues,*" *John Gardner: Critical Perspectives,* eds. Robert Morace and Kathryn VanSpanckeren (Carbondale: Southern Illinois University Press, 1983), 33, 39; and Cowart's *Arches and Light,* 59.

14. See Cowart, esp. 67.

15. Morris, "Babylonian in Batavia," 36.

16. For a thorough discussion of these points see Paul Piehler, *The Visionary Landscape* (Montreal: McGill-Queens University Press, 1971), esp. 4–5, 62–63; and Angus Fletcher, *Allegory: The Theory of a Symbolic Mode* (Ithaca: Cornell University Press, 1964), 157–59.

17. *The New Fiction: Interviews with Innovative American Writers,* ed. Joe David Bellamy (Urbana: University of Illinois Press, 1974), 188.

18. Christian interview, 89.

19. Daniel Laskin, "Challenging the Literary Naysayers," *Horizon* 21 (July 1978): 32–36.

20. Bellamy, *The New Fiction,* 190–91. John Howell's "Chronology" dates the start of *Sunlight Dialogues* in 1964 and its completion in 1968. It is preceded by *Nickel Mountain* and *The Resurrection* and followed by *Agathon* and *Grendel.* See Howell, *Bibliographic Profile* (Carbondale: Southern Illinois University Press, 1980), xvii.

21. Bruce Allen, "Settling for Ithaca, The Fiction of John Gardner," *The Sewanee Review* 85 (Summer 1977): 520–31. Fredrickson argues that Gardner writes literature that "deconstructs itself" and "denies access to meaning," as if "it were redemptive to long for what we cannot have." Fredrickson too seems to mistake Tag's nihilism for the whole vision, and sees entropy as the victor rather than as one pole of a continuous dialectic between the entropic and the

regenerative. Yet Fredrickson oddly subverts his own argument that the novel is, therefore, "anti-intellectual and anti-art" when in his concluding paragraph he acknowledges that in *Sunlight* "human relationships, then, do counteract entropy," and art in this instance "draws meaning from the life to which we are returned." See Robert S. Fredrickson's "Losing Battles against Entropy: *The Sunlight Dialogues*," *Modern Language Studies* 13 (Winter 1983): 47–56.

22. Gardner, *The Wreckage of Agathon* (New York: Harper & Row, 1970), 209. Future references are parenthetical.

23. Ed Christian interview, 81. See also the Harvey interview, 75.

24. *Arches and Light*, 38.

25. Gardner, *Grendel* (New York: Ballantine Books, 1972), 16. Further references are parenthetical.

26. "Art of Fiction LXXIII," *Paris Review:* 44–45.

27. Gregory Morris, *A World of Order and Light: The Fiction of John Gardner* (Athens: University of Georgia Press, 1984), 55–56.

28. Gardner, *Freddy's Book* (New York: Alfred A. Knopf, 1980), 153. Future references are parenthetical.

29. Walter Cummins, "The Real Monster in *Freddy's Book*," in Morace, *Critical Perspectives*, 108–10.

30. Gardner, *Mickelsson's Ghosts* (New York: Alfred A. Knopf, 1982), 52–53. I purposely exclude from my discussion the two posthumous fragments published by Knopf in 1986. Judging a dead artist on work that he gave up in the early 1970s *(Stillness)* and another that he never shaped beyond, in Richard Gilman's just phrase, "a chaotic set of fictional swatches" without "imaginative control or coherence" would be to my mind even more irresponsible and gratuitous than publishing them. See Gilman's comments in "Novelist in a Mirror," *New York Times Book Review*, 20 July 1986: 11–12.

31. Morris, *Order and Light*, 116–42.

32. See Marshall Harvey interview, 81.

33. *The New Fiction*, 185. Compare one example of Mailer's assessment of his contemporaries: "Where the original heroes of naturalism had been active, bold, self-centered, close to tragic, and up to their nostrils in their exertions to advance their own life and force the webs of society, so the hero of moral earnestness, the hero Herzog and the hero Levin in Malamud's *A New Life*, are men who represent the contrary—passive, timid, other-directed, pathetic, up to their nostrils in anguish: the world is stronger than they are; suicide calls." From *Cannibals and Christians* (New York: The Dial Press, 1966), 100.

34. D. H. Lawrence, *Mornings in Mexico and Etruscan Places* (New York: Penguin Books, 1960), 158. Further reference is parenthetical.

Chapter 4

1. *Esquire*, July 1983: 116–17.

2. Leslie Fiedler, "Going for the Long Ball," *Psychology Today*, June 1983: 16–17.

3. See Manning's "Look upon this Work, Oh ye Mailer, and Despair," *Boston Globe,* 3 April 1983: A10-A11; and Chassler in *Ms. Magazine,* 12 August 1983: 33–34.

4. See Epstein's "Mailer Hits Bottom," *Commentary,* July 1983: 62–68; and Wolcott's "Enter the Mummy," *Harpers,* May 1983: 81–83. Epstein and Wolcott represent a host of negative reviewers who could not stomach the subject matter and who still believe Mailer's gifts are as a naturalistic, not fantastic, writer.

5. See Davis, "Excess without End," *The New Leader,* 16 May 1983: 14–16. This principle—the healthy confrontation with one's dark side—goes back at least as far as "The White Negro" (1957) and of course is Jungian in its implications. For Jung, individuation or the restructuring of the self comes about by the meeting of the "shadow"; that is, the patient meets the instinctual, irrational, primitive, and violent side of his or her nature, recognizes it for what it is, no longer represses it or totally capitulates to it, but learns to accept it and even use it in some healthy balance with the other elements of psychic life.

6. See DeMott's "Normal Mailer's Egyptian Novel," *New York Times,* 10 April 1983: 1, 34–36. That Mailer centered his narrative on the Night of the Pig is not arbitrary; it is directly related to his theme of rebirth. As Mircea Eliade points out: "The meaning of this periodical retrogression of the world into a chaotic modality [i.e., 'the extinction of fires, the return of the souls of the dead, social confusion of the type exemplifed by Saturnalia, erotic license, orgies, and so on'] was this: all the 'sins' of the year, everything that time had soiled and worn, was annihilated in the physical sense of the word. By symbolically participating in the annihilation and re-creation of the world, man too was created anew; he was reborn, for he began a new life." See *The Sacred and the Profane* (New York: Harcourt, Brace & Co., 1959), 78–79.

7. Peter Shaw, "Norman Mailer Turns Victim," *The American Spectator,* September 1983: 45–46.

8. The source of Mailer's comments here on the novel is Robert Begiebing, "Twelfth Round," *Harvard Magazine,* March-April 1983: 49, hereafter cited as "Twelfth Round."

9. Norman Mailer, *Ancient Evenings* (Boston: Little, Brown, 1983), 363, 365. Future references are parenthetical.

10. From page 40 of the full transcript of the interview "Twelfth Round" for *Harvard Magazine* (1983), which is available in the Harvard University Archives, Harley P. Holden, Curator. The statement that elicited this response was: "You've also made the argument that trying to understand fascism and Nazism leads one to the great questions of our century, the nature of the unconscious." George Steiner's quotation is from *In Bluebeard's Castle: Some Notes Towards the Redefinition of Culture* (New Haven: Yale University Press, 1971), 43–44.

11. See Richard Poirier in *TLS,* 10 June 1983: 591–92.

12. Harold Bloom, "Norman in Egypt," *New York Review of Books,* 28 April 1983: 3–5.

13. See Stade's "A Chthonic Novel," in *The New Republic,* 2 May 1983: 32–36; and Dick's review in *World Literature Today* 58 (Winter 1984): 102–3. For Mailer's complete discussion of dreamlike, robust art see *Cannibals and Christians,* 101–3, 214; and *Existential Errands: Twenty-Six Pieces Selected by the Author from the Body of All His Writings* (Boston: Little, Brown, 1972), 111–12, 122.

14. See Joyce Carol Oates, *New Heaven, New Earth: The Visionary Experience in Literature* (New York: Vanguard Press, 1974), 177–203; and Peter Brooks, "The Melodramatic Imagination," *Partisan Review* 2 (Spring 1972): 195–212. For a further discussion of the moral occult

principle that Brooks develops, see also Robert C. Post, "A Theory of Genre: Romance, Realism, and Moral Reality," in *American Quarterly* 33 (Fall 1981): 367–90. Post compares romance and realism and finds in Hawthorne a connection to this inward, spiritual realm of human value.

15. For a more complete discussion of these heroic themes in Mailer's previous work, see Robert Begiebing, *Acts of Regeneration: Allegory and Archetype in the Works of Normal Mailer* (Columbia: University of Missouri Press, 1981), esp. 113–31. The two quotations in this passage are from *Cannibals and Christians,* 100, and "Twelfth Round," 46.

16. "Twelfth Round," 48.

17. Eliade, 12–13, 146, 165, 168. Rene Girard's study of sacrificial violence makes a similar point relevant to Mailer's use of violence in the novel: "The Sacred consists of all forces whose dominance over man increases or seems to increase in proportion to man's effort to master them. Tempests, forest fires, and plagues . . . may be classified as sacred. Far outranking these, however, . . . stands human violence—violence seen as something exterior to man and henceforth as part of all the other outside forces that threaten mankind. Violence is the heart and secret soul of the sacred." *Violence and the Sacred* (Baltimore: Johns Hopkins University Press, 1977), 31.

18. See for example Mailer's development of these points in *The Presidential Papers* (New York: G. P. Putnam's Sons, 1963), 213–14; and *Cannibals and Christians,* 321–27. The Eliade quotation is from *Sacred and Profane,* 147–48. Future obvious references are parenthetical.

19. James Henry Breasted, *The Dawn of Conscience* (New York: Charles Scribner's Sons, 1933, 1968), 411–13. My previous summary of the rise of conscience is much indebted to Breasted's book.

20. "Twelfth Round," 49.

21. Jeffrey Burton Russell, *The Devil: Perceptions of Evil from Antiquity to Primitive Christianity* (Ithaca: Cornell University Press, 1977), 78, 80, 82.

22. Compare Barbara Mertz on this point in *Temples, Tombs, and Hieroglyphs* (New York: Coward-McCann, 1964), 99. Two sources come to mind for Mailer's narrator-hero. The first is Ramses II himself who speaks of one "Menena"—his charioteer and shield-bearer at Kadesh—who, alone with certain household butlers and his two steeds, was with the king at the outbreak of battle and who became "weak and faint-hearted." See the "Kadesh Battle Inscriptions of Ramses II, The Poem," in Miriam Lichtheim, *Ancient Egyptian Literature: The New Kingdom,* vol. 2 (Berkeley and Los Angeles: University of California Press, 1976), 68, 70. The second source might be an actual son of Ramses II, Khaemwise, a high priest whose celebrity as a learned man and magician carried his name into Graeco-Roman times. See Sir Alan Gardiner's *Egypt of the Pharaohs* (New York: Oxford University Press, 1961, 1980), 267.

23. "Twelfth Round," 45.

24. Mertz, 277–78.

25. *Ancient Evenings,* 587–88. Among Mailer's many sources we must certainly count Sir James George Frazer, especially when considering the nature of magic. On the point at hand, however, Frazer's description of Osiris-power and worship in the section on dying and reviving gods seems relevant to Mailer's depiction of the Sed Festival. Here Ramses seeks to renew what Frazer calls the power "of creative energy in general," represented in Osiris worship by the erect phallus, an "aspect of his nature . . . presented to the eye not merely of the initiated

but of the multitude." Village women, for example, would sing praises to his phallic image, "which they set in motion by means of strings." See *The New Golden Bough,* ed. Theodor H. Gaster (New York: Criterion Books, 1959), 345.

26. "Twelfth Round," 49.

27. See *The New Golden Bough,* 9, 31, 132.

28. MacIntyre, *After Virtue,* esp. 116–19, 122, 202–3.

29. See Traister, 52–53, 99, 133–52. A further connection between Mailer and this tradition is worth mentioning: the foundation for the rise of dramatic magicians is the Renaissance revival of Neoplatonism as a revival in the belief of a general animating spirit as, through Plotinus and the hermetic writings, a source of cosmic wisdom and energy. Mailer's magus, like Mailer the artist, seeks contact with the infinite and archetypal wisdom. See Traister's discussion on 5–6 esp.

30. *Criticism and Social Change,* 18, 22–27, 35–36, 61–62.

31. See Lichtheim's *Ancient Egyptian Literature,* vol. 2, 124–28, 220.

32. See esp. *Cannibals and Christians,* 274–86.

33. See Carl Jung's introduction to *Aion: Researches into the Phenomenology of the Self,* translated by R. F. C. Hull, Vol. 9 (Princeton: Princeton University Press, 1951); and Neumann, *The Origins and History of Consciousness* (Princeton, N.J.: Princeton University Press, 1973), 25–27, 288, 290–91.

34. "Twelfth Round," 47.

Chapter 5

1. "Twelfth Round," 50.

2. *The Contemporary English Novel,* 208.

3. Frederick Karl, *American Fictions* (New York: Harper & Row, 1983), 3.

4. See Lodge's "The Novelist at the Crossroads," in *The Novel Today: Contemporary Writers on Modern Fiction* (Manchester, England: Manchester University Press, 1977), 109.

5. See Waugh, *Metafiction,* on which this discussion is based.

6. See Barth, "The Literature of Replenishment," *Atlantic,* 24 January 1980: 65–71; Gardner in *The Art of Fiction,* 28–31; and Mailer in "Pontifications," *Pieces and Pontifications* (Boston: Little, Brown, 1982), 157.

7. See Willi Goetschel, Leslie Dunton-Downer, and Cyrus Patell, "Terra Fuentes: An Interview," *Harvard Review* 1 (Fall 1986), 151–52. Fuentes' theme of moral commitment is developed throughout the interview, 131–62.

8. See *Criticism and Social Change,* 130, 138.

9. Fowles in Carol Barnum's "Interview," *Modern Fiction Studies* 31 (Spring 1985): 203.

Bibliography

Allen, Bruce. "Settling for Ithaca, The Fiction of John Gardner." *The Sewanee Review* 85 (Summer 1977): 520–31.

Alter, Robert. "Deconstruction in America." *The New Republic*, 25 April 1983: 27–32.

Barnum, Carol, "An Interview with John Fowles." *Modern Fiction Studies* 31 (Spring 1985): 187–203.

Barth, John. "How Is Fiction Doing?" *New York Times Book Review*, 14 December 1980: 3.

_____ . "The Literature of Replenishment." *Atlantic*, 24 January 1980: 65–71.

Barzun, Jacques. *Critical Questions: On Music and Letters, Culture and Biography*. Edited by Bea Friedland. Chicago: University of Chicago Press, 1982.

Beebe, Maurice. "Reflective and Reflexive Trends in Modern Fiction." *Bucknell Review* 22 (1976): 13–26.

Begiebing, Robert J. *Acts of Regeneration: Allegory and Archetype in the Works of Norman Mailer*. Columbia: University of Missouri Press, 1981.

_____ . "Twelfth Round." *Harvard Magazine* 85 (March-April 1983): 40–50.

Bellamy, Joe David. "The Way We Write Now." *Chicago Review* 25 (1973): 45–49.

_____ , ed. *The New Fiction: Interviews with Innovative American Writers*. Urbana: University of Illinois Press, 1974.

Bellamy, Michael O. "John Fowles's Version of the Pastoral: Private Valleys and the Parity of Existence." *Critique* 21 (1979): 72–84.

Berets, Ralph. *"The Magus:* A Study in the Creation of a Personal Myth." *Twentieth-Century Literature* 19 (1973): 89–98.

Bergonzi, Bernard. *The Situation of the Novel*. Pittsburgh: University of Pittsburgh Press, 1971.

Bloom, Harold. "Norman in Egypt." *New York Review of Books*, 28 April 1983: 3–5.

Bourjaily, Vance. "Return of the Ancient Mailer." *Esquire*, July 1983: 116–17.

Bradbury, Malcolm, and David Palmer, eds. *The Contemporary English Novel*. New York: Holmes & Meier, 1979.

Bradbury, Malcom. "John Fowles's *The Magus.*" *Sense and Sensibility in Twentieth-Century Writing*. Edited by Brom Weber. Carbondale: Southern Illinois University Press, 1970.

_____ , ed. *The Novel Today: Contemporary Writers on Modern Fiction*. Totowa, N.J.: Rowman and Littlefield, 1978.

Breasted, James Henry. *The Dawn of Conscience*. New York: Charles Scribner's Sons, 1933, 1968.

Brooks, Peter. "The Melodramatic Imagination." *Partisan Review* 2 (Spring 1972): 195–212.

Bruss, Elizabeth. *Beautiful Theories: The Spectacle of Discourse in Contemporary Criticism*. Baltimore: Johns Hopkins University Press, 1982.

Chassler, Sey. *"Ancient Evenings*—Modern Menace." *Ms. Magazine*, 12 August 1983: 33–34.

Christian, Ed. "An Interview with John Gardner." *Prairie Schooner* (Winter 1980–81): 70–93.

Coale, Samuel Chase. "The Design of the Dream in John Gardner's Fiction." *Thor's Hammer: Essays on John Gardner*. Edited by Jeff Henderson and Robert E. Lowrey. Conway: University of Central Arkansas Press, 1985.

———. *In Hawthorne's Shadow: American Romance from Melville to Mailer*. Lexington: University of Kentucky Press, 1985.

Conradi, Peter. *John Fowles*. New York: Methuen, 1982.

Cowart, David. *Arches and Light: The Fiction of John Gardner*. Carbondale: Southern Illinois University Press, 1983.

Craige, Betty Jean, ed. *Relativism in the Arts*. Athens: University of Georgia Press, 1983.

Davis, Robert Gorham. "Excess without End." *The New Leader*, 16 May 1983: 14–16.

DeMott, Benjamin. "Norman Mailer's Egyptian Novel." *New York Times*, 10 April 1983: 1, 34–36.

Dick, Bernard. Review of *Ancient Evenings* in *World Literature Today* 58 (Winter 1984): 102–3.

Eliade, Mircea. *The Sacred and the Profane*. New York: Harcourt, Brace & Co., 1959.

Epstein, Joseph. "Mailer Hits Bottom." *Commentary*, July 1983: 62–68.

Federman, Raymond, ed. *Surfiction: Fiction Now—and Tomorrow*. Chicago: Swallow Press, 1981.

Fiedler, Leslie. "Going for the Long Ball." *Psychology Today*, June 1983: 16–17.

Fletcher, Angus. *Allegory: The Theory of a Symbolic Mode*. Ithaca: Cornell University Press, 1964.

Fowles, John. *The Aristos: A Self-Portrait in Ideas*. Boston: Little, Brown, 1964/70.

———. *Daniel Martin*. Boston: Little, Brown, 1977.

———. *The Ebony Tower*. Boston: Little, Brown, 1982.

———. *The French Lieutenant's Woman*. Boston: Little, Brown, 1969.

———. *A Maggot*. Boston: Little, Brown, 1985

———. *The Magus*. Boston: Little, Brown, 1977.

———. *Mantissa*. Boston: Little, Brown, 1982.

Frazer, Sir James George. *The New Golden Bough*. Edited by Theodor H. Gaster. New York: Criterion Books, 1959.

Fredrickson, Robert S. "Losing Battles against Entropy: *The Sunlight Dialogues*." *Modern Language Studies* 13 (Winter 1983): 47–56.

Gardiner, Sir Alan. *Egypt of the Pharaohs*. New York: Oxford University Press, 1961, 1980.

Gardner, John. "The Art of Fiction LXXIII." *Paris Review* 21 (Spring 1979): 37–74.

———. *The Art of Fiction*. New York: Alfred A. Knopf, 1984.

———. *Freddy's Book*. New York: Alfred A. Knopf, 1980.

———. *Grendel*. New York: Ballantine Books, 1972.

———. *Mickelsson's Ghosts*. New York: Alfred A. Knopf, 1982.

———. *On Becoming a Novelist*. New York: Harper & Row, 1983.

———. *On Moral Fiction*. New York: Basic Books, 1978.

———. *The Sunlight Dialogues*. New York: Alfred A. Knopf, 1973.

———. *The Wreckage of Agathon*. New York: Harper & Row, 1970.

Gass, William, and John Gardner. "William Gass and John Gardner: A Debate on Fiction." *The New Republic* 180, 10 March 1979: 25, 28–33.

Gilman, Richard. "Novelist in a Mirror." *New York Times Book Review*, 20 July 1986: 11–12.

Girard, Rene. *Violence and the Sacred*. Baltimore: Johns Hopkins University Press, 1977.

Goetschel, Willi, Leslie Dunton-Downer, and Cyrus Patell. "Terra Fuentes: An Interview." *Harvard Review* 1 (Fall 1986): 131–62.

Graff, Gerald. *Literature against Itself*. Chicago: University of Chicago Press, 1979.

Harvey, Marshall L. "Where Philosophy and Fiction Meet: An Interview with John Gardner." *Chicago Review* 29 (Spring 1978): 73–87.

Hassan, Ihab. *The Dismemberment of Orpheus: Toward a Postmodern Literature*. New York: Oxford University Press, 1971.

Howell, John. *Bibliographic Profile*. Carbondale: Southern Illinois University Press, 1980.

Jung, Carl. *Aion: Researches into the Phenomenology of the Self.* Translated by R. F. C. Hull. Vol. 9. Princeton: Princeton University Press, 1951.

Karl, Frederick. *American Fictions.* New York: Harper & Row, 1983.

Klemtner, Susan Strehle. "The Counterpoles of John Fowles's *Daniel Martin.*" *Critique* 21 (1979): 59–71.

Kroeber, Karl. "The Evolution of Literary Study, 1883–1983." *PMLA* 99 (May 1984): 326–39.

Laskin, Daniel. "Challenging the Literary Naysayers." *Horizon* 21 (July 1978): 32–36.

Lawrence, D. H. *Mornings in Mexico and Etruscan Places.* New York: Penguin Books, 1960.

Leitch, Vincent. "The Book of Deconstructive Criticism." *Studies in the Literary Imagination* 12 (1979): 19–40.

Lentricchia, Frank. *After the New Criticism.* Chicago: University of Chicago Press, 1980.

_____ . *Criticism and Social Change.* Chicago: University of Chicago Press, 1983.

Lever, Karen. "The Education of John Fowles." *Critique* 21 (1979): 85–100.

Lichtheim, Miriam. *Ancient Egyptian Literature: The New Kingdom.* Vol. 2. Berkeley and Los Angeles: University of California Press, 1976.

Lodge, David. *The Modes of Modern Writing.* Ithaca: Cornell University Press, 1977.

_____ . *The Novel Today: Contemporary Writers on Modern Fiction.* Manchester, England: Manchester University Press, 1977.

Loveday, Simon. *The Romances of John Fowles.* New York: St. Martin's Press, 1985.

McCaffery, Larry. *The Metafictional Muse.* Pittsburgh: University of Pittsburgh Press, 1982.

MacIntyre, Alasdair. *After Virtue.* Notre Dame: University of Notre Dame Press, 1981.

Mailer, Norman. *Ancient Evenings.* Boston: Little, Brown, 1983.

_____ . *Cannibals and Christians.* New York: The Dial Press, 1966.

_____ . *Existential Errands: Twenty-Six Pieces Selected by the Author from the Body of All His Writings.* Boston: Little, Brown, 1972.

_____ . *Pieces and Pontifications.* Boston: Little, Brown, 1982.

_____ . *The Presidential Papers.* New York: G. P. Putnam's Sons, 1963.

Manning, Margaret. "Look upon this Work, Oh ye Mailer, and Despair." *Boston Globe,* 3 April 1983: A10-A11.

Mertz, Barbara. *Temples, Tombs, and Hieroglyphs.* New York: Coward-McCann, 1964.

Morace, Robert and Kathryn Van Spanckeren, eds. *John Gardner: Critical Perspectives.* Carbondale: Southern Illinois University Press, 1983.

Morris, Gregory. *A World of Order and Light: The Fiction of John Gardner.* Athens: University of Georgia Press, 1984.

Natale, Richard. "John Gardner: 'Great Age of the Novel Is Returning.'" *Women's Wear Daily,* 8 December 1972: 16.

Neumann, Erich. *The Origins and History of Consciousness.* Princeton: Princeton University Press, 1973.

Newquist, Roy. "John Fowles." *Counterpoint.* Chicago: Rand McNally, 1964.

Oates, Joyce Carol. *New Heaven, New Earth: The Visionary Experience in Literature.* New York: Vanguard Press, 1974.

Palmer, William. *The Fiction of John Fowles.* Columbus: University of Missouri Press, 1974.

_____ . "John Fowles and the Crickets." *Modern Fiction Studies* 31 (Spring 1985): 3–13.

Piehler, Paul. *The Visionary Landscape.* Montreal: McGill-Queens University Press, 1971.

Poirier, Richard. *Norman Mailer.* New York: Viking, 1972.

_____ . Review of *Ancient Evenings* in *TLS,* 10 June 1983: 591–92.

Poirier, Suzanne. "*L' Astrée* Revisited: A Seventeenth-Century Model for *The Magus.*" *Comparative Literature Studies* 17 (1980): 269–86.

Post, Robert C. "A Theory of Genre: Romance, Realism, and Moral Reality." *American Quarterly* 33 (Fall 1981): 367–90.

Rogers, Pat. "Left Lobe and Right." *TLS,* 20 September 1985: 1027.

Rubenstein, Roberta. "Myth, Mystery, and Irony: John Fowles's *The Magus." Contemporary Literature* 16 (Summer 1975): 328–39.

Russell, Jeffrey Burton. *The Devil: Perceptions of Evil from Antiquity to Primitive Christianity.* Ithaca: Cornell University Press, 1977.

Scholes, Robert. *Fabulation and Metafiction.* Urbana: University of Illinois Press, 1979.

———. *Textual Power: Literacy and the Teaching of English.* New Haven: Yale University Press, 1985.

Shaw, Peter. "Norman Mailer Turns Victim." *The American Spectator,* September 1983: 45–46.

Stade, George. "A Chthonic Novel." *The New Republic,* 2 May 1983: 32–36.

Steiner, George. *In Bluebeard's Castle: Some Notes Towards The Redefinition of Culture.* New Haven: Yale University Press, 1971.

Tanner, Tony. "The Agent of Love and Ruin." *Saturday Review of the Arts,* 6 January 1973: 78–80.

Trachtenberg, Alan. "Intellectual Background." *The Harvard Guide to Contemporary American Writing.* Edited by Daniel Hoffman. Cambridge: Harvard University Press, 1979.

Traister, Barbara Howard. *Heavenly Necromancers: The Magician in English Renaissance Drama.* Columbia: University of Missouri Press, 1984.

von Glasersfeld, Ernst. "Reflections on John Fowles's *The Magus* and the Construction of Reality." *Georgia Review* 33 (Summer 1979): 444–48.

Wade, Cory. "Mystery Enough at Noon: John Fowles's Revision of *The Magus." Southern Review* 15 (1979): 716–23.

Waugh, Patricia. *Metafiction: The Theory and Practice of Self-Conscious Fiction.* New York: Methuen, 1984.

Wilde, Alan. *Horizons of Assent: Modernism, Postmodernism, and the Ironic Imagination.* Baltimore: Johns Hopkins University Press, 1981.

Wolcott, James. "Enter the Mummy." *Harpers,* May 1983: 81–83.

Wolfe, Peter. *John Fowles, Magus and Moralist.* Lewisburg, Pa.: Bucknell University Press, 1976.

Woodcock, Bruce. *Male Mythologies: John Fowles and Masculinity.* Totawa, N.J.: Barnes & Noble,

Index